D1356165

"Chris's theorem of why digital banking is not only here to stay, but critical to the survival of the retail bank as we know it, starts with some pretty basic assertions, but is backed up with his usual scholarly approach. Chris compares the likes of Apple and other industries and businesses that have adapted to digital by taking a revenue-led and customer-led approach to reform and innovation. He starts off by saying we have to wipe the slate clean.

"The key problem for retail banks right now is that they don't capture revenue effectively through mobile, web, tablet and other channels like most other industries. While there is a role for the branch moving forward as Chris points out, the bias that exists in serving and selling to a customer through the branch is still alive and well. That distribution channel is hopelessly inefficient and overburdened with a ton of process and complexity that simply adds to the cost structure. However, there is strong defensibility of that model because there's no commitment to alternative revenue streams.

"Chris defines the causes of this intractability well. From the problems of skill sets ('...you firstly need to rehire'), through to the design of processes and interactions, and the very understanding of consumer behaviour. I think Chris has added tremendously to the conversation with this book and I highly recommend it."

Brett King,
author of *Bank 2.0* and founder of Moven

"It's always tough to read and review a book where (a) you know the author and (b) you read his daily blogs fairly regularly. Liking him slightly diminishes his authority and daily reading means you're sure you know what he'll say.

"Well, Chris Skinner has done a great job here. This is very much an up-to-the-minute look at the challenges banks face as the information age goes into overdrive. And it's not pretty. Banks are unprepared, incapable and slow.... If banks can't handle information—the core of money—then perhaps they should get out of the game. A genuinely valuable read for anyone who thinks banks can return to the same old after the financial crises since 2007."

Michael Mainelli,
Emeritus Gresham Professor of Commerce at Gresham College, London

"There are very few people in the financial services industry who can cut through the complexities of the business to provide truly valuable insights. Chris has a strong track record for understanding the present and accurately predicting the future in financial services. The combination of his knowledge of changing customer preferences and his understanding of the strategic priorities of the financial services industry results in highly valuable insights."

Debbie Bianucci,
president and CEO of the Bank Administration Institute (BAI)

"Chris is perhaps the first writer I know who successfully captures the pulse of the financial services industry not from a European or American but from a truly global perspective."

Emmanuel Daniel,
founder and editor-in-chief of *The Asian Banker*

"In *Digital Bank*, Chris Skinner shows why he is considered the foremost financial industry scholar. As the banking world is being transformed from a world of branches to digital financial experiences, with new partnerships, new forms of commerce and even new currencies, Chris captures the scope and impact of these changes in an easy-to-read format. While nobody can be sure exactly how all these changes will impact tomorrow's financial landscape, Chris combines his perspectives with interviews of some of today's most innovative FinTech leaders into a book that no traditional or digital banker should ignore."

Jim Marous,
senior vice president at New Control

"Way too many business books blather on about how the world will be different because of emerging technologies. Way too few go into details about the how and why to create that future vision. This book belongs in the latter category. The depth of examples the Skinner offers up on how digital technologies is transforming banking is staggering. More importantly, though, is the in-depth analysis of how banking will change from how data is the new competitive battleground to the impact of data on bank processing to the new economics of banking. This is not simply a must-read book for financial services execs. It should become a discussion tool for management teams, who should be assigned to read chapters to be discussed in management meetings."

Ron Shevlin,
Senior Analyst, Aite Group and author of the Snarketing Blog

"Chris's call to arms for the banking industry to embrace its digital future. What does the future hold for existing banks and can they transform their operations and relationships to compete successfully against digital newcomers? Will legacy bank customers trust them with their data and permissions, given the lack of confidence and trust in banks and bankers, and the search for a new banking? *Digital Bank* brings these, and many other dilemmas out into the open. One of the greatest strengths of the book is the wealth of examples and case studies from around the world, showing just how much of the future is already here, now. A very useful resource for bankers, would-be bankers and business students alike."

Simon A. Thompson,
Chief Executive, Chartered Bankers Institute

DIGITAL BANK

STRATEGIES TO LAUNCH OR BECOME A DIGITAL BANK

CHRIS SKINNER

Marshall Cavendish
Business

Cover image by zentilia/123RF Stock Photo

Published by Marshall Cavendish Business
An imprint of Marshall Cavendish International
1 New Industrial Road, Singapore 536196

Other Marshall Cavendish Offices:
Marshall Cavendish Corporation. 99 White Plains Road, Tarrytown NY 10591-9001, USA • Marshall Cavendish International (Thailand) Co Ltd. 253 Asoke, 12th Flr, Sukhumvit 21 Road, Klongtoey Nua, Wattana, Bangkok 10110, Thailand • Marshall Cavendish (Malaysia) Sdn Bhd, Times Subang, Lot 46, Subang Hi-Tech Industrial Park, Batu Tiga, 40000 Shah Alam, Selangor Darul Ehsan, Malaysia

Marshall Cavendish is a trademark of Times Publishing Limited

National Library Board Singapore Cataloguing in Publication Data
Skinner, Chris.
Digital bank : strategies to launch or become a digital bank / Chris Skinner. — Singapore : Marshall Cavendish Business, 2014.
pages. cm.

ISBN : 978-981-4516-46-4 (paperback)
Internet banking. 2. Electronic funds transfers. 3. Electronic commerce. I. Title.

HG1708.7
332.024002854678 — dc23   OCN873962825

Printed in Singapore by Craft Print International Ltd

THIS BOOK IS DEDICATED TO MY MUM,
SOMEONE I'VE NOT SPENT ENOUGH TIME WITH
OVER THE PAST TWENTY YEARS BUT
SOMEONE WHO NURTURED MY SUCCESS
AND HAS BEEN MY INSPIRATION.

ACKNOWLEDGEMENTS

This book is an amalgam of ideas, insights and thoughts written on my blog since 2007. The blog is fed by lots of news from around the world thanks to the Financial Services Club, a business I created with my business partner, Andy Coppell, in 2004. It is because of Andy that this club exists and I am forever in his debt for his stalwart support.

So first and foremost, my utmost thanks to Andy Coppell and his family Margaret, Heather and Lynn. Without their unfaltering support of the Financial Services Club and our activities, I would not be doing what I am doing today. Equally, thanks to Michael Baume, Thomas Labenbacher, Lydia Goutas and Sandy Davison for all of their efforts in keeping this network alive. Words cannot say enough.

A specific group of people who are real movers and shakers are the guys at Moven, a bank start-up in the United States led by my good friend Brett King, author of *Bank 2.0, Bank 3.0* and more. Brett, alongside Alex Sion, Richard Nearn, Scott Bales and the team, is launching something really interesting and I am excited to be a small part of it.

Another group that has fed me so much good content are the guys at SWIFT who created Innotribe, an innovation stream within the industry group. I specifically would like to cite Matteo Rizzi, Mariela Atanassova, Konstantin (Kosta) Peric and Peter Vander Auwera for including me in their efforts.

There are a number of people in the banks that I would like to pick out but the list is too long. Given the chance, I guess I would start with the following as they have been particularly supportive in recent times: Amanda Brown, Andy Hutchinson, Darren Armitage, David Ellender, Ian Lloyd, Mark Mullen, Jim Marous, Jeffry Pilcher, Paul Smee, Roy Vella, Ruth Wandhofer, Tim Decker, Aden Davies, among many others who help me with my work.

Equally, there are others who feed me regular news about the banking markets and I need to give a specific nod to Anthony Thomson, David Birch, Michael Mainelli, Bob Fuller, Neil Burton, Edith Rigler, John Bertrand, Bonita Osgood, Bikash Mathur, Arun Jain, Jim Marous, Jeffry Pilcher, Kenneth Cline, Jim Bruene, Brian Caplen, Giles Andrews, Chris Dunne, Julia Whittaker, Tony Virgo, Bob Ford and Katie Gwyn-Williams, alongside many more, who provide me with the ability to blog and analyse this industry. I would like to name you all but this book would then be just a collection of names of thanks!

Finally, I would like to give a big thank you to Kamila Nosarzewska, my partner, for putting up with me and my passion. Yes, banking and technology and the future are my passion, and I hope this book will provide you with some useful insights.

CONTENTS

PART 2: INTERVIEWS

INTRODUCTION

I've called this book *Digital Bank*. I did want to call it *Data Wars* but this book is about banking. Nevertheless, calling it *Data Wars* would have made more sense. This is because the book is about the battle for the future of banking, which is all about data. In fact, it is already about data, it's just that some banks are yet to realise this. I find this somewhat surprising as the battle over bank data has been bubbling away for over thirty years.

Around thirty years ago, a visionary bank CEO articulated what we all knew then but many dared not say: "Banking is just bits and bytes." John Reed, the then chief executive of Citibank, is credited with this quote and over the past three decades we have seen the import of this statement become clearer and clearer.

Back in the 1980s, when John Reed made this statement, banks did not have call centres or Internet banking, just branches. Even then, the processing of data and the importance of data to the bank were prescient. This is because banks had moved through the 1960s and 1970s automating back-office functions using mainframe computing and were heavily processing data in the back office.

The first—and largest—processor of data about money was Visa, the commercial organisation spawned by BankAmericard, the credit card that stormed the United States in the 1960s. The company automated the paper and carbon billing processes that hampered the industry back then. Fast-forward to today and Visa processes billions of trillions of bytes of data every day.

Things changed very slowly, from the large-scale mainframe automation of Visa and the banks in the 1970s to where we are today, and are all a result of revolutions of compute power. Bear in mind that the automation that put a man on the moon in 1969 was more basic than the automation you now hold in your hand in the form of a smartphone, and you can pretty much see why.

Compared to forty years ago when banks were automating the back office and becoming large-scale data processors about money, Visa is now processing 100 billion transactions a year whilst currency traders trade over $5 trillion[1] a day, and this amount of trading is growing exponentially.

These numbers reflect the explosion of data around the world thanks to the ubiquity of technology. The fact that the majority of people on the planet have a mobile telephone, tablet computer, laptop or other form of technology in their possession is part of the reason for this change.

Today, we talk about more data being produced in a year than in the whole history of mankind but what does this actually mean? In practice, it can best be illustrated by thinking about the complete works of Shakespeare.

William Shakespeare, the bard and playwright, produced magnificent plays, dramas, tragedies, sonnets and poems. If you were to look at the total output of his work as a computer file, his complete works would amount to about 5 megabytes of data. Today, we produce 500 billion works of Shakespeare every day. Yes, that's right, 500 billion works of Shakespeare or, if you prefer the computer number, 2.5 exabytes of data per day. An exabyte is a 1 with 18 zeroes after it, or 1,000,000,000,000,000,000 bytes. That's a staggering amount of information!

Much of this data is erroneous or irrelevant, coming in the form of updates on Facebook, Twitter, Tumblr, Flickr and other social media.

---

1   Unless otherwise stated, the currency used throughout this book is the US dollar (US$).

Nevertheless, the rise of the Internet to the mass deployment of mobile telecommunications has resulted in a world where every single one of the seven billion people living on the planet can now communicate, share, transact and trade with each other electronically, one-to-one, globally.

That is the transformation of today. It is the reason why exabytes of data are being produced every day and why data is the new battleground for commerce. From retailing to banking, every aspect of how we live is being targeted by data. Data analysis, data mining, data leverage and data detail is the criticality.

It is the reason why data is described as the new oil, greasing the flow of business, commerce and economics the world over. It is the reason why thieves target the theft of data as data is where the money is. It is the reason why data is the gold for everyone trying to win mindshare, wallet share and attention from their target audience.

We live in a world where everyone is data rich but time poor, and that creates the real issue: How do you sort through all of this data to find the gold? How do you analyse all of this information to provide insights? How do you find the unknowns from the data in order to provide knowledge? And how do you wrestle with all the bits and bytes to find wisdom?

Again, this is not new. As Michael Douglas noted when he played Gordon Gekko in the 1987 film *Wall Street*, "The most valuable commodity I know of is information." The difference today is that data has just become far more of a centrifugal force for change thanks to the rise of the mobile Internet where ubiquitous technologies connect everything everywhere.

As we all move towards wearable computing through the Internet of things, we see a fundamental transformation of society, government, economies, business, commerce and banking.

This book focuses upon what these changes mean to banks but it could equally apply to any other business being transformed through digitisation. For example, the revolutions in retail through the rise of Amazon and in entertainment with Apple have resulted in the death of traditional retailers such as HMV, Jessops, Comet, Blockbuster and more. This is the challenge we now face in banking.

In banking, these changes mean a complete rethinking of customer relationships and the method of delivering value to meet customer needs. It has created non-stop debate about whether banks need branches, whether there will be a cashless society, how to bulletproof banks from cyberattacks, how to keep up with customer demands as they move to mobile and tablet banking and so on. In fact, digitisation has meant that banking is no longer about banking money but about banking data and keeping data secure.

All of this is radical change and requires radical action in order to keep up with such change. Unfortunately, this is where banks are failing. They are too slow to change and, in some cases, downright resistant to the changes demanded by the digital age. In fact, for some banks, it is plain scary as it is hard to change when you do not know what you are changing into.

For those banks floundering with the future and for those engaged in change for the future, this book provides a blueprint guide to the journey. It provides direction and guidance as how to re-engineer products, services, processes and structures in order to become a Digital Bank.

Rich with case studies, commentary, knowledge and facts, this book is indispensable for anyone working with strategies for dealing with the digital age—not just banks—as it will give you the critical insights required to understand how money, value, commerce, trade and economics are being reshaped and re-engineered for the digital age.

I hope you find this useful and look forward to engagement in future dialogue.

Chris Skinner, March 2014
chris.skinner@fsclub.co.uk

PART 1
DIGITAL BANKS

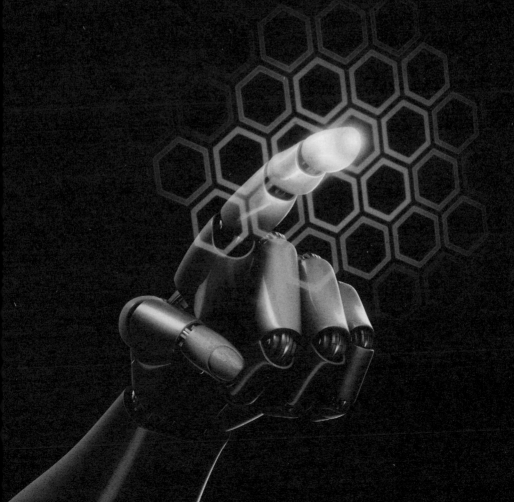

WHY WE NEED DIGITAL BANKS

For half a millennia, retail banks have worked on the basis of physical distribution. For half a century, that model has been challenged to move towards electronic distribution. At the end of the first decade of the new millennium, we have finally reached the point where electronic distribution has matured, works and is proven. Unfortunately, most banks are stuck in the 20th century. It's time for banks to turn their model on its head and focus on electronic platforms, where physical distribution is the cream on the cake, rather than the other way around.

This occurs regularly as a debate around the future of retail banking. The discussions go something like this: "So are things like Second Life and Facebook just passing fads or are they really important to the future of retail banking?" My response is that the question is flawed because it shows that the person who asked the question is a digital alien.

"Digital aliens" and "digital natives" are terms coined by Marc Prensky and refer to different generations of digital usage.[2] In Prensky's definitions, a digital alien is an adult who is comfortable using the newest Internet-based technologies whilst digital natives are the younger generation who have grown up with the Internet as an integral part of their lives. The people

---

2   Prensky, Marc. "Digital Natives, Digital Immigrants." *On the Horizon 9*, no. 5 (October 2001)

who fall into the category of digital natives are Generation D, the i-Pops ... whatever you call them. They don't think of the Internet; they just get on with their lives and see online, mobile and all other digital channels as being seamlessly integrated into their world. These people do not think about branches, call centres, the Internet and so on. They just think of these things as *life*, and this is where retail bankers are getting it wrong because they are run by digital aliens or immigrants who do not get the *digital life*.

For example, retail banks have a historically strong branch network. They added ATMs in the 1970s, call centres in the 1980s, the Internet in the 1990s and are now adding mobile in the 2000s. Each channel is added as an extra layer on the foundation of the branch distribution cake. Branch networks are the foundations whilst electronic distribution is the cream on the cake.

This is why retail banks talk about multichannel strategies whereby they try to integrate their call centre channel with their Internet channel. They attempt to deliver mobile banking interoperable with the call centre channel. They mess about with customer relationship management (CRM) to ensure consistency across branch and Internet channels.

My problem is this: banks only have one channel. They do not have multichannels, call centre channels, Internet channels, mobile channels and so forth. They just have an electronic channel that underscores and provides the foundation for all end points: mobile, telephone, Internet and branch.

The electronic channel is based on Internet protocol (IP) technologies, as is the branch as it happens. And this is the big change: banks should stop thinking of channels and just recognise that they are digital enabled. Call centres, ATMs, the branch, Internet, mobile ... everything is digital enabled and, therefore, the bank has become a Digital Bank based on digitised platforms that reach into every nook, cranny, sinew and synapse of the bank.

Thinking this way demonstrates the fundamental flaw in much bank logic because many banks still have everything built in layers of complexity and legacy. The ATM, call centre and Internet channels were all built as layers of cake and created when the physical branch was the foundation. The electronic channels were built as ancillary to the core branch channel. That is why they were often separated and have this chasm of non-integration between each other, as banks were built on a physical distribution model where electronics were layered on top.

However today, and certainly tomorrow, the population has moved to a world in which the majority are digital natives. As this Digital Generation grows up and matures, and as the world becomes populated solely by digital natives, what role will there be for banks that have been built upon the basis of a physical distribution model with electronics layered on top?

It's time to turn all of this on its head. It's time to think about banking as an electronic structure. It's time to bite the bullet and admit that retail banking is not a physical distribution structure with electronic channels on top but, instead, an electronic distribution structure with electronic and physical channels on top. It's time to become the Digital Bank.

This means wiping the slate clean and starting afresh.

How would you build today's bank if digital networking is its foundation, and call centre, Internet, mobile and the branch are just the cream on the top of the cake? Where would you build branches, and how would you build them, if the branches are ancillary and perfunctory to the electronic foundations? Who would you employ, and how would you employ them, if the core differentiation of the bank is its digital base rather than its branch structure?

The fact is that any bank launched today as a greenfield operation would think this way and, with the right leadership and implementation, would thrash the weak competition existing in most markets that are based on legacy structures and legacy thinking.

Start thinking about the bank being a digital network at its core, with layers of distribution on top and branch as the cream on the cake.

It's time for change.

DESIGNING THE DIGITAL BANK

As banks design their new generation Digital Bank, the starting point has to be customers and employees. Using this as the start, banks then need to consider how to build the processes and organisation structure using digital resources in an optimal way to reach and support those customers and employees. Finally, the bank needs to consider how traditional bricks and mortar fits in with this new digital structure in order to support the physical organisational structure that will be using the digital network.

Banks are trying to do the latter and, with greenfield operations, could do so brilliantly. Instead, due to the fact that they started building using physical structures years ago, they have to find a path to marry the two worlds. They are achieving this by building their digital architectures around the rewiring of the existing buildings that they want to keep in play, as part of this process.

The most important consideration here is the building of the digital architecture. What does this mean in practice? It means that banks need to recognise that they have been deconstituted in the digital process and need to consider how to reconstitute themselves.

As a digital business, all banking can be broken down into pure bits and bytes but, more than that, a bank can be seen as three digital businesses in one. It is a *manufacturer* of products, a *processor* of transactions and a *retailer* of services.

In this context, the digitisation of banking becomes more interesting at a strategic level. First, the products have been deconstructed. Every bank product can be deconstituted into its lowest common denominator of components, and then reconstituted into new forms of use and structure. This component-based bank demands that every bank capability is put into a basic widget form, or object form if you prefer, and then offered to customers to put together as they see fit. In other words, there are no integrated product sets any more, simply banking as apps that customers put together to suit their needs.

Moving onto processing, we build upon the app-based product view and begin to consider processes as open-source code. The open sourcing of digital processes is rife and has disrupted and changed everything from how operating systems operate, vis-à-vis Linux, to how Google develops its omnipotent reach.

Learning from such open-source processing, PayPal launched X, a developer-based service for PayPal processes as application program interfaces (APIs), or forms of packaged functionality. APIs allow anyone to pick up and drop PayPal into their systems and, like banking products as apps, allow PayPal to be reintegrated by third parties into any code and operation desired. The result is that PayPal's relevance increased greatly overnight and led to Citi following a similar approach when it announced that its transaction services would be offered as APIs at the SWIFT International Banking Operations Seminar (SIBOS) in 2013. In other words, all bank processing is just open-source coding, offered to anyone to plug and play with their offerings through APIs.

Finally, the customer relationship has also changed. The customer relationships used to be human, one-to-one. Then it became remote, one-to-many. Now it is digitised, one-to-one.

This is where Big Data[3] comes into its own as we are now trying to manage remote relationships leveraged through mass personalisation. Mass personalisation can only be achieved by offering contextual servicing to each and every customer at their point of relevance. This means analysing exabytes of customer data to identify, on a privacy and permissions basis, what contextual service customers may need as they live their lives.

If they are walking past a car showroom, do you promote cheap motor insurance or a car purchase scheme? If they are leaving a casino, do you offer a loan or a referral to an addiction clinic? If they are leaving the maternity clinic, do you offer child investment services or a referral to an abortion clinic?

Some of these may seem controversial but we are already seeing contextual offers through finance coming into play in the form of Google

---

3   For more on Big Data, *see* pages 151–153.

Wallet. And the aim of such contextual offers is to track your digital footprint, using Big Data analysis, to gain intuitive service offers relevant to your point of living.

For example, as Google tracks your searches for plasma TVs, you get an offer for £200 off the TV you spent the longest time studying online as you walk past an electronics showroom. However, the offer is only good for an hour, and only as long as you are in proximity of that electronics showroom.

This is the new augmented reality of customer intimacy through Big Data analysis, and bank retailing will be based on the competitive differentiation of analysing mass data to deliver mass personalisation.

In summary, the digitisation of banking is now mainstream, and all bank capabilities will be packaged as digital structures whereby products will be apps, processes will be APIs and retailing will be contextual, delivered through mobile Internet at the point of relevance.

Having said this, what happens to the physical structures of banking, as the digitisation of everything takes over, will be the biggest challenge of all.

WHAT DOES THIS MEAN FOR THE PHYSICAL BANK?

To become a Digital Bank, with digital networking at the core of the bank, is a real challenge as it means moving fundamentally away from placing branch networks at the core. Some people believe this is purely academic as we have branches today and can't get rid of them, so the question is how to use the branches we have today. My contention is different.

It is obvious that branches are critical sales centres and, in the future, they will not be transaction centres. However, as they have served as transaction centres historically, this is what everyone is struggling with today: how can tellers be turned into sellers and branches into sales operations?

It is incredibly difficult to turn tellers into sellers. It's a bit like turning credit risk officers into customer service reps. It might work with one or two people, but most would rather be tellers. So you first need to rehire.

If you are going to do that then you also need to ask, in the transformation process, if you are going to turn your old transactional branches into sales operations. If yes, do you need so many of them? After all, if you can get rid of the transaction focus and move it to machines, how many branches do you need?

Equally, if you are moving branches away from transactions, which are now managed through remote telephone and Internet connections and other self-service machines, all of which are digitally enabled systems including the branch ATMs, then how do you rethink the network?

This is why some bank strategies are fundamentally flawed as those who think branches are the starting point will throw good money after bad. In contrast, those who think digital networks are the starting point, and then build the end points on top, including bank branches, will be much nearer the right strategy for the future.

So here's the bottom line: those who think digital networks are just layered on top of old infrastructures, networks, distribution strategies and organisations are wrong. Believing this is precisely why we have ended up with silo structures, painful processes and inappropriate skills.

A bank strategy today needs to start around a digitally enabled bank. If you were designing that bank, then here's the question to ask around the branch focus:

How many branches would you layer on top?

- How many of those would be self-service automated branches and how many would be sales centres?
- How many members of staff, and what sort of staff, would you hire for those sales centres?
- What would be the customer demographics for each sales centre, and how would those staff skills fit with those customers?
- What will happen to the existing staff and who do you need to retrain or offer severance to?

- What are the technological aspects of the digital enabled branch in this context, and how much technology should you put into the branch?
- What is that technology doing and how does it profile against the staff skills and customer demographics?
- Is the technology future-proof and how engaging is this going to be versus putting that service into other channels such as online or through contact centres?
- How does the underpinning of the new digital enabled branch fit with the digital enabled alternative contact points?
- Are they fully consistent with a single electronic digital enabled service?

These are all questions retail banks are asking, and some are answering ... and it isn't easy. But it has to start with the network being the IP network of the 21st century and not the high street bricks-and-mortar network of the 20th century and before.

BANK DESIGN VERSUS ARCHITECTURE

The reason why the focus on becoming a Digital Bank is such a difficult one is that often people confuse design with emotion, architecture with distribution and channels with infrastructure.

The design of a Digital Bank begins with architecture, which is why I keep referring to foundations. The discussion often gets confused with bank design, which is different. Architecture is about materials, dimensions, frictions and structures; design is about the user experience, customer engagement, the human connectivity and whether it is face-to-face or screen-to-screen. The two go hand-in-hand.

The bank designer would start with the customer and how to focus on customer emotion and behaviours. I call this buyology.

BUYOLOGY: THE SCIENCE OF UNDERSTANDING BUSINESS RELATIONSHIPS

Buyology is a core science for designing banking in the new world of freakonomics, where everyone is struggling to understand the methods to get customers buying, and is defined as the science of understanding business relationships. It is all about knowing why people buy and how to create business encounters where purchases are made that can be replicated over and over. In other words, it is the ability to create long-term business relationships, not just a one-sale stand.

Bankers are learning about buyological processes because traditional selling and advertising no longer work. People don't want to be sold to and they certainly don't believe corporate speak. What they really want is to deal with businesses that demonstrate a true understanding of their individual wants and needs. That is buyology. Buyology then targets customer experiences through the customer's channel(s) of choice.

Banks' understanding of buyology is a clear strategic imperative because business has become so transparent thanks to blogs, Facebook and other social media. These networks now ensure that any cover-up of any issue is going to be exposed. That is 21st-century Internet-enabled consumer power. Social networks mean that banks must start demonstrating clear integrity that can be trusted or the truth will come out.

In effect, you cannot have a relationship without trust, so banks that don't demonstrate clear integrity will only have the one-sale stand or the partner abuser. Buyology is therefore the sharing of a meaningful trust.

Bank relationships are based on trust and trust is easily broken. This is just as true in the investment markets as in retail for, in the investment markets, buyology has been moved to another extreme. Buyology for investment banks means creating services that the customer needs and wants but doesn't understand.

Consequently, the relationship has become one in which the trust is in ignorance. A little like a father-child or priest-confessor relationship, the institutional buyer has to believe the broker-dealer is looking after their best interests. Unfortunately, this is being called into question thanks to the new regulations around best execution and transparency, which implies broker-dealers don't always act in their clients' best interests (really?!).

This trust has also been tested by companies like Enron, WorldCom and Parmalat and is being tested again in the credit crunch. In fact, the recent admission by the Bank of England that it no longer understood the financial markets, in light of the Northern Rock collapse, is shocking. When the regulators and coordinators of the financial markets lose their understanding, something has to change.

Buyology therefore means knowing the why, how, what and when ingredients of buying, and ensuring you position your business to always be there *at the right time, with the right words* ... there's a song with those words and the next line is "and you'll be mine".

Creating strong relationships is a tough call. Future buyers will not buy from anyone they do not trust or understand. They will instead use the power of social networks to find the truth and will morph towards those who deal with integrity. In other words, buyology means knowing your customer so well that they are no longer a customer, they're a partner.

In relationships, you cannot have one side treated unfairly. Although you may not know each other on the first date, if you don't get to know each other well sooner or later, the relationship will end. That's the one-sale stand approach to business. It's a bit like a one-night stand. If you have no interest or empathy, then the relationship stops there.

Relationships are based on understanding and compromise. We talk CRM, but you don't have relationships with customers. Customers are sold to; partners have relationships.

Banks that turn tellers into sellers or have big swinging dicks in the dealing room will soon find that the truth will come out. Instead of sustainable sales, they'll get lots of one-sale stands. The real partnerships based on fair dealings with trust will prove to be the long-term sustainable relationship businesses.

DIGITAL ARCHITECTS REQUIRED TO BUILD DIGITAL DESIGNS

If you accept that the future of banking will be based on whichever banks are the best buyological scientists, then that is the premise that the bank designer would use to build the Digital Bank. The bank would be based on digitised techniques of customer understanding in order to build processes from the customer viewpoint. At the end of designing, they would then go to a digital architect to build the digital design.

This goes to the core of business process re-engineering (BPR), which is why we talk about process redesign when we're designing, and process implementation when we're architecting.

The architect has been called in recently because the bank's foundations are suffering from subsidence. The foundations were built on bricks and mortar, and those foundations have cracked due to the revolution of technology in the last fifty years. Most banks got away with painting over the cracks but, today, they are finally saying they want to replace the brick foundations with technological foundations in the form of digitised architectures. The architect is there to replace the physical foundations— process implementation—and the designer is there to work out what the new bank house should look like—process redesign.

Likening this to the building trade illustrates the point well. A house or building has foundations. My point is purely to say that the bank architects of the last few decades used branches as those foundations but today would use IP infrastructures.

This does not mean that branches or people are irrelevant. The branch and face-to-face discussion is more to do with what type of house you want to build. In other words, it's the design, the vision, the interior decoration, the furniture and all the other bits.

The designers may say, "I want to build a high net worth house, with sales advisory centres for people who want face-to-face engagements." In this case, you would build your bank house with IP foundations and lots of snazzy advisory centres, or branches, in the physical world. Others may say,

"I want to build a low-cost high volume processing house, with minimal physical contact" in which case you would build your bank house with IP foundations and hardly any branches in the physical world. Either way, the IP is the foundation, and that is where the architect will start.

There may be some confusion about the fact that I am starting with a technology focus, rather than a customer focus. As an architect of today's bank, an implementer, I would start with technology because technology, especially IP networking, is my raw material for the building. As a process designer, I would start with customers and staff because people are my core differentiation for populating my building.

From an architecture and implementation viewpoint, I would look at the IP network and how to build upon that network. From a design and process redesign viewpoint, I would start from the statement: "Design for the customer experience you want to deliver to the customers you want to engage by creating processes and touch points that those customers want to engage through and with you."

In other words, work out what customers you seek and what those customers want. Build your bank and design it based on desired customer experiences. Build those customer experiences to appeal to the customer behaviours of your targeted audience. Address the needs of digital natives and digital immigrants or aliens, and work out how your designs address this mixture of customer types. What experiences and behaviours will these different audiences require and how is it best to deliver them?

These are all designer questions and nothing to do with architecture. Once you have your design, you can then give this to the architect to work out how to build it … and the architect will begin with a base design using IP as the foundation.

So we have a critical segregation between the designer, who will focus on processes, interactions, people and customers, and the architect, who will focus on building materials, infrastructures, networks and technologies.

The fact that people get confused about this segregation—the channel mix, the house design, etc. versus the foundations of the bank—is because they mix up process redesign and process implementation. The channel strategy is the house design; the building strategy is the architect's digital materials.

The focus must move to a strategy whereby the architect lays the digital foundations, rather than tries to maintain the old brick foundations. It's to do with the materials at the base of the bank and the fact that these materials are fundamentally different today because they are digital rather than brick-based. This is why banks need to fundamentally redesign.

This redesign is to replace the building foundation. In replacing the foundation, the strategy for the design of the house itself may also change, but this is still very much open to the designer's competitive strategy. It is a separate discussion that has nothing to do with architecture.

The architect is purely working out how to replace the foundations with IP. Therefore, the designer's role is to tell the architect what the designer wants to build on top of the foundations—branches or multichannels or electronic connections.

The two roles—architect and designer—go together but are very separate and distinct roles. The reason why the redesign started in the first place, however, is because the foundations are crumbling—the branch bricks-and-mortar model—and need replacing through a new architecture, namely IP networking. And, as I keep saying, architecture is related to, but separated from, design.

In conclusion, the issue today is that most banks have their foundations in branches as the raw material, and that is forcing them into poor designs that do not match the way they want to behave. That is why they are hiring architects to replace those foundations with IP. The architects are then asking the bankers, "What design would you like to have on top of these foundations?"

Some bank designers want redesigned branches. Some want to close down branches. Some want to integrate branches onto common platforms with their electronic channel connections. Some just want electronic connections.

It's all a matter of choice but, as you have to replace the foundations, you might as well rethink, re-engineer and re-energise to exploit the new foundations effectively.

THE DIGITAL AGE DEMANDS A DIGITAL BANK

Throughout this chapter, we have focused on designing the Digital Bank, evolving from the Physical Bank, and recognising that the new bank is very different. It is deconstituted and needs to be reconstituted. It is modular and plug-and-play and no longer integrated and end-to-end. It is remote and human rather than local and face-to-face. And most of all, it has digital at the core and the flow of logic flows from that core.

This then leads us to a very different but clear challenge for the future Digital Bank. This bank has the challenge to turn a vertically integrated business—one that owns the customer process end-to-end and organises itself around products and channels—into a horizontally structured business. The new business is designed to provide functionality to the customer at their point of need and organises itself around the customer's data.

That's a big problem for many. As it is so fundamental to the subject matter, it would be beneficial to break it down step by step.

First, banks were created to look after all the financial needs of people and businesses. They were licensed to live in their own segregated world of operation and completely owned that piece of turf. Everything from taking deposits to giving loans was the banks' domain and they were organised to do just that. As a result, most banks created operations based around products: money transmissions, mortgages, cards, loans, insurances, etc. These were delivered through one channel, the branch.

Over time, another channel appeared, the direct sales representative. These sales people resided in branches and were served by the branch system. Then, a new channel emerged, the call centre.

The call centre was like one massive remote branch and required a new structure to operate. But the underlying data could be delivered through the branch-based systems so the new structure was primarily designed to sit on top of those systems, offering scripts into the various products the bank offered. The call centre people struggled with this, sometimes operating six or more windows of screens at any one time to get a competitive picture of the customer's needs, but they lived with it.

Then, another channel popped up—the Internet. At first, banks thought this could lead to branch closures and started to invest heavily in moving from branch to Internet services. However, the underlying data was still held in product silos and the Internet was not responsive to customers' views of the world. Broadband had yet to appear and customers were reluctant to lose their branch connection.

So, the banks left the Internet as another layer on top of the branch-based systems, alongside the call centre spaghetti. Banks had become locked into vertically integrated processes, structured around product silos that were ill-suited to the multichannel world they now served. But it was okay. Using middleware, fudge, smoke and mirrors, it did the job.

Then this perfect storm of mobile, cloud (a large number of computers connected through a real-time communication network such as the Internet) and Big Data appeared, augmented by customers tweeting and socialising 24/7 and most bankers went, "What the hell?"

Now here's the challenge. The bank cannot leverage data; it's locked in product silos. It cannot serve the customer's needs. Banks layered channels over products. Now, they need to leverage data over mobile. And banks lost the end-to-end process as customers moved to apps and pieces of process and functionality as needed. Now there's a need to organise the bank around the customer's data and then leverage that data through the cloud to mobile devices as apps.

No way. Way. There is a way.

The way is to completely rip out the old systems and replace them with new core banking that can service the bank, and therefore the customers, in the way that is appropriate for the 21st century. How do you do that?

Changing core systems is like changing the engines on an aircraft at the height of 9 miles … you just don't do it. Well, more and more banks are doing just that. Some are having problems, but that is precisely why banks are changing the core systems. You cannot restructure a bank around customer data if that data is locked into legacy systems that are product siloed and channel handcuffed.

DESIGNING DIGITAL BANKS WITHOUT BRANCHES

It is clear from all sources of statistics that bank branches are no longer as relevant in the distribution mix as we move towards Digital Banks. For example, the European Central Bank (ECB) produced figures in 2013 that indicate significant branch closures, particularly in countries affected by austerity measures like Spain:[4]

"Banks have shut about 20,000 branches across Europe in the last four years, including 5,500 last year and 7,200 in 2011. That represents the closure of about 8 per cent of Europe's branches since the financial crisis, and the cull is expected to continue for many years."

"The cuts have been most severe in Spain, unravelling years of expansion by regional savings banks, which had landed it with the biggest network in Europe. Its branch numbers were down 17 per cent by the end of 2012 from four years earlier. But at just over 38,200 branches, Spain still had more branches per head than any country in Europe—one for every 1,210 people."

4   "All aboard for Europe's shrinking bank branch network," Reuters, 11 August 2013

"France had the most branches in Europe by the end of last year, with nearly 38,450, or one for every 1,709 people, behind only Spain and Cyprus per person. Cyprus had one branch per 1,265 people."

France "shed less than 3 per cent of its network in the four years to the end of 2012, while 5 per cent of UK branches and more than 8 per cent of German ones pulled down the shutters for the last time. The number of branches plummeted by a third in Denmark and by a quarter in the Netherlands."

British "banks have almost halved branch numbers since 1990. Senior bankers privately say a network of 700–800 outlets would be an optimal size for a bank covering all of Britain. None of the big five have so few. Lloyds has three times that (2,260), and Royal Bank of Scotland more than twice (1,750), excluding almost 1,000 branches they are already selling between them."

British banks closed 557 branches over the last four years resulting in 11,713 branches in 2012, compared with 12,270 in 2008. Between 2008 and 2011, HSBC closed 181 branches, NatWest 135 and Barclays 99. The British Bankers Association (BBA) provides statistics which show that a further 68 branches were closed by HSBC in 2012, 60 by Royal Bank of Scotland (RBS)/NatWest in the first half of 2013 and 30 by Barclays. HSBC has announced another 25 closures are anticipated while HSBC pushes more focus on its partnership with Marks & Spencer and banking through post offices.

The figures are more dramatic in the United Kingdom if you dig deeper. According to a recent study by Nottingham University,[5] nearly 7,500 branches closed between 1989 and 2012, accounting for 40 per cent of all branches in Britain.

The United States is the one country that has consistently refuted the need to close branches, expanding the branch footprint from around 80,000 in 2000 to over 95,000 in 2012. Even there however, we are seeing a final day of

---

5   "UK has lost '40%' of its banks and building societies," BBC News, 19 August 2013

reckoning with branch closures rising in the last twelve months. From a recent article in *St Louis Today*, "Bank branches in the U.S. fell to 97,337 this year (2013), reflecting a loss of 867 branches in 2012, according to SNL Financial. From 2010 to 2011, branches nationally declined by about 315."[6]

The writing is on the wall, as illustrated by the *Motley Fool* which has pointed out that bank branches are going the same way as bookshops and record stores:[7]

"With a 4 per cent average annual decline in branch traffic over the past 16 years, banking is the natural next domino to fall ... the competition among online banks, particularly from names like Ally Bank and ING and Everbank, is likely to cut into margins—but Bank of Internet does have admirably high Return on Equity (ROE) and a high earnings growth rate compared to all of the more traditional banks I looked at (their ROE is around 16 per cent, even great banks like Wells Fargo are down around 13 per cent and most are closer to 10 per cent or less, sometimes far less)."

This is supported by further research by AlixPartners, a New York consulting firm, which is quoted in the *Wall Street Journal* as estimating that American banks will cull one in five branches over the next decade, putting the total closer in line with 2000 levels.[8]

Perhaps this is further illustrated in the same article by comments from William Demchak, the president of PNC Financial Services Group. This Pittsburgh-based bank operates 2,900 branches but aimed to close 200 by the end of 2013 as the bank's focus going forward "will be weighted far more in the direction of technology than teller lines." Each time a PNC customer deposits a cheque by snapping a picture on a mobile phone, it saves the bank $3.88 per transaction compared with a deposit at a teller window.

---

6   "U.S. Bank bucks branch-closing trend," *St Louis Today*, 3 October 2013

7   "Big Banking's $20.8 Trillion Secret," Pick from David Gardner, *Motley Fool*, October 2013

8   "After Years of Growth, Banks Are Pruning Their Branches," *Wall Street Journal*, 31 March 2013

There are other statistics worth noting in the *Wall Street Journal* article, such as:

- The number of U.S. branches doubled over the past three decades, and the industry has reduced branches just three times in the 77 years since the FDIC started keeping track.
- Online banking now accounts for 53 per cent of banking transactions, compared with 14 per cent for in-branch visits, according to research from AlixPartners.

All in all, the writing is clearly on the wall when you see the statistic that the Top 30 American banks spend $50 billion a year on their branches.

This is well illustrated by the *Financial Times* which stated that Bank of America "had cut the number of its branches to 5,243 in the third quarter, a 6 per cent decline from the same period last year" while Citigroup, the third-biggest US bank by assets, has reduced its branches aggressively over the past seven consecutive quarters, reducing outlets to 3,777 from 4,069 a year ago."[9]

So here's the bottom line: If you are not aggressively looking to migrate customers from physical to digital distribution, you're a dead bank.

DO CUSTOMERS WANT BRANCHES?

Many bankers believe that branches are the foundation of a bank, and critical to its future, as they grew up in the bank with this channel reach at its core. Why the branch is so critical is because it provides a physical point of interaction. That physicality acts as a security blanket because, when push comes to shove, people want a place to go to and see someone to talk to and make sure that their money is there.

---

9   "US banks automate as they cut branches," *Financial Times*, 16 October 2013

A branch provides a place for service, and that is critical when you need that service. For example, when a family suffers a bereavement, the branch is a key support mechanism to sort out the financial affairs of the deceased. And it's also a case of choice. Some people may not want to visit branches, but they want them to be available. For example, 88 per cent of customers are more likely to choose a bank with multichannel capabilities including branch. Moreover, the real reason why branches are required is because customers want to engage in a human dialogue. You could do business via video, but most do not want that. They want to sit and talk and network and engage with a human, face-to-face. That's why they want branches.

In particular, customers want branches because dealing with money is frightening. It's not an easy thing. It's scary. People need help with managing their money and for them, the branch is the place to go. Not everyone will do this online and remote these days because they want to have someone to talk to about money, and that's what the branch gives them. It is the reason why Virgin acquired Northern Rock's branches, why Marks & Spencer is opening branches with HSBC and why Tesco is opening branches. Without branches, you cannot grow a banking business, and you wouldn't pay millions for bricks-and-mortar branches if the bricks-and-mortar branches did not matter.

This is all well and good, but those who are anti-branch say that branches were designed in the 18th century for a market of three hundred years ago and are not fit for purpose today, as the world has become digitised and the next generation customer does not think in the same way. In fact, many of the reasons why bankers state that branches are needed are pure fallacy. For example, most bankers believe that branches are needed for sales, service, advice and information, but that is surely wrong when we live in a world of information overload. There is no information scarcity. We are producing more knowledge, information, advice and support online than ever before.

As Google CEO Eric Schmidt said in 2010, "There were 5 exabytes of information created between the dawn of civilization through 2003, but that much information is now created every two days, and the pace is increasing."[10] That's why all the statistics show that the number of transactions and value of services in branches are falling rapidly, being displaced by online and telephone services.

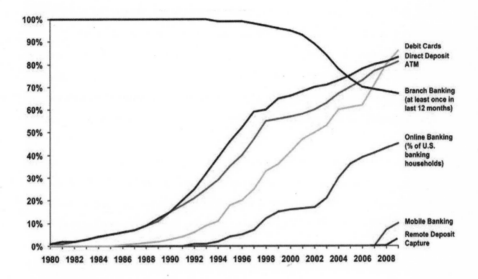

Source: From the Investor Presentation reporting the acquisition of ING Direct by Capital One, June 2011

Furthermore, a basic metric of banking is that a branch is a high cost overhead that is city-focused. The city customer is in fact subsidising the rural customer, by supporting low traffic branches in more suburban areas to be provided at the cost of the high traffic branch in the city centre.

It is also worthy to note that the industry is in terminal decline. For example, most banks are afraid of meeting customers in branch because there is no audit trail of what happens. That is why we can fall into the trap

---

10   Techonomy conference, Lake Tahoe USA, August 2010

of mis-selling, vis-à-vis the United Kingdom's £20 billion plus Payments Protection Insurance (PPI) scandal, especially when the person in a bank branch is a low paid teller and not a highly informed advisor. These exposures will only grow as face-to-face interactions take place with no record. This is why remote digital service is so much better, as you can keep a full audit trail of the telephone calls and clickstream of the customer. Add on to this the fact that you can delight a customer through a remote digital experience, and that is the reason why you find the advocacy of remote banks, like USAA and First Direct, being far higher than branch-based banks.

Thanks to this rapid transition towards continuous digital, remote access, branches are clearly becoming less important today and customers are voting with their feet by not visiting branches anymore. This was clearly demonstrated in a presentation given by Eric Mackor, head of Channel Development at the Netherlands Retail Bank ABN AMRO at a European Financial Management Association (EFMA) conference in Brussels in June 2013.[11] The changing dynamics of channel usage within the bank clearly showed that mobile is now its dominant contact point with customers. ABN AMRO Netherlands now receives over a million interactions per day with customers via mobile, representing three out of every five customer contacts and far outweighing Internet and call centre services.

This statistic is backed up by others. For example, Barclays Bank took thirteen years to achieve two million customers using Internet banking but took just two months to reach that number for mobile banking. Société Générale took ten years to achieve twenty million contacts per month through Internet banking but took just eighteen months to achieve that number through mobile bank services.

With this rapid transition from bricks-and-mortar contact to remote, digital contact, it is not surprising that branch numbers are declining, although this varies by region. For example, over half of all the bank branches in the Netherlands have closed in the past decade. You will find

---

11   "Proof that mobile banking is killing the branch," the Finanser, June 2013

similar numbers in many other developed economies. For instance, Danske Bank noted in a presentation in 2011 that teller transactions declined 32 per cent between 2009 and 2011 as mobile Internet banking increased.[12]

On top of this is the fact that Danish banks, along with others in the Nordic nations, have focused on using digital identities to avoid having to on-board customers using a traditional paper-based process. "On-board" is the term used by banks to manage the account-opening process and is incredibly difficult due to the regulatory requirements of Know Your Client (KYC). KYC demands that new customers opening accounts at a bank must prove their identity with various documentation, such as a passport or driving licence as well as proof of address through official letters sent to them recently at that address, such as a utility bill. In contrast, digital identities allow customers to be recognised without the need for such physical documentation, and are the likely way in which banks will manage the KYC process in the future. Nordic banks were the first banks to accept such digital identities for two reasons. First, the governments and banks worked in collaboration to create such capability and, second, because Internet banking became so dominant in the region over the last decade. For example, 80 per cent of the Danish population use Internet banking—double the average in the European Union (EU)—and hence a public/private partnership of development between government and finance was created to develop e-identities. Once created, the e-id can be used to open new financial accounts, without the requirement for a branch visit.

The Nordic countries' use of a digital identity program that is used and shared by both government and banking is to be admired as it means that welfare, health care, benefits and banking are all harmonised and standardised. That is a dream for all.

As part of that dream, Danske Bank closed over one in ten branches (11 per cent) between 2009 and 2011, and that number is increasing. Even

---

more notable, mobile Internet banking is impacting call centres, with calls to the contact centre at Danske falling 14 per cent during this period. This is because balance checks and payment transfers can be achieved easily on a mobile device with an app; who needs to make a call?

All of this is reconstructing the core structure of the bank, its channels and products. ABN AMRO Netherlands states that, on a weekday, a small branch welcomes twenty customers per day. Each of these small branches has an average of two employees servicing twenty customers in an eight-hour day. That's just over one customer served per staff member per hour. That's either amazingly personal service or an awful lot of thumb twiddling during the day waiting for something to happen.

The punch line, however, is that although the bank can see more and more ways to service the customer out of branch, the customer won't let the branch go. For example, ABN AMRO organises its customers into five distinct categories:

- **Intensive channel users** who use all channels regularly
- **Personal contact seeking customers** who want advice and face-to-face service
- **Self-directed people** who think they can do everything themselves
- **Passive hybrid customers** who only talk to the bank when they have to
- **Inactive channel users** who never talk to the bank via any channel

The last two categories represent the least profitable and smallest sector for the bank. In contrast, the first two are the targeted "mass affluent" whilst the mid-category is the majority of the client base.

Amazingly, the majority of those falling into the first three categories answered the following two statements in the affirmative: (1) I prefer to discuss more serious banking issues in person (89 per cent) and (2) In case of problems, I want to be able to go into a branch and speak to someone (94 per cent). In other words, although the bank knows the branch is dead, the customer does not.

This is why, according to research by Forrester in 2012, 80 per cent of all current accounts are opened in branches, 75 per cent of Gen Y customers conclude their product purchases in a branch and 67 per cent of all product sales are made in branch.[13]

This is regardless of the fact that many customers are visiting branches less, but bear in mind this varies from country to country. For example, only 7 per cent of banking customers in the Netherlands visit a bank branch once a month, down from 9 per cent in 2011, while, in Spain, 49 per cent of banking customers still visit a branch once a month.

BRANCH-BASED BANKING IS DEAD

The critical point is that, however long it takes and however slowly, branch-based banking is dead. It is not dead because of technology but because of what technology can do for society. People are not jumping on mobiles and PCs because they want a mobile or a PC. No, they are using mobiles and PCs because of how it provides them with new relationships and connections. People get technology today not because of its gadgets but because it connects their lives to the lives of countless friends and strangers. This is why Facebook went from nothing to a place with the population of the United States in just a few years, and why Twitter went from off the radar to on everyone's radar in just a few months. It is precisely because these media help people to manage, share and organise their lives and loves. That is what banks have to do if they are to reconnect. They must connect people to their money and finances in a simple and easy way, especially if they are to appeal to the new generation of bank consumer.

Today's new consumers see the computer and its operating system as a history lesson. They don't care how technology works, just as I don't care how electricity works. I just like what it can do, and that's how most see technology. They also see banks as a history lesson. Their grandparents went

---

13   "Is there a future for bank branches?" Forrester Research, 9 October 2012

into branches, their parents used ATMs and they just think of banking as an Internet service that organises their finances for them. Tellingly, over half of Americans use Internet banking today while a third use mobile banking.[14]

WHAT IS THE PURPOSE OF A BANK BRANCH?

If banks are starting to completely rethink the bank around social technologies and the reach of mobile and the Internet, then you have to ask: what is the purpose of a bank branch? The mobile Internet and social media have combined to squeeze the bank into a complete rethink of the branch network. These joint pressures are forcing the bank to consider closing most of this network down and reinvesting what it saves into mobile, social finance. If they don't, they're dead. Give it less than a decade, and they'll be dead.

Mainstream media fought this battle ... and lost. That's why television stations and newspapers are shutting down as today's media is created on YouTube and Tumblr.

This means that banks face a lost bank cause of the branch network and will have to rethink it by keeping open the branches needed for sales, and shutting down the rest. There are a number of banks that get this such as eBank and Jibun Bank in Japan, Wells Fargo and Bank of America in the United States and BBVA, Caja Navarra and a few others in Europe. Such banks though are few and far between.

The bank of the future will connect intimately via mobile 24/7. It will not only be proactive, but predictive of customer needs and provide a connection not just to a payment or to money but to a financial lifestyle. And its branches?

Well, the branches are not entirely eradicated. In fact, some branches are very much alive and kicking ... just not as transaction centres. Branches as retail stores are definitely not dead and are unlikely to be for some time. It's just the concept of branch-based banking per se that is dead. Banks will still

---

14   "51% of US adults bank online   Pew Research Report, 7 August 2013

need some branches for sales and relationships, and it is for this reason that the current branch system is dead. Long live the new branch system.

This is very much in keeping with the realignment of other industries. For example, book, record and travel shops have been closing faster than a racing rocket in recent years because such stores had yet to realign to accommodate the new Internet age. Customers had gone online and were self-serving, so the traditional retail stores needed to do something different. That's why most book and media stores are now coffee lounges that encourage reading and entertainment.

Banks tried to do the same thing in terms of becoming coffee lounges that encouraged people to talk about money. That didn't work well; there were simply too many coffee shops around to begin with and customers didn't trust going into bank branches for a free cup of coffee. The few that did then found the staff grimacing as they served it. What this demonstrated is why it is better to wipe the branch slate clean and start all over again. How would you build the branch and the branch network if you were starting all over again?

First, you would probably look around and ask, "Who's got the best retail network?" Your answer might be Marks & Spencer, John Lewis, Tesco or Walmart, all large retailing stores in hypermarkets and shopping centres. Consequently, you would select the largest shopping areas and locate your main stores there. These would be the biggest shopping centres, and the towns and cities with the largest populations.

Then you would ask, "Who has the coolest shops?" Your answer to this question would probably be Apple. Therefore, you would design your mega branch stores to be cool Apple-style sales and advisory centres in the largest locations for shoppers and workers. Would Apple build a store in every city, town, suburb and high street? Of course not. So why did banks do just that and, even worse, still maintain that structure? Because it's their legacy. It's the way things were done in the past. And it's a lesson banks are learning. The lesson is that this is broken, very much like the old record store and bookshop distribution system, which is now dead.

The result is that most banks will eventually rationalise down to just one store for every 250,000 people—or one store for every large town, city and shopping centre—rather than the current structure which allocates about one store for every 20,000 people. The question then is this: What do you do with the 80 per cent of stores that are no longer needed? The ones in the suburbs and smaller high streets? The answer is that you replace them with satellite self-service hub stations, which allow people to self-serve with ATMs and deposit machines. Contrary to what this may imply, these hubs would not disconnect the customer from the human face of the banks as, if you wanted to talk to a human, there would be a remote advisor video terminal for access to advice and, if you wanted to talk face-to-face with a human, the bank would offer an appointment making facility that would enable someone from the bank to visit the customer either at home or at work.

That is bank distribution of the future. In other words, 80 per cent or more of existing branches are closed down and replaced by machines while the remaining 20 per cent are relocated into the best shop and work locations, and become cool mega branches for sales and advice, modelled around Genius Bars, and, yes, a place that encourages you to come in and relax over a cappuccino whilst talking about your money. That still holds true.

Many banks are implementing the above strategy as we speak although this is mainly in economies where the cost of physical distribution is high due to staff and building costs. It does not necessarily apply to countries where it is cheaper to run a branch operation than an IT operation.

BANKS DESIGNED FOR HUMANS, NOT MONEY

This brings us to designing banks for humans. That's what Apple realised early in the day with computers. It is not about computers, but about designing technology for humans. Thus, the design agency that created and designed the Apple stores has always talked about designing branches for people, not money. That's what we want to do with banks, and most of us take Apple as the master class for such designs.

This focus on humans rather than money is best illustrated by the Apple store concept, which was the first to include the Genius Bar, a children's play area and other features that critics thought were a waste of time. When the first Apple store designs were announced, Bloomberg reported: "(Steve) Jobs thinks he can do a better job than experienced retailers. Problem is, the numbers don't add up. I give them two years before they're turning out the lights on a very painful and expensive mistake."[15] However, after opening, it was obvious that the stores were engaging customers in an even more immersive, brand building experience. Eight years later, Apple's New York store became the highest grossing retailer on Fifth Avenue.

In other words, retailing has moved from selling products or services in stores to using the stores as a method of building a sense of community around the brand. A sense of belonging. A sense of ownership. A sense of loyalty.

These are all things that banks aspire for, and some think they have found, but it goes far beyond the traditional retail experience. It's about being part of an immersion in the community. This is the answer to the question: what are branches for? Branches are banks' retail stores to engage their community.

The issue today is that branches were not designed for this purpose. They were designed to look after money and process monetary transactions. They were designed to handle physical forms of cash and cheques, as secure transaction centres. This is the core reason why everyone thinks that branches will disappear because they are not retail stores, engaging the brand community, but instead transaction centres run like some administration process.

So let's start to imagine how the branch experience can become a retail experience fit for 2014 and beyond. I've known for a long time

---

15   "Sorry, Steve: Here's Why Apple Stores Won't Work," Bloomberg, 20 May 2001

that branches were changing as I saw banks like Washington Mutual in the United States deploy its new branch design called Occasio in the mid-2000s.

The radical news about this bank branch design is that it removed the teller counters—the traditional barrier between customer and agent—and started to open the dialogue towards a more human, face-to-face conversation. This new engagement is allowed because the cash disappears, as does the security issue, and far more of the branch front-office focus is allowed to focus on the customer dialogue and interaction.

It then struck me that banks like Caja Navarra and ING Direct were instigating community engagement by having open house sessions. Caja Navarra in Spain offered evening classes in its stores (branches), including hair styling and flower arranging, while ING Direct in the United States offered sessions where anyone could ask questions like "How does a mortgage work?" Umpqua Bank in Oregon did something similar, where the bank could be booked in the evening for cocktail parties or business meetings, rather than leave the branch space dead during those hours. This is because there is no money in the branch anymore; the money is in the data.

Now let's start thinking about the remote experience and the fact that most techno geeks believe no one wants to visit a retail store, or branch, anymore because they can do everything remotely. This may be true but, when we talk about designing banks for humans rather than money, we also want to design banks that engage with humans, not distance them. So the bank that moves to remote servicing must still find ways to get the customer to feel a relationship, and you don't feel or have a relationship with your mobile or tablet computer. You have a relationship with the apps on your mobile and tablet, and with the people you socialise with through those apps. You have a relationship with the friends you call, and some of those friends might even work for your bank.

This is the secret sauce of remote banking leaders like First Direct (*see also* the interview with Paul Say of First Direct) and USAA. They designed their operations specifically on the basis of being remote but want you to feel a relationship with their brands by the amazing service you receive. Their remote services are designed to be as simple, easy and convenient as possible, and when you need to talk to someone, the someone you talk to is amazingly impressive. They are customer focused and engaged, and deal with you as a human and not an account number. They work without scripts and think on their feet, and on their handset. That is why these financial providers consistently get stratospheric customer service results.

Let's now combine the two worlds: the retail store and the remote experience. Can we bring those together into one? Yes, we can. This is precisely what Apple has successfully achieved through stores and online services like iTunes and the App Store with its appcessories. If you ever get confused, you can just go and ask a Genius how it works in the App Store on the high street.

Applying this to the financial sector, the bank designed for humans will not have retail stores that are geared for transactions but instead will have retail stores that reinforce a sense of belonging to their brand community online. Their brand community will be the community of people who are fans of their apps and services on mobiles, tablets and laptops. They may be fans who use the brand in augmented services, like Google Glass, to see if they can afford things as they cook, commute, shop, search, work and exercise. These fans see their financial service embedded in their daily lifestyle, not as something that is transacting but as something that is advising them at their point of living. And every now and again, they feel prompted to go and ask "How does this work?" or "What do I do when ...?" and this puts them into human contact at the bank's Genius Bar in-store or on the telephone.

It's about designing banks for humans, not money or data. That's the secret sauce for today's 21st-century bank, and the core of this design is using data to service humans.

BUILDING A CUSTOMER ADVISORY BANK

In reality, the only reason why digital customers still go to branches is because the bank needs them to visit for regulatory purposes. KYC rules state that customers have to physically go to the bank to show their passport and utility bills in order to open an account. The truth is, therefore, that in today's world of digitisation, people only visit a branch because the rules make it that way. If you stripped away a lot of the rules, then no one would visit a branch. In fact, most would avoid the branch, given the chance.

So here is the challenge for a Digital Bank: how can new customers join with proof of identity, such as a passport, when there aren't any branches? The obvious view might be to have the customer scan and email a picture or send a picture of their passport from their phone but, for most banks in most economies, that is not acceptable by law. The bank has to physically see the passport for KYC and money laundering rules. This is at the heart of the debate about why banks need branches but there is another solution.

If it is inconvenient for the customer to physically come to the branch, why can't the bank go and physically see the customer? This is another alternative for the branch closure discussion, where we will see banks switch from a branch structure to a direct customer advisor operation. In this new digital world, customers handle all of their transactional needs via direct, remote self-service. Cash is all automated via ATM infrastructure and the only residual service is sales and advice.

If the only residual need for face-to-face human interaction is for sales and advice, then why not take the best branch advisory people and give them a car, an iPad and an iPhone (or Android if you prefer) and send them out on the road. Whenever a customer clicks or touches "Make an Appointment" on their online or mobile banking service, they can immediately see a schedule of available times from the direct advisor group and, like booking an appointment with the Genius Bar in the Apple store, you choose your time and location.

Automated online appointment systems have been around for a long time, although many banks still have not deployed such systems, and the biggest gain here is that you would no longer need branches. Or not as many.

This future view would mean that 90 per cent of all bank operations would be managed by the customer and, whenever they needed help, they would still deal with humans either remotely via telephone or direct via an advisory visit to their home or office or, if more convenient, by visiting the bank's überbranch in the nearest city centre. By eradicating most of the branch overheads, a bank could offer this to the mass market and make two strategic gains overnight: cost reduction with increased customer centricity. Now that's what I call building a customer advisory bank.

A TRULY SOCIAL BANK ADVISOR IS THE KEY

When we talk about a customer advisor in the bank who can visit the home, we must also remember the power of today's social media as an advisory tool. We all talk about Facebook and Twitter in the abstract whilst, for most banking people, it's a world in which they are not necessarily engaged. For many bank decision makers and management, using Facebook at work is seen as "wasting time".

This is not the case, however, as some financial firms like AMEX and ICICI Bank are making incredible headway with social media. A bank that truly engages with advising customers via social media is different today, but will be the norm tomorrow. Banks will become part of the social community, not just using these capabilities as public relations or marketing mechanisms, and that really is the difference. If a bank viewed social channels to be of equal importance to their call centre and branch, then they could really engage customers as a remote trusted advisor.

Imagine if you will the bank that picked up on your everyday financial needs as you text, tweet or status update. "Oh I wish I could go to the Scissor Sisters concert tonight," you say on Facebook and your bank says, "You can afford a ticket, and we've found one for you." Wow. Or you tweet "thinking about buying this used Aston Martin" and your bank sends you a direct (private) message saying, "Are you mad? You're already $20,000 overdrawn." Shucks.

Now I know some of you will say, "This is awful. It's big brother bank in reality." The answer here is that this has to be based on permissions-based marketing. If I, for instance, accept that my bank can share my personal updates for "concierge services", then sure, the bank can proactively and contextually advise me.

"Just arriving in Rome," you comment on Foursquare and the bank responds, "Enjoy your stay and our best exchange rate is €1:25. Here are the nearest ATMs to where you are staying."

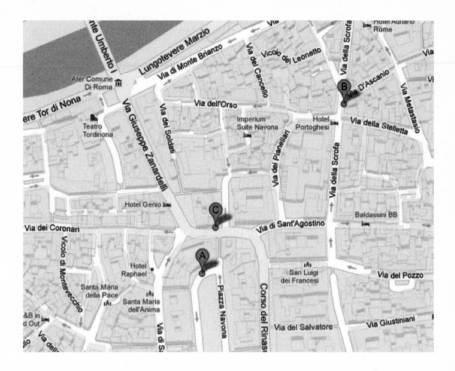

This is really getting my bank to advise me on my spending and saving, and it also shows that I have a truly engaged, permissions inclusive bank relationship, socially enabled through remote channels. And so, if you want to see how social media can move from social marketing to social advisor, then banks that leverage these remote social channels for social relationships will be the ones that really excel.

DIGITAL BANKS DO NOT HAVE CHANNELS

One of the key things that comes along with the branch discussion is the old multichannel nugget. Frequent research shows that the top strategic priority of retail banks is to harmonise and improve cooperation and consistency between branch, Internet and call centre channels. Part of the reason for this, as already shown, is that branch sales are declining, thus the relevance of the branch is decreasing, whilst Internet sales of bank products are increasing year-on-year so, consequently, the focus on mobile Internet is increasing too.

However, talking about channels in this way is wrong because it diverts attention from integrating digital servicing with human services.

"We've got our contact centre, then there's our Internet banking division and now we have to integrate these mobile thingamajigs. These channels are never-ending, wail, wail, sniff, sniff."

Banks that think this way think the wrong way as mobile is *not* a channel. Internet banking is *not* a channel. Call centres and ATMs are *not* channels. Nothing is a channel. Things have changed.

Our planet is populated by people who have digital personas that are tightly integrated with their physical lives. We walk the street texting, talking, surfing and interacting. We geolocate our address and are smart navigated to our destination via the My Maps app. We check what's on TV whilst reading newspapers on digitised screens. We transact with each other person-to-person, face-to-face, end-to-end.

In the very near future, every single person on the planet will be connected this way and, in that same near future, they will think differently too. In fact, we are already starting to do so. This is why we don't think, i.e. "I'm on my mobile channel and I shall switch to my Internet channel later." We don't think "Now I'm doing digital stuff and, shortly, I'll do some physical stuff." My digital stuff is my physical stuff. It's all tightly coupled into my, and everyone else's, life.

This is why we have to stop thinking of channels and multichannels. It's a fundamental flaw in bank thinking. There are no channels. Just everyday lives that are highly digitised for the 21st century. We talk about multichannel, or omnichannel as people prefer to call it today, strategies, but I do not believe in a multichannel or omnichannel strategy, just a strategy of how to deliver augmented service to the customer at the point of relevance. For me, that is a digitised delivery of service, proactively via my mobile today and soon through my watch or glasses. That's what I want, but not everyone wants that. Some people want branch-based service and some want contact with the call centre. Not everyone wants to have a pure remote service that is digitised and augmented to serve at the point of relevance.

TALK ABOUT CUSTOMERS, NOT CHANNELS

In fact, the whole omnichannel thing really does not exist. Channels are what banks deploy to reach customers. Customers are looking for service that is relevant to their needs, such as buying a home. Customers want service delivered in the way that is relevant to them and in the way that they like. So it is not the bank reaching out to customers through channels, but customers reaching out to banks through needs.

That is why I much prefer talking about omnicustomers rather than omnichannels. The omnicustomer differs by segment, demographic, perspective, adoption of technology. Some customers want all digital, some want all face-to-face. The bank's challenge is to design the service for every customer so that they get the experience they want. Or rather, the challenge for the bank is to design experience for customers such that they get the experience they want through the channels the bank prefers to deploy. Thus the key is to get the omnicustomer to migrate to the bank's channels of preference.

This is the core of a debate that occurs regularly with banks when I discuss the role of branches with them. For example, in a recent conversation, a bank argued that small- and medium-sized enterprises (SMEs) need branches. Yes, some do. Some SMEs deal in lots of cash and coins, and that creates a real need for a branch-based bank service as there is a physical need for deposits. But do SMEs need branches to get a loan? Not necessarily. I'm an SME, and my bank manager comes to my office once a year for a review of my financial needs. Branches can be replaced by direct sales and direct service managers.

So then we get to the core of the discussion: Who needs branches? People who like their contact with the staff in the branch? People who want to feel there is a physical space to see where their money is? People who are resistant to change? People who have not been introduced to the alternatives? People who are unsure of the alternatives and need to be educated to discover what they can do?

A little like the many people who resisted getting a mobile phone as they were just for yuppies (young, upwardly mobile professionals) but now depend on them or the people who thought they didn't need the Internet until it became a consumer proposition. Those who still do not use mobile or Internet banking do so for a variety of reasons: fear, insecurity, distrust, lack of access, lack of knowledge and more.

My suspicion therefore is that if banks put in concentrated programmes to migrate customers from branch to remote channels, with immersion workshops and programmes offered to show people how they work, then they would find far faster take-up of their remote channel offers and far simpler abilities to reduce branch-based costs and operations.

It reminds me of the experience I had working with a bank in the 1990s when it tried to migrate customers to the self-serve machines in branch for deposits and cash withdrawals. The bank had made this huge investment in automating the transactions in branches but only a small percentage of customers were using the self-serve machines. Therefore, the bank started a programme of focus to get customers to use them.

Members of staff were deployed as concierges in all branches to greet and meet customers and ask if they would like to see how the machines worked. And the programme worked. Mature customers were delighted to have the chance to try the machines with assistance, as were busy mothers. Both consumer groups had previously shunned the machines because they did not know how to use them or did not have the time.

The only customer group that proved to be truly resistant to the programme were male account holders. Yep, the testosterone-driven male felt that no education was needed and no bank could force him to use a machine if he didn't want to use it. Young males being the most resistant by the way. I suspect this would be the same if banks pushed mobile banking heavily, but at least it would get a further third to two-thirds of customers out of branches.

THE DIGITAL BANK IS THE AUGMENTED BANK

Therefore, as we see customers migrating to digitised service, we can find in the designs of new banks that there is a realisation of banking not being fit for today's digital customer—unless it becomes the Digital Bank.

The Digital Bank does not believe in channels, and any mention of multichannel strategies is outlawed in the Digital Bank. In fact, the Digital Bank wholly focuses on customer lifestyle, how they choose to relate to and communicate with their financial provider and how to deliver augmented digital servicing as part of their customers' day-to-day lives.

This is proactive fulfilment at the point of life, rather than reactive services at the point of interaction. Proactive fulfilment is all about recognising customer activity through opt-in services, and enriching a person's or corporate's day-to-day financial needs as they arise. This is what we get today from Amazon and Apple. I don't need to fill in multiple forms to order that book or song, just click-to-pay or confirm. But proactive fulfilment in the Digital Bank goes far further than this. It will recognise my movements through global system for mobile communications (GSM) tracking and provide me with alerts and offers as I live my daily life. The Digital Bank will recognise that I looked at a new LCD TV on Google last night for $499 and, as I walk past the electronics store, will offer me a coupon with a quick response (QR) code[16] to buy that TV now for $449 at a saving of $50.

The Digital Bank is already here, in fact. Just look at Google Wallet and Apple Passport, neither is a bank. It is a bank-like service that leverages data at the front end and financial transaction processing at the back end.

The Digital Bank goes further than proactive fulfilment, as it can actively seek to direct customer behaviour through rewards. Buy your goods with this retail store, and we will automatically give you an extra 5 per cent discount if you use our bank to pay as they are our bank's loyalty programme sharing partner. Save more than 10 per cent of your earnings per month and we will give you a "Saver King" or "Saver Queen" badge to share with all your friends on Facebook.

In fact, the Digital Bank will be the Augmented Bank as it will recognise that anything can transact with anything person-to-person, person-to-machine or even machine-to-machine. Transactions become embedded in everything from underpants to escalators through the placement of Radio Frequency IDentification (RFID) chips inside everything. This means that everything will be intelligently and wirelessly communicating with everything through what is now called the Internet of things. The Internet of

---

16   A quick response (QR) code is a barcode that is readable by camera telephones. The code consists of black modules arranged in a square on a white background and can be linked to text, URL or other data.

things delivers a new wireless augmented world of digital reality where, in the very near future, fifty billion devices will be communicating with each other.

THE INTERNET OF THINGS

The Internet of things is where Internet communication—both wired and wireless—is placed into everyday objects from cars to refrigerators, keys to key rings, jewellery to watches and more. Basically, anything that can have a chip placed inside it. We will all soon be wearing and watching and being monitored by chips in everything, and the vision of the Internet of things is just that: ubiquitous connectivity with everything communicating and transacting non-stop.

The key point about the Internet of things is that it will be the next big wave of change. It may take ten years or so but, just as we were talking about Internet banking in the early 1990s and it became the next big wave of change in the 2000s, the Internet of things is going to be our next big wave of change and opportunity. This everything, everywhere connected world where everything can trade and transact is a huge opportunity and change for banks, and the banks that change today will win.

When you can put a chip inside anything and everything, you can track, trace, communicate and trade with anything and everything. Cars, phones, walls, ceilings, books, posters, glass, bricks and even babies.

This means that banks today should be trying to work out exactly what form of trade and transaction they will be offering and enabling when anything communicates with everything, everywhere. Questions that should be asked and answered include:

- What will be the process?
- Who will be the providers?
- How will security and authentication work?
- When will banks start deploying products and services that leverage this capability?

We can see the opportunity this change offers today, thanks to Near Field Communication (NFC), and RFID will provide the Internet of things with the ability to transact. When we talk about chips inside everything, so that they can wirelessly communicate, those chips in everything will be RFID chips today. As RFID can only hold a small amount of intelligence right now, it needs something to receive the RFID information and that something is NFC. Hence, NFC will become the reader mechanism in phones and other devices for RFID in the Internet of things.

Today, you buy things by taking them to the cashier; tomorrow, if you want to buy something, you will just have to read the QR code or hold your phone over its RFID tag. In addition, in the near future, the Internet of things will be driven by the mobile Internet of things, where everything is geolocated and identified by the network.

It is this network- and chip-driven transaction system that is the point. The network-centric view, where everything is monitored real time via the network, is the more sophisticated, intelligent and likely future scenario but the chip-based transaction system may well play an enabling short- to medium-term role in allowing the network to track the transactions.

THE REASON WHY THE CHANNEL DISCUSSION IS WRONG

As can be seen, the near future will be driven by Digital Banks that use augmented realities to track and trace their customers and deliver proactive, location-relevant servicing. The Digital Bank will be pervasive and not recognise channels as it purely exists in every digital space that its digital customers live in. So why do we talk about channels? Why do we talk about multichannel, omnichannel banks? Why do we try to deal with channel integration? Because of history.

The first new bank channels were introduced in the early 1990s. Back then, call centres were a problem and the ATM was being discussed as something that might be used as a marketing channel. Then the Internet hit and email rose as a communication tool with the banks. Yes, amazingly, this was an issue way back in the dim, distant past.

As a result, technology companies started to talk about multichannel because there was now the branch, call centre, ATM and the Internet. Even television was being considered a possible channel as interactive TVs were on trial. Multichannel tried to address the issues of the separation and gaps between channels, and technology firms offered integrators and middleware to try to create a single customer view on a single platform. The concept was to enable bank consistent interaction across branch, ATM, call centre and the Internet.

Just to emphasise the point, I delivered a presentation back in 1997. Even then, we were talking about the rise of 24/7 mobile and wireless banking. We called it Martini Banking back then because the summer party drink branded itself with the tagline "anytime, anyplace, anywhere". Now we are talking about *everything, everywhere banking*, and still having the same discussion as back then. Today we talk about social media but, back then, we also talked about online communities and the experience economy based on increasing consumer demands.

In fact, looking back at those old presentation slides amazes me as much of what we talked about then is still being talking about today: customer experience, loyalty, advocacy, service, data mining for personalisation and, yes, multichannel integration. Except that today, as I've already said, we prefer to call it omnichannel, but it's essentially the same discussion.

Back in the 1990s, multichannel was an issue as customers were starting to interact over many channels and consistency was a big challenge:

- Could the branch tell the customer the same thing the customer read online yesterday?
- Would the call centre know what the branch said?
- Could the ATM be used to provide advisory notes on receipts?

All of these issues needed some sort of multichannel integration. Indeed, these issues remain today but the difference is that we are now in an even bigger dilemma as answering emails and phone calls has escalated to sending and responding to text alerts, blog comments, tweets, Facebook and more.

The issue is clearly highlighted by the rise in user-generated data with the amount of global digital information created and shared exploding in the 2000s. In fact, from 2005 to 2011, the amount of information being created and shared, from documents to pictures to tweets, rose ten-fold to almost 2 zettabytes (2 trillion gigabytes), and is increasing every day. Equally, the demand for remote access to services via the Internet is increasing fastest in emerging, developing and growth economies.

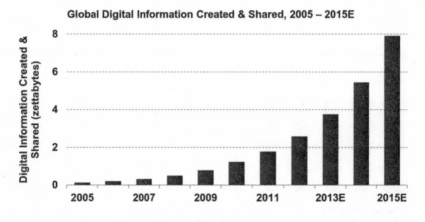

Global Digital Information Created & Shared, 2005 – 2015E

Source: Gantz, J. and David Reinsel. "Extracting Value from Chaos." International Data Corporation, June 2011

The immensity of demand over remote channels has significantly changed the mix and complexity of handling multichannel interactions, and handling them consistently is now even more key. After all, I wouldn't want the branch to say it couldn't offer me a loan after going through an online self-assessment test the previous evening at the end of which I'm told it's no problem. Similarly, I wouldn't want a call centre to ring offering a loan when I'd just paid one off the previous night through my mobile payments app.

CONSISTENT CHANNELS IS A CRITICAL PART OF THE DIGITAL BANK

As mentioned, Digital Banks do not separate their channels but view their combined digitisation as a way of providing augmented and consistent servicing. When the human elements are combined with the digitisation, it creates an augmented whole of holistic service. This is a challenge for incumbent banks but I have found one or two examples of banks that are evolving and adapting their offers to support the augmented digital realities of today.

For example, Wells Fargo in the United States provides personalised ATM messages. Its ATMs include customised screens based on customer preferences, and favourite activities are highlighted on screen based on previous usage of the ATM by the customer. There is also a tool called ATM Cash Tracker that allows customers to visually track their monthly withdrawals. The tool allows customers to set a monthly withdrawal target and see details about how much they withdrew the previous month, as well as their average withdrawals per month over the past year. This delivers consistency across channels from personalised ATMs to personal financial management.

Another example of leadership in innovation can be seen at Alior Bank in Poland. Alior Bank was launched in November 2008, with the aim of gaining market share of 2 to 4 per cent of the retail banking sector in Poland by 2012. By November 2012, the bank had more than achieved this aim with 4.0 per cent market share in mortgages (new volumes), 3.2 per cent in consumer loans and 3.8 per cent in current accounts. It has 1.4 million clients and is the number one bank by new client acquisition, breaking even after just 22 months. By comparison, the branch-based bank start-up in Britain, Metro Bank, made losses of over £100 million in its first three years of operation.[17]

---

17   Metro Bank's losses exceeded £100 million in May 2013, three years after its July 2010 launch. The bank made pre-tax losses of £45.7 million in 2012 but the bank's expansion plans will not be affected as it has the backing of deep-pocketed shareholders including hedge fund giant Steve Cohen and the billionaire Reuben Brothers.

Alior Bank made its debut on the Warsaw Stock Exchange in December 2012, with an initial share offer valued at 57 zlotys ($18). The bank's share offer proved to be the largest initial public offering (IPO) by a private company on the Warsaw Stock Exchange ever and, by August 2013, the shares had almost doubled in value, trading at 100 zlotys ($32) each.

One of the keys to Alior's success is its virtual bank offer. This is a fully virtual, 24 hours a day, 7 days a week online bank branch, with a complete variety of contact options including video conversations and video chats. The virtual branch not only offers conversation and advice; customers can also buy products and request consultants to complete application forms for them. The forms are displayed on screen as they are processed, enabling the customer to easily follow the progress of the application.

There are dedicated mobile applications for these features available at the Apple and Google stores, providing full accessibility and integration of the bank's services through smartphone devices. The mobile applications offer a number of additional features such as:

- looking up personal saving status by shaking the smartphone
- quick domestic transfers (also instant transfers) via mobile
- using social networks such as Facebook to transfer money
- money transfers with the use of the camera on a smartphone (by simply taking a photo of an invoice)

The bank's entertainment zone offers free music, movies and cinema tickets. Furthermore, you can buy smartphones, holidays and other products with a special discount and 0 per cent instalment plans. This bank is on the leading edge of innovation and other banks, such as BRE Bank in Poland, have been forced to transform to compete (see "mBank, Poland: A Bank that Killed Its Parent" later in this chapter).

What both Alior and Wells Fargo show is that banks need to deliver social mobile personalisation and virtualisation to compete today. That is fine but it goes further than this. The Digital Bank goes further than just having consistency across channels and interactions. A Digital Bank needs deep data mining and intelligent data mining to compete in the age of the Digital Bank.

Mining customer data intelligently is going to be critical and banks should be personalising services based on the customer's digital footprints. Customers' digital footprints can easily be followed as the bank knows the address of the computer or mobile device that they are using from their IP address, chip or SIM card. From this identification, my bank, for example, would soon discover, on a permissions basis, that I had been looking at its mortgage offers. Would it not then be great marketing if someone from the bank were to call the next day and ask, "Can we clarify anything related to our mortgage offers? Is there anything you are considering specifically and did the online service answer all of your questions?"

I know that some may find that scenario scary but it will all be based on accepting terms and conditions to allow the bank to have that marketing capability. In other words, it is permissions based, and some will accept this and some will not. I personally like it and, as a bank service, believe this will again become more predominant and notable.

After all, it's all about happy people = happy customers = happy business, and the more that technology can manage and bridge those gaps to create consistent service, responsive people and profitable products, the better.

THE MULTICHANNEL MYTH

As mentioned, I've worked with banks regarding multichannel integration and adding new capabilities to the core traditional channel of branch operations for years, and the mistake we made was building from history rather than revolutionising for the future.

We added ATMs because they reduced costs. We added call centres because new competitors were eating our lunch. We added the Internet because we thought we could close branches. And now we're adding mobile because it's the latest fad for customer service.

For all those years, we did the best we could to keep up but we failed. We failed because multichannel simply does not work. Instead we created mixichannel. *Mixi* meaning "mixed up". Instead of focusing on these new channels of innovative offers for new products and services, we added these channels as cost reduction programmes for self-service and branch rationalisation. As a result, call centres, Internet and mobile services have been added onto existing operations rather than engineered specifically for these services.

There are exceptions.

In the case of the call centre, First Direct was one of the first movers to make this channel work, and is the United Kingdom's leader in this area. First Direct built its bank around a remote telephone based centre rather than adding call centre to branch operations. Therefore, the difference is that First Direct has processes designed for remote customer reach rather than a process designed for administering customer service when the branch is closed.

In the case of the Internet, the United Kingdom's leading Internet bank is Smile. Smile is a bank designed to exploit Internet self-servicing rather than adding traditional bank processes to a home-based self-service channel.

And in the case of mobile, we now have a new dedicated mobile bank, Moven, which recently opened in the United States and is soon to launch in the United Kingdom.

What's the point?

The point is this: the banks that automated in the 1970s are still banks of the 1970s. The reason why their call centre operations ask for name and account number, and focus on balance and transaction statements, is because they view the branch as the key contact point. The reason their Internet services are dull and boring is because they are just automating statements online, rather than leveraging and using broadband-based social media, and their mobile services are often the same. This is because technology is being added to the bank focused around operations dating to the 1970s, rather than using the technology to design a new bank specifically for that technology. Given this, when a bank is designed around the technology, it wipes the floor of the competition.

First Direct is not only the United Kingdom's largest call centre based bank, it's also one of the country's favourite banks. Smile is not only an Internet designed bank for Internet access but, again, also one of the United Kingdom's favourite banks. According to a BBC survey of 13,000 UK viewers in 2010, these two banks were the top banks for customer satisfaction and service in the country. To make my point once again, if I may, both of these are banks without branches designed for the channels of today, rather than banks with branches that added these channels onto their traditional structures.

In Japan, Jibun Bank and eBank are similar, and yet more innovative because of their use of mobile services. eBank has half of the Internet banking market in Japan, as a bank designed for the Internet. Jibun Bank has also stormed up the bank charts, as a bank designed for the mobile.

Interestingly, it's not about banks closing down and being eaten by new competition because all of these banks, other than eBank, are owned by traditional branch-based banks. What it says is that a bank is far more likely to be successful with a new channel if it designs a bank for that channel rather than tagging on the technology as another layer at the top of its branch operations. In other words, to create a multi-branded bank. This is because banks are not great at multichannel but usually excel in a single channel. So the answer here is to create a separately branded bank for each channel.

Some banks have already started such a process—HSBC with First Direct being a case in point—but the idea of a bank that brands by channel is not yet a clear strategic market move, but maybe it should be. A bank that has a branch-based bank brand (HSBC), a call centre based bank brand (First Direct), an Internet-based bank brand (Smile) and a mobile-based bank brand (Moven).

Now that flies directly in the face of my earlier assertion that there is no channel separation, just digitally augmented realities. The challenge with that assertion is that each bank brand is launched at a different moment in time: branches (pre-1970s), call centres (1980s), Internet (1990s) and mobile (2000s). Each launch therefore has a layer of legacy, which is the challenge for the traditional bank to keep up.

The pre-1970s bank is hamstrung by heritage. Even the Internet-based bank of the 1990s is challenged by mobile as its existence is not designed for that channel. For example, one UK bank launched its Internet bank service in 2010 and has already dropped it and reinvented for mobile.

Branding by design for channel is possibly a way to ensure that banks can keep up with innovations, as each iteration of the bank will be launched with fresh infrastructure and a fresh start. The downside is obviously that the cost overhead of new brands and new banks is onerous but at least it means that each bank is fit for the future and, as old parts of the bank decline, the bank can close down the failing parts far more easily.

BRINGING DESIGN THINKING INTO BANKS

As part of this change, banks need to bring creativity into banking and bank design. If the customer is refreshed and has new technology, the bank needs the same but, in many cases, the bank is not. The bank is hamstrung by heritage technologies, and technology is not about interacting with organisations but interacting with people as they live their lives. That is why the core systems of banks need changing.

After all, twenty years ago, banking was all about an account number. That is how banks managed their customers, as numbers. In the space of two decades, banks have moved from *account numbers to relationships*, and the focus of their systems today needs to be on building relationships with customers through remote, digitised processes.

There cannot be systems designed for the internal organisation when the customer is renewed and when their technology has been refreshed. There cannot be old style systems when customers have refurbished. That is why so many banks are changing core systems today.

Banks are doing so because they are trying to focus on how customers want to communicate and consume services, which is predominantly through mobile and IT, and this complex interaction between humans, organisation and technology is the friction we live with today.

Within this however is the greatest unknown quantity, which is the human capacity for design and creativity. The world has given the customer the ability to create and share their lives through technology, and it is their creativity in design that is changing the process, the system, the structure and the interaction.

Banks should give thanks to Google, Apple and Facebook for enabling customers to create and share anything at anytime with anyone. Anyone can create anything and, if it's popular, it is valuable. By way of example, software and information design companies like Polaris are now able to design and create anything for banking. In fact, they have the ability to disintermediate IT. They can design new services for banks, they can create and they can put it out there before banks are even thinking about it. The biggest challenge then is:

- How to convert the business?
- How to persuade the bank to change?
- How to get the organisation to move?
- How to make the elephant dance?

The only way to do this is to cannibalise the organisation and create friction within the bank to renew the bank. Freedom fighters are needed to bring down the old and create the new. This freedom force is effectively the innovation group who are there to destroy the old bank organisation. That is why this group has to be separated from the existing organisation, as the existing organisation wants to keep the business as it is. In other words, the innovators fight the Business-as-Usual.

Business-as-Usual will fight any change, as they created what is there today. It is almost like going to the Business-as-Usual people and saying,

"What you built was wrong." This is why Business-as-Usual is not interested in destroying the existing organisation. That is why the innovators are needed to challenge all aspects of the Business-as-Usual, and work out how to regenerate the organisation. The core direction to the innovators is to focus on the outcomes.

- What are the key outcomes for the customer?
- What does the customer want from the bank?
- How do they see the bank?
- How do they want to deal with the bank?

This is precisely what Poland's mBank recently strived to do and, in so doing, it cannibalised the bank.

mBANK, POLAND: A BANK THAT KILLED ITS PARENT

mBank is owned by BRE Bank and, in 2013, BRE bank determined to rebrand the bank entirely as mBank. mBank was a sub-brand of BRE Bank for its Internet banking and launched in 2000 to support its online activities. How come the Internet bank has taken over the core bank? Because it makes sense.

BRE Bank was launched in the 1980s and is now Poland's fourth-largest bank. In 2000, with the rise of the Internet, BRE Bank launched mBank, a pure-play online bank. As an Internet-only bank, it rose rapidly to become Poland's biggest online bank and its third-largest retail bank. Thanks to its success, mBank expanded into neighbouring markets in the Czech Republic and Slovakia in 2007.

In 2012, the bank realised that there were significant changes taking place in the banking markets due to the use of mobile social media. Consequently, it decided to redesign the bank from scratch based on four key tenets:

- real-time marketing
- personal financial management (PFM)
- mobile banking
- social media

This was not a lightly made decision as it involved investing over $30 million for a complete redesign of the bank. On top of this, it resulted in the bank dropping its original brand—BRE Bank—and replacing it with the mBank brand, complete with a new logo and refreshed look and feel.

The transformation took fourteen months, with the transactional service built from scratch by a team of 200 bank employees in collaboration with partners including Accenture, Artegence and Meniga. The website, mBank. pl, is the main communication vehicle of the new brand and was designed and developed by Artegence and Intercon Systems.

The new service offers over 200 new functions and improvements including the following:

- Customers can use a smart transaction search engine, which is as easy as using Google on the Internet, to search through their transaction history, with results displayed in real time.
- Paying for things can be done the usual way or customers can make direct payments to friends and family via Facebook and text messages.
- Customers no longer need to remember or ask for account numbers and can use phone numbers or social network connections instead.
- Facebook transfers appear on the home page of the person who is sent the money and are just messages sent with cash attached.
- PFM is provided to allow budgets and alerts, in which the system clearly explains when money was spent and what for, along with a forecast of overall spending by the end of the month.
- An online expert is available 24/7 via a video or voice connection.
- Gamification in the bank's transactional service encourages sensible spending and saving.

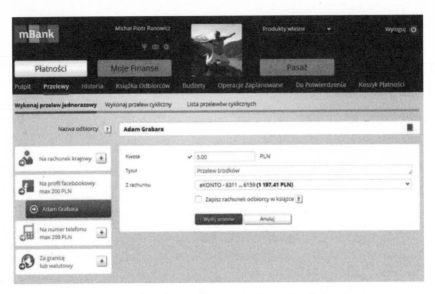

mBank's online services include being able to make payments via Facebook.

The bank has already won several awards for these innovations and it is no wonder as it's the first bank mobile social solution that comes close to delivering the new retail banking reality.

DIGITAL BANKS ARE HERE AND NOW

In reality, the Digital Bank is already here with banks like mBank and others such as FIDOR, Moven, Simple, Jibun, eBank, ICICI Bank and Deniz Bank. Each of these is delivering different versions of new business models for today's 21st-century customer.

All of these banks recognise that the basis of competition is not related to their digital channel, but their digital service. It is not a channel play but an augmented customer service play that will define their competitive success. They all are focused on the customer's point of existence, and delivering digitised financial services that are highly personalised at the point of relevance to those customers. This is the objective that these banks are striving to achieve by incorporating augmented servicing through the Internet of things.

This is the core change that the Digital Bank demands of the traditional banks. While most traditional banks are working to get there, they are hamstrung by their heritage systems, heritage structures and heritage thinking. That has to change if they are going to be capable of competing in this digital world.

BUILDING RELATIONSHIPS THROUGH DIGITAL BANKING

One of the big things about the Digital Bank is that it must be a human bank. Just because the bank is digital does not mean that it is automated and robotic. In fact, it means the opposite. A Digital Bank actually has to be more human than a branch-based bank because it needs to exude intuitive and intimate customer understanding through technology. In order to do that, it must really understand its customers and the human interaction with technology. This is the secret sauce that makes the Digital Banks of the 21st century far more competitive in their execution of technology than the banks that simply add the technology as an adjunct to their branch operations.

Specifically, Digital Banks need to advise customers about finance by providing strong customer engagement through remote channels and so, rather than KYC, Digital Banks need to focus on Know Your Customer's Context (KYCC). This is the leverage of location-based services combined with data leverage of the customer's needs, wishes and challenges.

The Digital Bank therefore engages with the customer through the customer's preferred access. That may mean that the bank offers sign in using Facebook, Twitter or LinkedIn, where opening an account takes place in under a day using the KYC from the customer's existing bank. Bearing in mind that customer interfaces have changed from keyboard to touch, this also means rethinking the bank offer, moving from click-to-see to scroll-to-see. This is a key point in the tablet age: touch screen users do not click. They scroll and slide.

Mobile tablet computing has made Digital Banking far more focused. For example, placing a clear contact telephone number on all web and mobile pages is critical as you want to encourage the customer to call and have a conversation, not just be left to scroll, slide, touch and type. After all, if you want to encourage customer interaction, what better way than making sure they can call you from their mobile screen than by providing a one-touch to call?

These nuances are all part of the theme of designing the Digital Bank from a human perspective, and designing the bank for the way in which the customer wishes to interact.

In fact, a good way to contextualise this is to view how mobile adoption has taken place in five waves:

- **The first wave** involved people using mobiles to find information.
- **The second wave** used mobiles to transact.
- **The third wave** allowed interaction with the financial provider through remote services.
- **The fourth wave**, where we are today, allows anyone with a mobile smartphone to manage everything on the move, 24/7, 365 days a year.
- **The fifth wave** will arrive in the very near future where everything communicates in the Internet of things to find you.

Regarding the fifth, and last, wave, it will mean you no longer search for things on the net but things find you through the net. That is a critical point as it means the customer will no longer be reaching out to the Digital Bank, but the Digital Bank will need to reach out to the customer by being relevant at their point of life.

This is why we do not have channels today. As stated in the previous chapter, there's no such thing as multichannel, let alone omnichannel; we just have a reality augmented by digital services. This is why the Digital Bank has to go further than just allowing customers to design their financial management as they see fit, to banks applying different views for account management by account segment.

Each account segment of the bank's customer base should be able to design their own way of viewing their money from young to old, male to female, Caucasian to Indian, Catholic to Jew and so on. By doing so, it provides skins, or personas, for each customer's user experience with the bank in a way that suits the customer. The customer designs the bank for them rather than the bank designing one size fits all.

Everyone should be able to have a view of their account management by age, sex, ethnicity and religion and more, as they see fit. This goes beyond the old way of doing Internet skins, where we just change the front end view of an account, to being the core of how we structure and present account information. It means the bank has componentised so that customers can allocate and integrate components of the bank in a way that suits them.

But that's a long way off as most banks today have transactional style systems presenting transactional style statements. Many banks have yet to move beyond a credit and debit view of a personal financial management view to a mobile financial management view. In fact, only a very small number of leading-edge banks are offering the true view: a view that suits the way in which each and every customer uniquely wants to see their money.

And the core of everything comes down to human design, which is why we have human interaction at the heart of everything. Human interaction is the reason why 90 per cent of account openings come through branches whilst 90 per cent of account services are self-served.

And if we can design more of the humanity into those remote transaction services, then eventually we may just be able to design customer experiences whereby 90 per cent of account openings also come through remote services.

BANKS DESIGNED FOR HUMANS BY GEEKS

When designing our Digital Bank with a human touch, the processes need to be designed by true designers who understand anthropology, empathy, engagement and the human experience of technology. The objective for the Digital Bank being to get to the customer 24/7 as they have financial needs, wants, desires and thoughts.

This is all about deep data drilling and the reason why banks are engaged in data wars, with the data being the key. Nevertheless, deep data drilling to proactively, predictively serve the customer could be creepy. That is why the starting point of the humanised Digital Bank is to ensure that this is all performed on a permissions basis. The permission is upfront and easily accessible at any time, and tells the customer that you are using their data to give them the best service possible. This means analysing the data, leveraging the data and potentially sharing the data with other divisions of the bank, partners and service providers. In return, this means that the customer will get better service with offers and discounts. It is a value exchange where the customer shares personal data to get more value from the bank in return and, as mentioned, the customer can easily opt out at any time. The key is getting the permission of the customer to leverage their data to give them better service.

Once a bank has the customer's permission to leverage their data, then the core message is about designing for humans rather than for money. Designing a bank for humans rather than money also challenges traditional bank operations because these operations were built for one point of emphasis— the branch—and are now struggling because banks no longer deal with that person face-to-face. Instead, they deal with a human at their point of need or want or desire or thought remotely. This is what the data geeks are really drilling for: to get to the customers 24/7 as they have financial needs, wants, desires and thoughts, and that is then all delivered remotely.

Now that sounds a bit creepy—not the geek thing, but the deep data drilling—and it could be, but you have to remember that this is all performed on a permissions basis. The idea would be that you could track a customer's mobile digital footprint in real time and, using geolocation, deliver proactive offers to that customer at their point of context.

Take the following example. I'm looking to buy a house. First, I do some searches online. The bank does not know about these searches but Google does and tips off the bank—on a permissions opt-in basis, of course—to let them know that I am house hunting. By coincidence, I get an email offering a great mortgage deal but I'm not that serious yet so I just ignore it.

Then I go into an estate agency and discuss what type of house I'm looking for. I see a few houses but I'm not sure that I can afford any of them so I bring up the bank app and look at how much a month I would be paying on a higher loan-to-value mortgage, and whether I could get one. Of course, the app lets me do the calculations and, just as I'm closing the app, it gives me a reminder that the bank has that great mortgage deal waiting for me if I want it. I don't. Yet.

I then find the house I want and am now getting serious. Time to look for a mortgage. Of course, I'm not going to take the bank's offer. Instead, I do a search on a comparison site to see what the best mortgage deals are. I find a competitor's rate is better and start to fill in its application form online. Now here's where it gets creepy—and maybe interesting. Before I process my application with the competitor, my phone receives a text message. It's 10:30 at night. Who's texting? It's Nitin, my bank relationship manager. The text reads: "Hi Chris, Nitin here from D-Bank. Can we talk about a mortgage tomorrow morning? We'll give you a better deal." Sure, I think. Let's wait till tomorrow.

Nitin calls me at 9:30 the following morning and tells me about the deal he can do. It's good. The interest rate is 0.1 per cent lower than the best rate I could find online, and a longer term. I ask him why the bank didn't offer me that rate upfront, and instead led me to believe the previous offer had been the bank's best rate. It was, he tells me, but the bank wants to keep me as a customer and recognises my loyalty (it's actually in order to cross-sell me all the other things that will make up for the 0.1 per cent loss of margin but I don't know or care about that as a customer).

As UK regulations require all mortgage applications to be signed in person before they are approved, I arrange to meet Nitin in branch to sign the forms. And by happening into the branch, I suddenly realise how much more the bank can do for me.

First, I'm amazed by the cappuccino that I'm served. Next I'm amazed at how lovely the branch feels. Then I'm more amazed at how much Nitin knows about me. He's aware of my salary increase two months ago, the fact that I do my shopping at Tesco, the news that my car loan with Ford Finance will finish in October, making me £500 a month better off, and more. It's almost as though Nitin is me.

As I leave the bank, I start playing with my PFM app on my mobile, looking at the balance of money between the mortgage I'll be taking out and the car loan that comes to an end in October, and realise that I could have afforded the slightly more expensive house that I hadn't looked at because the mortgage payments would have been £250 a month more than I could afford. From October, I could afford them. Wow! So I start heading for the estate agency to arrange a viewing on that house.

I've only taken a few short steps from the bank when I get an alert from Nitin via text again: "Yes Chris, we'll keep the same mortgage over the same term at £2,750 a month"—I had been looking at paying £2,250 a month— "and will reduce rates by a further 0.15 per cent if you can conclude the application process before the end of the month."

I could keep this scenario going further, but you get the idea. Yes, it may seem creepy but equally some would call it service and, in order to get that service, I've given the bank and Nitin permission to mine my data. Does it seem creepy to you when Apple recommends songs you might like or Amazon suggests books you might want to read? No, so why is it creepy when banks recommend things? Mainly because we don't trust banks in the same way because banks deal with our ability to pay while Apple and Amazon deal with trying to get us to buy.

We like buying things, we just don't like paying for them. That gets me to the real point, which is that the digitisation of the relationship needs harmonisation with the real world. We do have real-world needs for advice and support and always will. We just need to marry those real-world needs with the fact that our digital footprint today can augment and enhance our relationship with money and with our bank far more than it ever did before. And, for a bank, the biggest problem is how to harmonise the data and digital analysis across its legacy, which was built for channel silos rather than omnichannel integration.

DEALING WITH CUSTOMERS THROUGH REMOTE CHANNELS

When discussing the challenges and opportunities related to dealing with customers through remote channels, we often start with how this improves the customer experience. Everyone agrees that we live in a highly volatile period, where customers can interact in any way they want, and it will take some years for financial institutions to find the right way to reach the right customer through the right channel.

Nearly all of the banks that I talk to deal with customers through call centre, Internet and mobile channels, as well as through direct store operations, and the majority view is that delivering a fantastic customer experience is a real challenge.

It is more of a challenge for existing operators than new entrants because the incumbents have the issue of a variety of different platforms and technologies that have been built up over time. There is then the extra confusion of various acquisitions and mergers, which is the reason why many firms suffer from legacy spaghetti infrastructures that constrain them from change and flexibility.

That is the barrier to delivering great customer experiences through remote channels, as there is a huge mixture and diversity of customer types with different needs, particularly as economic migration has been a global trend over the past decades. In other words, the customer is not homogenous but has various ethnic, religious and attitudinal backgrounds that determined their channel choices in very different ways, and how to service each one to a level of true satisfaction is the ultimate goal.

This is as true for the retail banking operation as the commercial banking service, as two thirds of the transactions being processed by corporate clients is on behalf of consumers. This means that the consumer experience is just as important in commercial banking as in retail, as improving the consumer's experience in relationship with a corporate client also helps to differentiate the bank. The way to do that is to recognise that consumers want to serve themselves for sure but, when it goes wrong, they want someone to sort it out fast.

The real issue of having customers self-serve through remote channels, however, is that it opens the market to new competition. After all, if the customer never needs to talk with you and purely deals with you on an app, then firms such as Apple and Google enter into the game.

This is why the technology and telecommunications firms (telcos) are developing more and more partnerships and joint ventures with firms such as Visa and MasterCard and the like, and why financial institutions need to think more carefully and proactively about the relationships they are creating. In particular, banks need to analyse the information they have about customers in more depth. As people are so strongly connected electronically, banks need to be more aware of the fact that they can record, analyse and understand every customer attitude, behaviour and view in a multichannel environment.

If banks do not do this, then the likes of Apple and Amazon will, and the key is to recognise and deliver service across those channels in a consistent way, recognising the customer value through those channels, and leveraging the relationship by engaging the customer to switch from one channel to another as appropriate.

For example, if it is known that a customer is looking for a mortgage online, then the bank needs to encourage a switch to engage in a remote discussion either through live chat or telephone and then a store visit. Critically, the bank needs to recognise that as the customer moves through those channels, all the information related to the mortgage enquiry is carried across consistently through these channels.

THE IMPACT OF MOBILE

All of the banks recognise that the world is moving rapidly to mobile wireless devices, and this means that the traditional banking model is changing. Although banks see this as an obvious development, it still raises challenges as consumers do not switch off their old behaviour when new ones are introduced. Therefore, mobile channels may be pervasive but customers will still expect or demand to access old channels, particularly call centre and branch. In fact, they will not only want all of these choices but also have the same level of experience with each, which brings it back to how firms evolve their legacy to innovate their future.

The challenge is how to develop new business models and what these models will look like. The starting point is already here. Card processing firms are fully aware that cards will be displaced by mobile wallets and are developing new business structures with Google, Apple and Facebook as a result.

This is key for these firms as the likelihood is that less than half of payments will be through cards by the end of the decade, and therefore card processing firms will no longer be around. Instead, there will be transaction processing companies that allow consumer to corporate payments to flow easily through any electronic channel. It also means that the traditional card processors may potentially be a utility that competes against or partners with other transaction processors, from traditional clearing companies to the global transaction banks.

This leads to a debate about the relationship and the brand in that, as you move across channels, who do you have the relationship with? The online retailer, the card company, the financial institution or the mobile carrier? The real challenge here being how to keep your company's brand with the customer if you never see them?

That is a double-edged sword as some banks do not see themselves as the brand to the consumer, but they are the brand for the mobile carrier.

Taking it from a bank's viewpoint, does a licensed bank really want a relationship with a million people it does not know and have to face all the industry's requirements for client on-boarding—notably, KYC and Anti-Money Laundering (AML) rules—or does it want one relationship with the telco that looks after the one million for it?

It is a clear choice about whether a bank needs to extend its brand to its client's customers or focus on the client, and in order to determine which one to opt for, the bank just needs to work out where it sits in the value chain.

It is clear that the point at which a customer buys and the point at which a transaction takes place has changed and is getting even more complex. In the near term, you might be buying an Apple download using a Zynga credit through an O2 wallet backed by a PayPal payment which is on a Visa card issued by a bank.

As already stated, the model has changed and the real question of dealing through remote channels in this way is this: Whom do you trust to pay and process the money? Will people trust a payment if they don't see a bank or a bank's brand in the process?

Interestingly, most people do not even realise they are making a payment in this effortless, secure and convenient new world. One bank carried out a survey among young people asking if they had ever made a payment on their mobile. Over half said they had not, but when asked if they had ever downloaded something from iTunes to their mobile, most had and yes, they had paid for it on their mobile through iTunes. So it comes down to how you ask the question and how you offer the functionality. Apple offers everything bundled in such a way that it's very easy to use and convenient. "Fast", "effortless" and "secure" are the keywords here.

Certainly, Amazon's "1-Click" process and Apple's "confirm" in iTunes have made the process of payment fast, effortless and secure but if you were asked to bank with Amazon or Apple, that's not the same thing. The fact that you have a secure account that is regulated and managed by a bank behind the likes of Amazon and Apple and, in the future, behind your online and mobile wallets is the key here.

Another key change to the complexity of this process is that there are also multiple strategic parties moving in multiple strategic directions in the value chain, each trying to understand their position, virility and viability in that value chain with the consumer. Does a consumer think that when they buy from an online retailer that it is the retailer who processes their payment or that it's Visa or their bank? Ultimately, with more and more payments processed without any logo or brand, do they really care? All they want are the goods and services; the financial process within that is irrelevant to them.

This is easily illustrated by the fact that most people do not even read the terms and conditions—the Ts and Cs—of an online purchase anymore. The Ts & Cs agreement is just an autoclick. Similarly, people do not want the Verified by Visa or MasterCard SecureCode getting in the way. They just want the end result: the goods, products or services they are buying. Does this mean that a new structure of payments processor will emerge that is purely mobile-based, a new PayPal if you will? Possibly, as processing to date has all been built upon the traditional and current banking infrastructure, including PayPal, but it will not stay there. The speed of change is too fast. For example, over a million people downloaded a Person-to-Person (P2P) payments app in less than three months. The service then starts to grow virally as a million people start sending several hundred pounds a day through those apps.

This means the regulator and other organisations have a challenge to see what both the movement towards m-wallets and virtual currencies cross borders and P2P means. It may be irrelevant now, as it is tiny, but that will change. The adoption rate is too fast and the regulatory process needs to keep up. The regulators are relaxed about this right now, as these transactions run on traditional bank infrastructures, but if it bounces off those rails, things will change.

Would consumers adopt this technology as quickly if it weren't in a regulated environment? That's a question but when you see Facebook,

Google, Apple and RIM announce that they want to work with one telco, as they recently did, then they are working outside every scheme and you don't get four organisations of that size wanting to get into the business without a good reason.

The challenge of remote channels is around change therefore. It is around how to evolve a business model through many significant technological, behavioural and customer changes whilst retaining what is already there, as not everyone moves at once. This is where strong leadership is needed in order to be organisationally aligned. Product, marketing, sales and service and working together in a coordinated fashion are needed to allow this to work.

A good example is social media. You cannot roll out an app, launch a blog or establish a Facebook presence if you are not committed to interaction and dedication of agents to these areas, as these are now channels just as much as mobile, branch and call centre. Customers will demand responses when these services are launched and will expect interaction. This means that these media channels cannot be opened without the right structure to respond.

Most banks know that we will eventually be in a position where no physical contact will be required for financial services or servicing, but they also believe that the physical channel needs to remain in place. This may seem strange in that, if banks all believe that remote channels augment and eventually replace physical channels, what is the physical channel there for?

The answer: it is critical for customer acquisition.

TECHNOLOGIES CREATE A DIGITAL BANK STORM

During the past few years, the world has moved into something loosely described as 2.0. Web 2.0 is applied to the age of the easy generation of content, media, activity, networking and more. These combined developments of technology are impacting banks in the 21st century to create the Digital Bank.

The technologies themselves have been emerging for decades but they are especially hot now because they are reaching maturity. The technologies fall into four major categories:

1. mobile networking
2. social technologies
3. data analytics
4. unlimited networking and storage and modular computing

These technologies will be explored in depth in the following chapters but, in order to introduce them effectively, let's briefly look at what these technologies mean in totality.

Mobile networking is all about the emergence of the mobile Internet, and the combination of telecommunications with information technology.

While social technologies build on this networking, they are focused more on the developments of consuming content on the Internet in the 1990s to creating content from the 2000s onwards. Fuelled primarily by Twitter and Facebook, the social Internet is not just about these platforms but about the plethora of methods of creating content from consumers to corporates in a simple, interactive, social manner using 21st-century technologies.

Data analytics is briefly labelled "Big Data" today but evolved from the data analytics and data mining techniques of previous decades.

Unlimited networking and storage applies the idea of Moore's Law—double the power at half the price every eighteen months—to all areas of computing. This has led us to the cloud-based structures of today, where anything can be stored in any file size anywhere on the Internet, with easy access in nanoseconds.

Leading on from this, modular computing points to the developments of object orientation and plug-and-play computing to enable banks to become component-based APIs.

Although we will explore each of these in depth later, the core of this discussion about converting the bank into digitised pieces is that we talk about mobile social in a cloud of Big Data today because this is fundamentally transforming banking, finance, government and, on a larger scale, the world. Here are a few illustrations to highlight why they are such transformational technologies.

Mobile is truly transformational as it has moved us from having to go somewhere to do something—a physical place or a desktop screen—to having connectivity in all of our pockets and handbags. This means the 24/7 availability of service is now the optimal state rather than the dream. It goes beyond this, however, as mobile delivers two further transformational moments.

First, it gives everyone on the planet the ability to communicate. In the farthest reaches of the world, people are communicating wirelessly in a way they never could before. You may think that these remote corners of the world just have simple dumb 2G phones, but you would be wrong. The fact that most affluent consumers change their mobiles every eighteen months means that emerging markets are getting smartphones sooner than you think. For example, in the remote village of Kisama, Nagaland, India, inhabitants are now taking photographs on their smart mobile handsets during celebrations. In other words, everyone is socialising via mobile. Anyone, anywhere can now relate socially and communicate globally. Seven billion people globally are connecting one-to-one, person-to-person, peer-to-peer.

Second, mobile provides a transactional infrastructure that was non-existent just a few years ago. It is the reason why Africa has seen the most rapid transformation through mobile, with M-PESA in Kenya cited as the most revolutionary change (*see* Mobile Fuels Digital Banking for more on this). This means that communities that only had physical connectivity now have digital connectivity. Communities have exploded from local to global, and the wireless transmittance of anything to anyone, anywhere is a reality.

Mobile is part of the reason why social is now a major shift. After all, communicating with friends and family is what most people use a mobile phone for, and the ability to create and share photographs, updates, news, links and more via mobile is the truly social hemisphere of technological change. On top of this, mobile allows you to locate anyone, anywhere, anytime, provides a further dimension of change and brings in the importance of Big Data and cloud.

Geolocating targeted consumers with offers at their point of consumption is a big piece of change. This is the dream of marketers and is now a reality. Forget mailing coupons in the post, you just say at the point of retailing, "Here's the deal." But you cannot do this without having massive analytical capability of data to dig out what is relevant to whom at what point of time. Big Data, cloud and mobile bring all of this together, and they deliver.

Obviously, Big Data and cloud also do a lot more than this. After all, cloud provides the ability to analyse unlimited amounts of data for any purpose. It is the antidote to Big Data. Big Data is all about drowning in exabytes of bytes whilst cloud provides the magic capability to gain access to unlimited power and storage to analyse that data.

So these four technology shifts were centrifugal forces of change in 2012, as they are hugely complementary. Mobile allows anyone to socialise with anyone on the planet while cloud allows companies and government agencies to sift through the massive amounts of data that the mobile, social world is creating.

The perfect technology storm.

STOP TALKING ABOUT MOBILE, SOCIAL, CLOUD AND BIG DATA

Even though I have outlined that this is a perfect technology storm, it's already a dull storm due to overhype by technologists and under-delivery. For example, so many vendors talk about mobile and tablet computing in banking, Big Data, cloud and the like, and I'm fed up with it. Not of the vendors, but of this bandwagon hype around jargonised words that are meaningless. They were meaningful five or ten years ago, when no one knew what they were or what they meant, but now everyone throws these buzzwords into their presentations and you find yourself saying, "Oh jeez, shut up and show me something useful."

Big Data, cloud, mobile, social ... it's like watching the news. The first time you hear about a major issue, you think "That's interesting." When that issue is aired over and over again, day in and day out, you eventually switch off and wait for something else that's interesting to come along. That's how many of us feel about vendors and their mobile Big Data cloud dialogue.

What we really want to hear is something new. Tell me about the Internet of things and wearable computing, and how that's going to change banking. That's a far more interesting dialogue because I'm not hearing enough of that. That's future positioning.

This is why solutions providers need to talk about what the world will look like in three to five years and, if they're confident about their vision, bet the farm on it. After all, vendors who poured their money into mobile Big Data cloud stuff five years ago should be making a mint today. Five years ago, the mobile Big Data cloud conversation was interesting because it was new and unknown. But now? Yada, yada, yada, tell me something else. Tell me about how you have implemented a solution for a bank that allows them to pinpoint a customer, anywhere, anytime with a relevant offer.

That's a Big Data conversation but just don't call it Big Data. Call it Small Data. It's small in that the exabyte stream of data has been taken and converted into this really small moment of truth where the customer gets an amazing experience that is completely personalised. Now you've taken the dull conversation and turned it into a story with benefit and relevance.

This is why it is important to either talk about long-term vision or short-term illustration. The vision is the three-to-five-year away concepts; the illustration is the here and now. That's why I no longer want to hear about mobile, social, Big Data or cloud but about how banks are using the mobile network to identify where the end customer will be in the next ten minutes and, by using the GPS network combined with small data, making them an offer they cannot refuse.

Solutions providers just need to get detailed when things are here and now, and macro when they are yet to come. With that clear challenge as background, let's now look at each of the technologies in turn.

MOBILE FUELS DIGITAL BANKING

We are seeing many changes in the world of banking but none as revolutionary as the mobile space—mobile telephony is revolutionising the planet. There are more telephone handsets in use on the planet than toothbrushes and developing economies, such as India, have more mobile telephone handsets than toilets.

In fact, the planet has a handset in existence for every person in the world. Although that doesn't mean everyone has a telephone, it does mean that everyone has the potential to access a handset. This is revolutionary. It means that the whole planet is wirelessly connected. Every person on the planet has the potential to electronically interact with someone else on the planet. That has never been a capability in our history of existence, and is the reason why this is such an exciting space.

For banks, this is a very exciting space as these changes are allowing many new and innovative services to be launched from direct P2P payments via text messages to contactless apps and dongles for payments to full-scale financial services delivered over tablet and smartphone systems. It is the reason why PayPal and Google have invested over $1 billion in mobile payments development between 2008 and 2012.

According to Gartner Group, the mobile-payments market is a hot space because it is a market that processed around $235.4 billion in global transaction values in 2013, up 44 per cent from 2012. That is why so many companies are investing in mobile payments and mobile financial developments. For example, between 2008 and 2013, venture capitalists invested over $1.5 billion into the mobile payments market. Interestingly, they have little to show for it, with only Square a major success so far.

Square was founded in February 2009 by Twitter co-founder Jack Dorsey. The system is a simple idea that entails putting a payments dongle into the earpiece of a mobile smartphone. Once inserted, it allows the phone to become a point of sale (POS) and take payments. Ideal for small merchants, the system slowly grew and then accelerated rapidly in 2011. For example, it took about 10 months from its launch for Square to reach $1 million a day in payments transactions going through its mobile app. This doubled to $2 million a day two months later and one month later, in May 2011, it was generating over $3 million a day, resulting in the card firm Visa making a major strategic investment in the business. By 2013, the company was valued at $3.25 billion, which is significant when most start-ups are challenged by heavyweight incumbents such as PayPal and, of course, the banks.

Banks have been active in the mobile payments space for almost two decades. Back in the 1990s, banks were playing around with Wireless Application Protocol (WAP) for account balance checking on mobiles. However, much of this was experimentation and it was not until the late 2000s that mobile became a really hot space.

SIMPLE MOBILE SYSTEMS

As mentioned, we have moved from a disconnected world, where few had access to technological links, to a world of connections where everyone can wirelessly communicate.

For Africa, Asia, Latin America, China, India and other developing markets, this is where we can see the true revolution in both society and banking. Cheap access to mobile communications has given Africa and other economies the ability to transform from a world where crime was simple and payments were hard to one where crime is tracked and payments are easy. This is because electronic payment processing is both traceable and immediate, with no challenge of distance, and the best example of such change is seen in M-PESA in Kenya, although this is not a typical implementation of mobile payments.

M-PESA—*M* is for "mobile" and *pesa* means "money" in Swahili—was launched in March 2007 when the Kenyan government asked Safaricom, a division of Vodafone, to help improve the way money was moved between citizens. At that time, most payments from towns to villages were made through the physical transportation of notes and bills using bus and taxi drivers.

Under the M-PESA system, agents manage the transfers with mobile text messaging, allowing simple and immediate real-time transfer. The result is that M-PESA has rapidly become the most trusted form of payment in Kenya and the mobile operator, Safaricom, is now the largest financial operator in the country.

By 2010, M-PESA had attracted 9.5 million customers. This figure had increased to 17 million by 2013, of which over 10 million make at least one transaction per month. Add on the other mobile money operators in Kenya and a large part of the country's gross domestic product (GDP) is now transacted over the mobile network. For example, 142 billion Kenyan shillings (Ksh) were transacted in the month of April 2013, or $1.6 billion, which would translate into around $20 billion a year processed via the Kenyan mobile payments network in 2013. Kenya's GDP was $37.23 billion in 2012, and so it is easy to see how a significant proportion of the economy is now dependent on mobile money.

In addition, M-PESA converted many unbanked into banked users, with around 2.5 million bank customers in Kenya when the system launched in 2007 increasing to over ten million today.

This success has led to many other mobile models from Standard Chartered Bank's partnership with MasterCard and airtel Africa to Easypaisa, which works with Orange in West Africa, Safaricom in Kenya and Tigo in other parts of Africa.

But there's more than just a mobile revolution taking place in Africa, a continent that had zero electronic infrastructure for mass payments ten years ago but now has coverage almost everywhere, as the developed economies' usage of mobile has exploded thanks to apps.

SOPHISTICATED MOBILE SERVICES

As you jump from the basic SMS telephone message through WAP to the iPhone and Android, you find more and more interesting uses of mobile and mobile payments and banking. These are also key as it is expected that the emerging economies will be at the same level of smartphone usage by 2015 as developed economies are today.

The smartphone enables touch-based access to the mobile Internet and has completely changed the whole thinking about how mobile telephony works. This is demonstrated by the sudden rise of apps and the implications of these.[18] What the app represents is a two-fold change to the way we think about the world and, in turn, the world of money.

First, the app makes everything simplified and highly functional. It overcomes the fat finger syndrome. It can be used by a seven-year-old or a seventy-year-old just as easily, without any training and just as consistently. In other words, it's foolproof. For complex financial processes, this makes the touch-screen tablet and smartphone ideal.

Second, the app breaks down functionality into pieces. As a result, banks can break down processes into bits and make them interchangeable and plug-and-play. You can have a payments app that has nothing to do with a bank app. You can have a balance and alerts app that has no

---

18   Apple launched the iTunes app store on 11 July 2008 with 500 apps. A year later, there were 55,000 apps and over a billion downloads. In an announcement in June 2011, Apple said it had reached over 14 billion downloads with 425,000 apps and then, by 2013, the store had surpassed 40 billion app downloads with a library of over 800,000 apps. http://en.wikipedia.org/wiki/App_Store

relationship with an account. You can deliver a micropayment and even a nanopayment.

The last point is the most important in fact, in that because you can deliver a nanopayment, the world of money changes. This is demonstrated by apps such as Angry Birds, which recently celebrated its 250 millionth mobile download,[19] and shows that a firm can make millions from charging just 99 cents a download.

In fact, this has led to an explosion of alternative payment options and virtual currencies. For example, in-app gaming on phones and tablet computers is becoming standard with Apple paying out $5 billion to its app store developers in 2012 and Google paying out a further $900 million.[20]

Bearing in mind that these billions of dollars are based on $0.99-cent downloads and in-app gaming updates of a few cents each via iTunes and the Android Store, you can see new forms of virtual currency in operation. You may disagree, but the aggregation of large amounts of small payments is effectively building a virtual currency system.

You don't believe me? Then take this personal experience that introduced me to gaming virtual currencies.

ZOMBIE MONEY IN A CHAINSAW HELL

During a quiet summer, I started playing zombies on my phone. It was an app that used the mobile Internet to connect me with my Facebook friends. I earned points by turning friends into zombies and could earn more points by fighting them but my friends weren't so engaged. Eventually, I stopped

---

19   "With 250 Million Downloads Angry Birds Moves Into Magic, Cookbooks, And More", TechCrunch, 14 June 2011, http://tcrn.ch/kR2GJY

20   As of summer 2013, Google dominated the smartphone mobile market with 900 million users while Apple had 600 million iOS and Microsoft a far third place with an estimated 12 million Windows Phones sold. For more information, see www.forbes.com/sites/tristanlouis/2013/08/10/how-much-do-average-apps-make/

playing, having reached the seventh level of zombiedom. After a while, one of my "friends" started killing me every day. Literally ripping me to shreds with a chainsaw. And it hurt. After all, I was meant to be the Zombie Priest in the Church of Goth, and no one had beaten me before. And where did that chainsaw come from?

I was mad and wanted to get a chainsaw myself. The problem was that I had to turn at least 40 friends into zombies too in order to earn enough points to buy a chainsaw and, so far, I had invited over 200 mates to become Zombies and only 12 had bothered to do so. How would I get forty of them to turn?

It was a problem but then I found zombie coins. Zombie coins is the in-app currency that can be bought through iTunes or the Android Store to buy chainsaws, shotguns and other in-game gadgets. I could purchase the coins either through my account or by PayPal or other services, and it allowed me to make microtransactions and buy things to spice up my favourite apps. For just $5, I could buy a chainsaw. So I spent $50 and bought two chainsaws plus a machete, shotgun, Uzi, meat cleaver and bazooka for good measure. Forget about turning mates into Zombies ... just kill them. Now I am the Zombie Pope in the Cathedral of Death and the idiot who attacked me with a chainsaw is dead meat.

This experience showed me the importance of these gaming tools, and gamification via mobile Internet is big news. For example, as of January 2013, Apple had more than half a billion active iTunes accounts linked to credit cards and this is likely to be a massive asset when the firm launches a mobile e-wallet.

But it goes further than this as these game worlds are big business. For example, the worldwide market for virtual goods was valued at $14.8 billion in 2012, with those in Asia being the largest buyers of virtual goods ($8.7 billion) and China leading the world's consumption ($5.1 billion). In 2011, American consumers purchased $2.3 billion worth of virtual goods, up nearly 30 per cent from 2009. The market is also growing fast, with TechNavio forecasting a compound annual growth rate

(CAGR) of 12.5 per cent for virtual goods between 2012 and 2016. In other words, we are looking at a $50 billion market in the near future.

It is also possible to build a business incredibly fast in this new world of global connectivity. For example, within 43 days of its launch in January 2011, game company Zynga's Cityville game on Facebook had garnered 100 million players, and analysts estimate that about a tenth of these players buy virtual goods. If a tenth of Zynga's 100 million Cityville players spend $5 per month, then Zynga is banking $50 million a month, or $400 million a year. All from a game that gained this audience in under two months.

This experience is replicated worldwide. DeNA in Japan found that its Moba-coin virtual currency was used in a record $689 million worth of transactions in 2012, representing half of its revenue stream. NHN Japan offers a global gaming virtual currency called Line Coins, KakaoTalk in Korea offers a virtual currency called Choco and Tencent's QQ in China is firmly entrenched as a virtual currency.

In fact, China has shown the new way in which money may evolve, thanks to the mobile Internet, through the experience of QQ. QQ is the largest mobile internet service in China, run by the firm Tencent, and has over a billion users worldwide, with more than 500 million active monthly users. In 2002, when Tencent was building its community, it launched the QQ coin to enable online purchases and downloads. This was important as most youngsters in China did not have credit or debit cards, so the coin became the de facto method of gaining access to online goods and services.

The basic operation of QQ coins is through retailers who sell QQ coins for the equivalent of 1 coin for 1 yuan ($0.16). Customers pay for the QQ coins with yuan in cash at the retail store and the retailer then transfers the QQ coins to the buyer's account or gives the buyer access to the QQ account, where QQ coins are stored, by giving them their username and password.

As customers purchased QQ coins, the virtual coin became a popular currency to transact for other services outside Tencent, such as call girls and gambling. According to a Chinese government estimate in 2005, the total volume of trading in virtual items in China was worth about $900 million. About 45 per cent of that went for items in the Tencent QQ world. That's why the People's Republic of China started worrying—almost a trillion dollars flowing through the economy going into illicit activities such as pornography and gambling is undesirable, to say the least.

This is a concern for all as, if a virtual coin really did succeed, it could change the dynamics of trade worldwide. This is what we have seen with Bitcoin (*see* "The Bitcoin Phenomenon" in the next chapter for more on this).

OTHER MOBILE FINANCIAL SERVICES

Another part of mobile worth noting is the use of mobile cameras. Mobile cameras are being used to eradicate cheque deposits in the United States as an image of a cheque is just as acceptable by law as the cheque itself. Therefore, customers can just take pictures of cheques and send them as multimedia text message to the bank, and that's the cheque deposited. This is one of the most talked about developments in mobile applications in the United States.

Meanwhile, in Asia, images are being used along with QR codes to support completely automated banking. For example, Jibun Bank and eBank in Japan both accept account opening on the basis of just a photograph of your driving licence via mobile. The driving licence is read by a character recognition system and checked with the government's driving database. As long as all is aligned, the account is opened.

More recently, Barclays Bank in the United Kingdom introduced QR codes to its P2P payments app, Pingit.[21] The app allows billing companies to send paper payment requests to customers with a QR code and, if the customer uses their smartphone to read the code, all of the billing

---

21   For those who aren't familiar with Pingit, it's like a PayPal for mobile and offers simple P2P mobile payments whether you are a Barclays' customer or not. Launched in February 2012, Barclays claimed after a year that the number one reason for new account openings was because of the experience of using Pingit and its ease of access, use and innovation.

information and customer account information is embedded with the code so that the customer purely has to confirm payment. Once this is confirmed, the complete transaction is performed electronically, radically changing the accounts payables and receivables cycle for corporates as this can now be automated end-to-end.

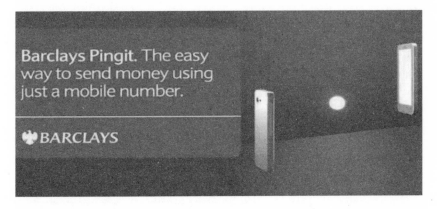

Mobile contactless payments are another major and growing area of interest for banks. Contactless payments are based on NFC chips, which are being integrated into nearly all new generation mobile devices. Apple has intimated that the iPhone will incorporate such functionality and Google estimate that every other smartphone will have an NFC chip inside by 2014. It is in Google's interest to push this capability of course, thanks to the launch of Google Wallet.

Google Wallet was launched at the end of May 2011 in partnership with Citi and MasterCard. The Wallet is a contactless mobile app that allows MasterCard's PayPass to work with Google Checkout to store credit cards, offers, loyalty cards and gift cards, but without the bulk of a traditional wallet. In addition, smartphones can automatically redeem offers and earn loyalty points synched with Google Offers.

Initially, Google Wallet was only accepted on approved telephones and networks, which limited its success, although the number of those installing the app surpassed five million in February 2013. Interestingly, Google has now integrated the payments capability into Gmail so the combination of the Wallet and Gmail should see Google becoming a serious player in the mobile Internet payments revolution.

THE BAD NEWS ABOUT MOBILE

As every bank is getting into mobile, there are issues. A good example is the coordinated ZeuS malware attack towards the end of 2010, where a web application supposedly from the bank asked the victim to input their mobile phone number. The victim was then asked via text message to install an application onto the phone and the application was then used to intercept any text messages the victim sent thereafter.

There are also numerous new man-in-the-middle and mobile malware attacks that are growing by the day such as a recent Facebook update about Justin Bieber, which resulted in over 100,000 views in 24 hours, with 27 per cent via mobile Facebook. Every viewing downloaded malware.

Then there is mobile hijacking, where you think you are on your mobile carrier's network but you're not. This is where a cybercriminal places a signal box near to the location of the person they are targeting. The person then sees their mobile signal disappear and come back stronger. What the mobile user does not realise is that their mobile service has been hijacked and all of their texts, apps and downloads are being filtered by the cybercriminal's service. This is something that is quite easy to set up and run by any average person with such criminal intent.

Although mobile attacks are increasing daily, banks are viewing this as something that is controllable today. The question is: with every person on the planet using or accessing a mobile device, will it be controllable in the future?

MAKING A PAYMENT BECOMES A BASIC HUMAN RIGHT

The fact that mobile phone ubiquity is creating a wirelessly connected planet is a key part of changing our world for more inclusion. To start with, six billion people now have 1:1, P2P connections. You only need to look at mobile densities by continent to realise how ubiquitous these devices have become.

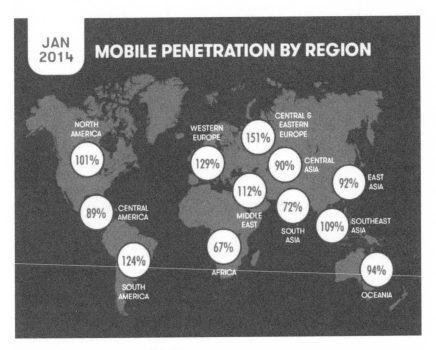

Sources: US Census Bureau, ITU, CIA

According to a 2012 survey by the Gates Foundation, the World Bank and Gallup, more than 10 per cent of adults said they had used mobile money in the last year and, of the twenty countries surveyed, fifteen were in

Africa. This is illustrated particularly well by Somalia, a country that lacks a functioning government but 34 per cent of adults use mobile money (often to receive remittances from family members abroad). The fact is anyone, anywhere can now send and receive money anywhere, anytime. In Kenya, it has created financial inclusion, where 2.5 million people had bank accounts in a country of over 40 million people in 2007 but this has increased to over ten million today thanks to mobile payments creating credit history and credit worthiness.

This revolution is not just down to emerging or developing economies, but also to developed economies. For example, the European Union is encouraging financial inclusion, as is the United States. P2P mobile money makes a difference here, but it's more than this. The real focus of mobile payments and mobile financial developments is all about the war on cash. Visa, MasterCard and the banks are all trying to encourage the move away from paper payments—cash and cheques—to electronic payments—card and mobile.

This is a transformation supported by the mobile revolution, but such a transformation does not take place unless people, process and technology change. This is the key to the mobile revolution as what we have here is technology transforming process and people.

The *technology* is mobile and contactless, but it's more than this— it's the connected planet. Until recently, businesses were connected with businesses and governments with governments via mainframe systems. That changed with the PC, but the PC only connected those with a lifestyle that covered the costs of the technology. That meant only those who could afford one, and limited the world of connections to consumers of the developed economies. Now, thanks to mobile ubiquity and low cost, every single person on the planet is connected wirelessly. Everyone has a connection to each other, P2P, in their pocket, handbag or loincloth. That's the big difference and, for finance, the huge difference is that we have reached a tipping point where transaction engines for payments are in the hands of every person on this planet.

That changes the *process*. The process changes because it is not just simple transaction engines that are in the hands of every person on the planet but also a whole range of mobile financial services: from mobile contactless to mobile proximity, from mobile money transfers to mobile bill payments, from mobile online payments for physical goods to mobile online payments for digital goods, from mobile as a point of purchase to mobile as a point of sale, from mobile as a loyalty programme for coupons and offers to mobile identity and authentication.

The mobile planet is a raft of innovation and change, and it is difficult for banks to keep up with all this innovation and change in their processes because they are hamstrung by their heritage. We embedded our world in old style business-to-business systems, and now the consumer-driven world is demanding rapid change to those systems that are hard to change.

There are many new forms of payment—contactless, QR, mobile—that challenges banks to know where to focus and invest. After all, changing processes means changing organisation products, services, structures and that's costly too. Or is it? Is this replacement, evolution or co-existence? Do you have to adapt processes to support some forms of mobile payment or all? Where do you place your bets?

Finally, if the technology and process change, so do *people*. We are told that Google, mobile and social media are rewiring our brains, resulting in all of us suffering from attention deficit disorder. Everyone is sitting there playing with their iPads, iPhones, Androids and blackberries, more interested in who's connecting virtually than who is there in reality. I don't blame people, I do the same, but the reason we are all here talking about mobile and new forms of payment is because customers are. Customers are more loyal to their mobile connections than their partners, so the debate is two-fold:

- Banks need to break the shackles of being hamstrung by heritage.
  As many bankers tell me, the only place where they engage with old technology is when they go to work.

- Banks need to work out how to keep information secure as, right now, it's not.

Banks also need to analyse customer data to sell more and service better, but the customer doesn't want to be digitally raped. We talk about permissions-based marketing, but the customer wants to keep their privacy. However, conversely, the customer then goes onto Facebook and gives away their email, mobile, relationships and more. In reality, there is no privacy or security, so how can we keep ourselves secure and private? This is the focus of the next chapter—making people secure in an insecure world.

DIGITAL BANKS ARE SOCIAL BANKS

First of all, let's define our terms:

- **Social media** is like mainstream media but user-generated. It's blogging instead of newspapers, YouTube instead of TV and podcasting instead of radio. It's media, but social media.
- **Social networking** is like real-world networking but online. It's where people date, talk, meet, relate and even work together, on occasion. It's networking, but socially and remotely.
- **Social banking** provides bank services but, in a similar fashion, through social methods. It is the process of personalising banking and enabling people and businesses to see the people and businesses they are saving and investing with. It's Zopa and Prosper, SmartyPig and Mint, and many more.
- **Social money** is the way to make payments peer-to-peer and has already taken off big time with PayPal and Square but now has many other pretenders, especially in the mobile space.

It is important to note that all of these services are based on IP as the platform, but may be delivered through any device including TV, PC, tablet or mobile. The above are brief definitions. Now let's look at each in much more depth starting with social media.

SOCIAL MEDIA

Social media replaces traditional media as a source of news, views and entertainment. This does not mean that the TV has been replaced by the Internet as the primary entertainment source but, for a large range of demographics, this may be the case. Meanwhile, how many of you pick up a paper every morning to read? How many of you pick up a *free* newspaper these days? It's free because print news is worthless. It's out-of-date by the time it hits the streets so you read it more for the tactile feel, because you don't have access to the net or TV and for the opinions and commentary.

When working at the home office—my usual office—my morning is typically made up of reading a number of daily alerts from news sources, including traditional ones such as the *Financial Times* as well as online. Many of these alerts are from blogs, Twitter and other sources however, so it's social. I read what the crowd I follow read. If my friends say a story is worthwhile, then it's worth reading. That's social.

Finally, I only really listen to the radio when I'm in the car. Otherwise, I'm on the train or in the gym listening to Spotify, podcasts or iTunes. This is the world of social media. So how does a bank make money out of social media? Bear in mind, I'm not talking here about social networking, banking or money, just media. I'll talk about the others later, and in sequence.

First, a bank should not try to make money out of social media. Social media is not there for money making but for customer engagement, which then leads to money making. And what does it mean for customer engagement? Well, on the one hand, it is understanding customer attitudes and ideas. If customers are saying that the bank is awful, horrible, difficult, complacent, arrogant, greedy or worse, then it's about the bank engaging with those customers to find out why they think that the bank is all of those things. This is what visionary banks like the West Coast American bank Wells Fargo and ICICI Bank in India recognise.

When Wells Fargo was asked why it blogged, the bank's answer was simple: "If you're not part of the social world of conversation amongst your customers, then they will talk about you negatively and you have no voice to respond. If you engage in the online conversation, then it becomes far more civilised, interactive and interesting." Other banks fear such activity, due to the negative feedback that they might receive. Initially, Wells Fargo did find that there was negative feedback but, by having a team monitor its social media 24/7, it always responded to any negativity straightaway with a response explaining why it had happened that way. Customers became far more polite and calm when they saw that their rude postings received civil replies; hence it led to being engaged in a conversation. Through conversation, the bank learnt a lot more about what frustrated customers. The result is better products and services.

However, it is quite clear that the bank cannot engage in such activity half-heartedly, as you need to be responsive and therefore have people dedicated to social media interaction. Like a call centre, it's a response team to online questions and issues. Interestingly, over time, customers often reply to rude postings and become the best advocates for the bank. Many other financial institutions have found the same results when using social media, where customers engage and manage other customers' feedback online.

For example, in 2012, ICICI Bank in India launched full-service banking on Facebook as an app. As there are over 80 million Facebook users in India, ICICI Bank believed there was an opportunity to engage those users for bank services. Thus, the bank service was launched in February 2012 and achieved a million Facebook Likes in just over ten months. After a year, the bank had achieved over two million Likes, and today its Facebook page offers full-service banking as well as lots of other services of customer engagement. The most recent innovation of the bank has been a service called iWish, a smart savings tool launched in partnership with the US firm SmartyPig.

SmartyPig provides a social savings tool for banks. The way this works is that you set a goal and then share that savings goal with friends and family to raise funds for your target. Your friends and family can then contribute and support your savings focus, as well as donate or gift you funds to assist if they feel it appropriate.

In terms of ICICI's Facebook banking service, the bank provides a secure link from Facebook into the bank's services. As Sujit Ganguli, head of Brand and Corporate Communications at ICICI Bank, said, "Our customers were worried about going into their bank services from Facebook but, as we made clear to them, you leave Facebook and are using our usual secure servers once you accept and install our Facebook app."

In other words, Facebook apps are like mobile apps for banking: it's just another app-based banking service, and ICICI Bank uses it to engage the customer by providing content, care, communication and creativity. In ICICI's case, it offers gaming and more to engage the customer and the neatest part of ICICI's experience is the impact of social media engagement with the bank's clientele.

For example, before using Facebook for customer engagement, 24 per cent of the online mentions about ICICI were negative and only 19 per cent positive. Now, 49 per cent are positive and just 6 per cent negative. That's a huge change and shows that a key part of the use of Facebook banking is for customer servicing, not just engagement. This is a key factor in using social media: customer engagement.

When Wells Fargo first entered into using social media for customer engagement, it was partly in response to one customer who had created a website called wellsfargosucks.com. Unfortunately, that website came up as the first result in any Google search. Therefore, in order to ensure the right image of the bank was presented, the bank sought to use social media as a key method of moving the right message to the top of the search results rather than leaving it to negativity from media or anti-bank activists.

It's more than counteracting negative views though; it's looking for ways to engage with people to create positive experiences. That's why banks should post stories that help people who are struggling with finance, for example, by proactively advising them. This tends to be the domain of independent blogs and aggregator sites today, although there are some great bank examples that already do this, such as Royal Bank of Canada's site aimed at students.

What these sites do is create a relationship with people, through news, views, advice and ideas. That's the point of social media: to create a conversation that leads to a relationship that leads to trust that, eventually, leads to business. In fact, there are many other new financial service operations emerging that use social media leverage across all areas of banking.

This is an unstoppable movement and therefore it is quite surprising that most banks and bankers do not even use Facebook and Twitter. A few do, such as the visionary banks already mentioned here, as well as others such as American Express, Commonwealth Bank of Australia, USAA and First Direct, but the point is that any organisation that ignores the fabric of society—bear in mind that over a billion people use Facebook, and it's already old—is missing a trick. In fact, more importantly, any such organisation would be missing the real point, which is that the world is changing and we need to as well.

This point is being missed by many banks because they are firewalled out of these changes. The workers spend all day working and do not see why social media is relevant because they cannot use it at work and are too tired to spend time at home on a social network when there are other things to do, like being a dad, mum, husband or wife.

I am sure many banks are changing their policies towards social media and no longer firewall everyone out ... but there are still far too many that are not and these are the ones that are starting to smell a little bit like nostalgic old worlds.

For example, search YouTube for "bank" or "bank advice" and you will find hardly anything worthwhile there. Under the search for "bank", the first page of results, in order of view count, contains music videos by Lloyd Banks, 50 Cent and Azealia Banks as well as a very juvenile cartoon of SpongeBob SquarePants robbing a bank. Mind you, with almost ten million views, the latter is popular with the social crowd. That's entertainment! Nevertheless, if you search further, there are then channels dedicated to advice about money that have been created by banks. The trouble is you cannot find them unless you purposefully seek to find them. That's a shame as it means that, even with a multimillion dollar spend on social media, most banks do not get social results.

What Has a Social Network Got to Do with Banking Anyway?

Quite a lot actually. Social media educates, advises and supports, which then builds relationships and trust. So do social networks. These days I might throw out the following question to friends and family via Facebook: "Does anyone know which bank we can trust these days?" Try it and see what happens ... mind you, if you're a banker reading this, you may not want to try that particular question. With banks no longer trusted thanks to the credit crisis, people are wondering who to trust, and the people they trust most are friends and family. That is why social networks are critical to banks to gain future business as recommenders will come through your network and their influence will be immense.

So how can a bank influence the influencers? Advertising? No. Investing in building its own social networks? Not really. Helping people to pay people? Yes.

The starting point of social finance is paying for things, and that is why the first financially related services appearing on Facebook are applications such as Pay Me, Spare Change and PayPal, although only PayPal survived this process of evolution. This is because PayPal is the incumbent, and paying between friends is what you focus on in social networks, not banking.

So I guess that's my conclusion in general. From a purely social networking viewpoint, banks need to focus on methods they can use to become friends with their participants in their networks. Friends advise and support, they don't sell, charge and make money out of you. By advising and supporting, banks can build relationships and trust. By doing so, just like social media, it will result in advocacy from "fans" who then become loyal and easier to do business with. That is the point: building trust and loyalty. This is something that very few firms really understand, although American Express does. American Express's Facebook page has almost three million Likes and around 20,000 people talking about its page at any particular moment.

With the average Facebook user connected to 235 friends, 20,000 discussions mean that American Express is exposed to around five million people at any time of the day or night via Facebook. And that exposure is not generic, but specifically 20,000 people influencing their friends and friends' friends.

How did American Express do it? It did it by focusing on the social interaction. It did it by focusing on its members and partners, rather than itself. It offers great incentives and promotions to build its fan base by asking people to Like its Facebook page in return for rewards. It did it by making sure its Facebook page entertains, rather than just informs. And finally, it did it because it had one of those lights-on moments that converted the management team within American Express to focus on social media.

What was that lights-on moment? It was back in 2010 when the firm launched a simple idea called Small Business Saturday. The idea was to encourage consumers to spend more money with local, independent shops on Saturdays. When it launched this idea on Facebook, the company was surprised at how popular it was, and particularly that it gained over a million fans in just the first three weeks of its launch. With that experience, American Express realised that the marketing potential of social media was huge, and it has since invested heavily in Facebook, as well as in Twitter and YouTube.

American Express really gets this space, but it is not the only one. For example, one new bank, launched in Germany in 2009, has been gaining a lot of attention as its interest rates are set by the number of Facebook Likes it receives. This bank is FIDOR Bank (*see* the interview with Matthias Kröner from FIDOR Bank for more on this). I've also been pretty impressed with card companies such as Visa and Barclaycard, as well as a few others.

What is it these guys get that the others don't? What they get is that it's not about Facebook and Twitter; it's about sales, service and relationships. In fact, the real thing they get is that Facebook and Twitter are not social media but a social platform for customer engagement, as are YouTube, Flickr, Tumblr, Foursquare and so on. Social platforms are like Salesforce.

com and the Internet. They are the building blocks of the new financial firms. They are not the end goals in and of themselves, but are the enablers towards real social connectivity. That is why when banks say "We've gotta getta blog out there" or "We've gotta build a Facebook page" or "We've gotta launch a YouTube channel" or "We've gotta engage on Twitter", it's actually not the answer.

Many firms believe that having a holding Twitter username @MyBank and a Facebook page are all you need. Some go as far as to populate their pages with links and news. But you still don't get it if you think along those lines because these are platforms, not websites. Facebook and Twitter have hundreds of specialist service providers creating new forms of social engagement from content curation to social marketing management, from social ads to social intelligence, from apps for gaming to apps for sharing to apps for commerce, the list is more or less endless. A good example is Instagram, purchased by Facebook for $1 billion in April 2012. Instagram is a photo sharing social service and provides an easy way to share such content via Facebook. In other words, Facebook, like the Internet, is a platform that provides the underpinnings for far more targeted and specialist social connectivity.

SOCIAL BANKING

It is quite clear that banks cannot ignore these developments and need to use social media communication capabilities to engage their audience in a conversation that advises, supports and educates potential customers in their financial capabilities.

This advice, support and education can build into a relationship and trust which might generate future account openings, but that is not the primary intention. The primary intention is to build trust. After all, banks have lost so much trust over the past few years that this alone must be a strong reason for social networks and media to be used as a critical platform for future business.

In addition, social media is creating new business models, some of which have already been mentioned such as SmartyPig. There are many new financial service operations emerging using social media covering capital markets (eToro, StockTwits, etc.), corporate banking (Funding Circle, Kickstarter, Market Invoice, Platform Black, The Receivables Exchange, etc.), retail banking (Zopa, Moven, Simple, Bitcoin, etc.), payments (Currency Cloud, Square, mPowa, etc.) and insurance (Friendsurance).

These sites have all been launched within the past decade and are firmly based on proven social models of finance. In general, the services fall into four categories of social finance:

1. social money and payments
2. virtual currencies
3. social lending and saving
4. social funding and investing

The rest of this chapter explores these areas in more depth.

Social Money and Payments

Social money and payments has been around for a while, with PayPal being a great illustration of the first entrant in 1999. PayPal is now the incumbent, with new start-ups like Square, mPowa, iZettle and more being seen as the innovators. This is because PayPal capitalised on the first wave of social money—P2P Internet payments—whilst the latter focus on the second wave—P2P mobile payments.

This is now a hot space with many different flavours including:

- mobile remittances changing the game rapidly, with Kenya's M-PESA copied into multiple geographies
- Square, launched by Twitter co-founder Jack Dorsey in 2009, being similarly copied into multiple geographies
- Google Wallet, an industry milestone when it launched in May 2011

- virtual currencies like Bitcoin nibbling away at the market and moving mainstream
- PayPal finding itself under attack from the card firms, as AMEX, Visa and MasterCard; likewise the banks with iDEAL and ePayo targeting their schemes for social payments

Out of the above, Square has been the main news story, mainly because of its phenomenal growth and charismatic founder. One of the key attributes as to why Square took off so quickly is that the sign-up process takes minutes. You download an app, put in your name and address, answer three security questions, link your bank account and that is all there is to it.

Just as Twitter democratised broadcasting, Jack Dorsey's new company democratised the credit card industry and is why Square, within two years, had signed up more than a million merchants. It is also why Square is being challenged by heavyweight industry incumbent PayPal, which launched PayPal Here in 2013.

PayPal Here is a mobile payment app and card reader for smartphones that lets users simply and securely accept multiple forms of payment including proximity payments, where the user and the merchant apps use the mobile network to transact the payment with no token exchange involved. In other words, a completely frictionless payment, with no action involved other than the use of app-to-app networking.

These players are also being challenged by suppliers like NCR, who are also getting in on the act with dongles and apps under the brand of Silver, as well as a whole raft of lookalikes including iZettle, mPowa and more. However, it's interesting to point out here that the models are different.

iZettle has struggled to get the right terminal out there because Chip & PIN is more challenging and costly than magnetic stripe payments while mPowa is focusing on empowering banks to engage merchants in its mobile payments revolution. This is why mPowa questions the Square and iZettle models, saying that if you seek small merchants, then the volume of transactions is too low to be a sustainable business model. It would certainly be true that if 90 per cent of your clients only make one transaction a month of low value payments, then the model is questionable. However, I am sure that Square would refute such critique by claiming that the long tail of payments creates enough volume to be profitable. It certainly seems that way, as there are a whole range of other companies competing in this domain such as Payatrader, Intuit with GoPayment, Bancard with PayAnywhere, Verifone, Payleven and Sumup. As many of these systems are reviewed in more depth in the chapter titled "Mobile Fuels Digital Banking", I do not want to repeat these in depth here except to focus a little bit on the virtual currency aspects of social money.

Virtual currencies have been exploding thanks to in-app gaming, discussed in the chapter "Mobile Fuels Digital Banking", but virtual currencies go further than this as they spawn a real contender for global commerce as an alternative to real money, namely Bitcoin.

Virtual Currencies

There are many examples of data as a currency arising, especially as the Internet era has taken off, and I referenced this earlier when I talked about zombie money in a chainsaw hell. For example, over a decade ago, numerous virtual currencies emerged for the Internet age including CyberMoola, Cybercash, Digicash and PocketPass, with the most successful being Beenz (1998–2001) and Flooz (1999–2001). These sites enjoyed brief but flawed success. Interestingly, the main reason for failure is attributed to the fact that none of these sites had enough availability, usability or recognition to gain critical mass and, therefore, widespread adoption.

Since then, other virtual currencies have arisen, specifically the Linden Dollar as part of the gaming world of Second Life. Again, these emerging digital systems failed, often due to a lack of governance or regulation. For example, the Linden Dollar failed because the developers did not regulate the managers of the currency.

The most recent attempt to provide a good alternative that gained significant traction is Bitcoin, and here we will spend some time looking at this development because, if it is successful, it will fundamentally change the nature of banking and finance.

The Bitcoin Phenomenon

Cash is one of the last bastions of the traditional financial servicing mix. Yet, with mobile wallets, e-banking, contactless everything and real-time transactions, does cash really have a future? Some say yes due to the unique attributes of cash, as noted in a 2010 Payments Council report titled "The Future for Cash in the UK":

1. Cash circulates and is reused limitlessly.
2. Cash is always valuable.
3. Cash provides full and final settlement of a transaction.
4. A cash payment is anonymous.
5. Once issued, the circulation of cash is uncontrolled.
6. It is regarded as a public good by its users.

These attributes have never been completely substituted by new forms of payment and, until they are, cash will always be prescient.

Bitcoin is providing people with a good alternative to cash, however, because it is critically changing the game for data as a currency by offering a cash equivalent for the digital age.

Bitcoin is the world's first, and so far only, decentralised online currency. Instead of a central bank issuing the currency, bitcoins are issued by anyone with a computer or smartphone and are issued using encryption algorithms. In other words, extremely difficult mathematical problems are incorporated into each coin and transactions are cryptographically authenticated. This makes bitcoins a combination of a commodity and a fiat currency, with the creation of Bitcoin dating back to 2008 when Satoshi Nakamoto published a white paper about a peer-to-peer exchange of value for the Internet age.[22]

22　"Bitcoin: A Peer-to-Peer Electronic Cash System", a white paper by Satoshi Nakamoto, 2008

The core features of Bitcoin are as follows:

- **Bitcoins can be sent** to anyone with a Bitcoin address.
- **Bitcoins can be accessed** from anywhere with an Internet connection.
- **Anybody** can start buying, selling or accepting bitcoins regardless of their location.
- **Bitcoins can be completely distributed** with no bank or payment processor between users (this decentralisation is the basis for Bitcoin's security and freedom).
- **Transactions are *free*** (for now but this will change).

It is possible to buy bitcoins quite easily through various exchanges, with the Japanese MtGox exchange being the most liquid during the early years of Bitcoin.[23] Other exchanges include Coinbase, Bitcoin-24 and Intersango. Many of these exchanges are talking to regulators to be recognised as official trading venues, with Germany and France providing official endorsement of bitcoins as a medium of exchange in 2013.

In order to buy coins, you send payment to the account that you have set up on the exchange of your choice in pounds, dollars, euro, yen or another currency, and then buy bitcoins at the strike price of the day. Once you have bitcoins, you can trade them with anyone who accepts the coins, with no charges for the transaction. This is the key attraction of Bitcoin; once purchased, you need never pay a cross-border or bank fee again because

---

23   MtGox suffered losses and eventual bankruptcy in 2014 due to hack attacks. The impact of its closure on Bitcoin is inconclusive at the time of this book's release.

no borders or bank are involved. In other words, it is a global currency for the Internet age.

You can buy all sorts of things with bitcoins from pizza to property, although the number of outlets accepting bitcoins has been limited to date. Nevertheless, it is gradually expanding in usage and you can use bitcoins at point of sale.

For example, VeriFone launched a POS system in 2011 that allows bitcoins to be traded on merchants' terminals in stores. The system is based on QR codes which are printed by the VeriFone terminal. The customer can then scan the code into their phone. Equally, they can make a Bitcoin payment by presenting the QR code on their phone for the merchant to scan. Technically, it's an open-source payment tool. Like BitTorrent, a peer-to-peer file sharing protocol, Bitcoin allows the peer-to-

peer sharing of value securely globally. The problem is that authorities do not like open-source P2P services like BitTorrent and Wikileaks because they undermine traditional forms of commerce as the currency can be used for both good and bad things.

In fact, Bitcoin is mainly associated with crime, being used for drugs and terrorism, according to government authorities. This is not actually the case as Bitcoin does not fuel crime, just as the Internet does not fuel crime. Just because the Internet enables links to drugs, gambling and pornography, it doesn't mean that the Internet should be banned. In the same way, if Bitcoin enables criminals to trade in drugs, gambling and pornography, it doesn't mean that you need to ban Bitcoin.

Precisely because bitcoins are digital tokens that can be traded anywhere by anyone without barriers is the reason why this method of payment concerns governments as most other forms of value exchange can be controlled. Visa, MasterCard and PayPal have offices in the United States, for example, and are therefore controlled by the American authorities. Bitcoin does not sit within American, Chinese, Russian or any other soil, it just exists across the worldwide web and is therefore uncontrolled. That is why Bitcoin's emergence into the public domain has not been without issue.

For example, one key challenge is liquidity and the fact that it is a limited market today. The average price to purchase a bitcoin was $70 in August 2013. In April 2013, the values peaked at over $250 per coin compared with $33 in June 2011 and under $2 in October 2011. As can be seen, the value of bitcoins swings wildly due to the limited amount of real money circulating through the system.

In April 2013, the total Bitcoin economy peaked at $2 billion. The question is: what would happen if there were $1 trillion in the Bitcoin system? It would be a mainstream currency and could even start to become a serious contender as a real reserve currency alongside the dollar and euro. This is a great concern for governments worldwide as bitcoins cannot be regulated like the dollar and euro because, as already mentioned, no government or central bank is involved.

Another key attribute is that only 21 million bitcoins will ever be issued. This cap was introduced in order to act as a currency control mechanism and ensure the stored value exchange would not break. Although there is this limit of 21 million bitcoins, the coins are infinitely divisible, with each bitcoin potentially being able to be divided to up to eight decimal places, resulting in an eventual total of 2.1 quadrillion units. By August 2013, of the 21 million coins that can be issued, just over 11.5 million had been issued. The aim is to limit the number of coins in existence because, unlike fiat currencies issued by government agencies, there is no centralised issuing authority in Bitcoin, just users. This is another reason why the cap exists and is one of the more contentious points of Bitcoin—those who own a whole bitcoin today will become billionaires tomorrow if it ever becomes a mainstream currency.

The Problem with Bitcoin

However, before getting too excited about Bitcoin, we have to remember that the ecosystem is still very fragile. Like Beenz and Flooz, the currency could disappear as quickly as it appeared if confidence dissipates. Let's remember that a currency not only needs to be a medium of exchange and a store of value but also secure and fully liquid. It is the latter attributes that have been questioned by many as Bitcoin's value is highly volatile—due to an illiquid market—and its security has been regularly compromised.

For example, Bitfloor, a former online exchange for bitcoins much like MtGox, was compromised in 2012 and forced to shut down for a while. Roman Shtylman, the founder of Bitfloor, announced the security breach on 4 September 2012 on BitcoinTalk, a forum dedicated to the discussion of the currency, as follows:

"Last night, a few of our servers were compromised. As a result, the attacker gained access to an unencrypted backup of the wallet keys (the actual keys live in an encrypted area). Using these keys, they were able to transfer the coins. This attack took the vast majority of the coins Bitfloor was holding on hand. As a result, I have paused all exchange operations."

In total, 24,086 bitcoins, worth around $250,000 at the time, were stolen. Although Bitfloor restarted operating soon afterwards, it encountered further issues in 2013 when its bank withdrew support for the exchange. The exchange has since completely closed down. This is an example of just one of several security breaches although, in almost all cases, it is not the bitcoins that were compromised but the systems and servers of the users.

Another challenge is that the total processing capability for the coins is seven transactions per second (tps). This is a false constraint created by validating the coins as they are processed, and creates a hard block size limit for coin traffic. Basically, this means that bitcoins cannot be used for more than about 360,000 transactions per day, or 2,500 transactions every ten minutes. By contrast VISA handles around 2,000 tps on average, with a daily peak rate of 4,000 tps. In fact, the company has the capacity for over 10,000 tps to handle the busiest holiday periods where transactions regularly reach 8,500 per second.

Bitcoin's 7 tps compared to 10,000 with VISA is a bit of a chasm, although Bitcoin does not claim to be a VISA. It does compare its targets to PayPal, however. PayPal handles around 4 million transactions per day for an average of 46 tps, or a peak rate of around 100 tps. That's what Bitcoin is aiming for, and the open-source community does say that if Bitcoin usage increases such that it needs to take the false 7 tps constraint away, then that figure could easily be achieved. Maybe that's why the value of bitcoins is rising, and rising fast.

Bitcoin Bubbles and Bursts

The Bitcoin phenomenon really hit the headlines in 2013 when the value of bitcoins rose from a steady $20 per coin to $266 in just a few months, only to crash to $100 by the end of April 2013. What caused this? The general consensus is the financial crisis in Cyprus.

In March 2013, Cyprus's government needed a bailout due to overexposures to Greek debt and agreed to a proposal to take money from citizens' domestic bank accounts as a tax to cover the exposure. This created a panic amongst many Europeans who felt that their banking systems were weak. Consequently, large numbers of people suddenly converted their euro savings into bitcoins. They even wrote a song about it to the tune of Swedish House Mafia's stomping summer hit "Don't You Worry Child".

The original lyrics go:

Upon a hill across a blue lake,
That's where I had my first heartbreak.

I still remember how it all changed.

My father said,

"Don't you worry, don't you worry, child.

See heaven's got a plan for you.

Don't you worry, don't you worry now."

The European Bitcoin version was released in March 2013 and went like this:

Just when the Cypriots were losing faith,

That's when I learned about the block chain.

I still remember how it all changed.

Satoshi said,

"Don't you worry, don't you worry, child

Bitcoin has got a plan for you

Don't you worry, don't you worry now."

This is not unusual as Bitcoin offers both a speculative investment and a potential safe haven for transacting online. For example, I presented to a conference in the Middle East in mid-February 2012 and, at the end, a gentleman from Iran asked me lots of questions about Bitcoin. As Iran's banks were thrown off the bank network by SWIFT in 2012, under severe pressure from the American government, the idea of putting all of their money into bitcoins would make perfect sense.

This particular Bitcoin bubble began in March 2013, with a massive rise in value from the stable $20 per coin mark in January to almost $100 per coin by the end of March. Then the Bitcoin bubble peaked at $266 per coin on Wednesday 10 April 2013, followed by a massive drop to just $55 in a few hours. It stabilised back at $100 and was consistently trading around $120 by the summer of 2013.

Then the Bitcoin bubble started to inflate again, peaking at a value of nearly $1,300 per bitcoin on MtGox Japan, the largest Bitcoin exchange, in December 2013, only for this to drop to under $300 in February 2014. Once again, this begs the question why? Well, it's all about trust and confidence. And the trust and confidence in the Bitcoin system is easily boosted or burst by media hype and the headlines.

Furthermore, exchanges like MtGox encounter technical and related issues that mean customers cannot withdraw funds. We also shouldn't forget about the challenges presented by distributed denial of service (DDoS) attacks,[24] such as the most recent one that targeted MtGox in February 2014, as well as the technical nature of Bitcoin itself.

In fact, the whole nature of these bubbles and bursts led to MtGox failing in February 2014, losing many Bitcoin enthusiasts thousands of dollars and causing major disillusion in the nature of this virtual currency.

Nevertheless, I've seen the bitcoin price bubble burst at least five times in the last three years, and I am sure we will see this happen again in the future, but the core of the above is this: what does Bitcoin mean to banking, trade, finance and commerce?

Much of the media use these bubble bursts to write off Bitcoin when, in fact, they have actually achieved the opposite. The media state that everything from the vulnerabilities of the Bitcoin system, the fragility of its system, the ease of hacking the system, its usage for dodgy purchases from drugs to weapons of personal destruction and more would kill the economy. It has not. It's just made the economy more robust.

Many of these accusations have been thrown at Bitcoin before, and it has survived all of these challenges to date. This is just symptomatic of a fledgling system and an economy that lacks mass liquidity. This is why Bitcoin is not robust today—the system has not got enough liquidity—but the fact that European savers, Iranian businesses and mainstream media are all now on the case of Bitcoin indicates that it will gain critical mass and potentially, over time, mainstream acceptance.

---

24   Such an attack targets the bandwidth of the website, sending TCP, UDP or HTTP requests to the site until it goes down.

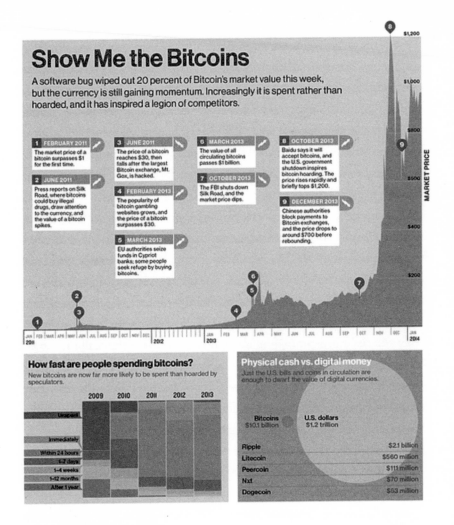

Show Me the Bitcoins

A software bug wiped out 20 percent of Bitcoin's market value this week, but the currency is still gaining momentum. Increasingly it is spent rather than hoarded, and it has inspired a legion of competitors.

1 FEBRUARY 2011
The market price of a bitcoin surpasses $1 for the first time.

2 JUNE 2011
Press reports on Silk Road, where bitcoins could buy illegal drugs, draw attention to the currency, and the value of a bitcoin spikes.

3 JUNE 2011
The price of a bitcoin reaches $30, then falls after the largest Bitcoin exchange, Mt. Gox, is hacked.

4 FEBRUARY 2013
The popularity of bitcoin gambling websites grows, and the price of a bitcoin surpasses $30.

5 MARCH 2013
EU authorities seize funds in Cypriot banks; some people seek refuge by buying bitcoins.

6 MARCH 2013
The value of all circulating bitcoins passes $1 billion.

7 OCTOBER 2013
The FBI shuts down Silk Road, and the market price dips.

8 OCTOBER 2013
Baidu says it will accept bitcoins, and the U.S. government shutdown inspires bitcoin hoarding. The price rises rapidly and briefly tops $1,200.

9 DECEMBER 2013
Chinese authorities block payments to Bitcoin exchanges, and the price drops to around $700 before rebounding.

MARKET PRICE

$1,200 — $1,000 — $800 — $600 — $400 — $200

How fast are people spending bitcoins?
New bitcoins are now far more likely to be spent than hoarded by speculators.

2009 2010 2011 2012 2013

Unspent
Immediately
Within 24 hours
1-7 days
1-4 weeks
1-12 months
After 1 year

Physical cash vs. digital money
Just the U.S. bills and coins in circulation are enough to dwarf the value of digital currencies.

Bitcoins $10.1 billion — U.S. dollars $1.2 trillion

Ripple	$21 billion
Litecoin	$560 million
Peercoin	$111 million
Nxt	$70 million
Dogecoin	$53 million

Source: MIT Technology Review

The Future of Bitcoin

Bitcoin's community liken Bitcoin to the development of the Internet. When the Internet began, it was difficult to use because you had to program it. Then it got easier with HTML (an Internet language) and the worldwide web, and now it's so simple thanks to social media that anyone can create, share, blog and inform. Likewise, Bitcoin started as a program, quickly became a form of exchange and very soon will become as simple as using PayPal or credit and debit cards online. Soon, it will be plug-and-playable into any form of transaction. Then it will be a serious contender to challenge traditional money. As Anthony Gallippi, CEO of BitPay, said at a conference I chaired: "Bitcoin is a new asset class where money can be stored in the cloud and accessed anywhere with any device for free." Now I like that. That describes it succinctly and perfectly as any money I can store for free in the cloud, use with any device and transact easily at low or zero cost makes sense to me.

Often though, people think bitcoins are some sort of dodgy Ponzi scheme used for money laundering and drugs, but that's because they don't understand what Bitcoin is all about. You see, Bitcoin is the Wikicoin for the Wikileaks world. As I keep saying, it is regarded as disruptive because it has no central issuing authority or control, and that's why governments, particularly the US government, view it as dangerous. As I write, dialogue between the US authorities and those promoting bitcoins is taking place regularly, and there will continue to be a long and arduous battle between the controllers and the uncontrolled. This is the nature of the Wikiconomy. Nevertheless, I have invested in bitcoins and suggest you do too, as it is very likely that they will be a major store of value for years to come in the near term.

Alternative Virtual Currencies to Bitcoin

As already stated, Bitcoin is not the only virtual currency out there and it still has to gain critical mass acceptance as a currency to buy and sell. This is the major hurdle that it has yet to overcome. For example, in a recent academic paper reviewing Bitcoin, several key inhibitors to data currencies were identified:[25]

- improper usage
- superior alternatives

---

25   Grinberg, Reuben. "Bitcoin: An Innovative Alternative Digital Currency" (9 December 2011). *Hastings Science & Technology Law Journal*, Vol. 4, p.160. Available at SSRN: http://ssrn.com/abstract=1817857

- government blockage
- abandonment due to deflation
- technology failures leading to theft or a loss of anonymity

Similarly, the ECB issued a report on Virtual Currency Schemes, with case studies on Second Life and Bitcoin. In the report, the ECB calls Bitcoin "the most successful—and probably most controversial—virtual currency scheme to date." The ECB goes on to say that the concept of Bitcoin stems from the Austrian school of economics, where the business cycle theory developed by Mises, Hayek and Bohm-Bawerk floated the idea that virtual currencies could be the starting point for ending central bank money monopolies.

Why did the ECB bother to write a report and an in-depth analysis of Bitcoin and other virtual currencies? Because it is worried that they are unregulated value exchanges that could represent a challenge for public authorities and have a negative impact on the reputation of central banks. On the other hand, the ECB does make note that "these schemes can have positive aspects in terms of financial innovation and the provision of additional payment alternatives for consumers."

To be honest, whether Bitcoin takes off or not, virtual currencies are going to explode thanks to in-app gaming on the mobile Internet, something the ECB report misses. Most of us already top up our gaming on our iPhones and iPads via iTunes. That is virtual currency in operation. You may disagree but the aggregation of large amounts of small payments is effectively building a virtual currency system. If you don't believe me, take note of the many examples of virtual currencies for gaming: NHN Japan offers a global gaming virtual currency called Line Coins, KakaoTalk in Korea offers a virtual currency called Choco and there's Tencent's QQ in China. There are other virtual coins around today including:

- Moba, Japanese social gaming firm DeNa's coins
- Facebook and Zynga credits

- World of Warcraft and Diablo Gold
- Amazon Coins virtual currency

All of these virtual currencies are driven by mobile Internet gaming services, with Amazon extending such services into book purchases and more. Once accepted as a currency of value, a virtual coin can then be traded anywhere, anytime, almost as if it were cash.

Then the real killer will be when the major payments processors move into the virtual payments space. For example, VISA recently acquired PlaySpan, a company with a payment platform that handles transactions for digital goods while American Express has purchased Sometrics, a company that helps video game makers establish virtual currencies and plans to build a virtual currency platform in other industries, taking advantage of its merchant relationships.

So it's the world of gaming that is developing our new world virtual economies into new world virtual payments processors and what all of these developments demonstrate is the rise of digital currencies offering real value in the same way as cash and other hard currencies. In other words, data is a currency and the Digital Bank needs to include data as a currency, virtual currencies, mobile money, proximity payments and more in their social money and payments plans.

The Drawbacks of Social Money

Having discussed virtual currencies and social money, there is one lesson that will be conciliatory for banks: they will always run the monetary network. This is a key area in banking as everyone always has the idea that others, such as Google and Facebook, will take over banking. They won't and the reason is best illustrated by the rise and fall of the virtual currency system in Second Life.

Second Life is a virtual world that gained huge popularity in the mid-2000s and then, just as quickly, disappeared off the radar. The reason Second Life's popularity disappeared was caused by the collapse of its banking system in the summer of 2007. The banking collapse was a reaction to Second Life being forced to close down gambling facilities in its virtual world in July 2007. Until then, the website had been a phenomenon, growing from virtually no users to over 10 million in a year.

This was incredible, and everyone felt it demonstrated the new emergence of business models. In particular, the fact that Second Life allowed real commerce to be transacted by converting real US dollars to virtual dollars meant that everyone started to test commerce in virtual worlds through the service. For example, several banks invested in major projects in Second Life, including ING, Wells Fargo, SAXO Bank and Deutsche Bank.

However, several banks also operated in Second Life that were managed by guys in their bedrooms. These included banks such as Ginko Financial, run by a Brazilian chap at home. Ginko Financial's troubles all began when Internet gambling was forced to close under US Laws. The management of Second Life decided that it also had to close access to gambling in virtual worlds in July 2007 to comply with this policy, which led to a major run on the virtual banks. Until this date, a lot of the commercial transactions taking place in Second Life, where people converted real US dollars to Linden dollars, had been for gambling purposes apparently. Therefore, the closure of gambling denizens in the virtual world meant that people immediately started to take money out of the virtual banks, a bit like Northern Rock but worse.

So imagine you are Andre Sanchez in Sao Paulo, the one-man band behind the virtual Ginko Financial. You have over a million real US dollars on account, translated into around 275 million Linden dollars, which you are managing for the Second Life community. Suddenly, your customers demand that their money be converted back into real dollars, and you drown in their demands so you close down the virtual bank, leaving punters with losses of around $750,000 in real life.

This led to calls for compensation from Linden Lab, which operates Second Life, but it said it wasn't its job to regulate the virtual banks. Result: Second Life's popularity collapsed and, in a desperate move to rebuild trust,

Linden Lab said that only real-life banks with real-world banking licences could operate virtual banks in future. Talk about virtual life mirroring real life ... mind you, I do note that Linden Lab didn't come up with a million dollar bailout fund, so maybe not.

This is one example of social money systems and how they can reflect real-world systems virtually and is the reason why the possibility of Google, Apple or Facebook opening a bank in the near future is unlikely. This is also why most of the innovations in banking and payments to date, such as PayPal, have been on the old bank plumbing in the past and will be in the future.

Banks are regulated and need licences and this is a key feature of the system from a governmental perspective in making them work. It is the reason why Linden Lab's Second Life had to regulate its banks in the virtual world with bank licences in the real world, and why QQ is regulated by the People's Republic of China. But this maybe ignores a basic tenet of the Internet: freedom.

So as we move into the melding of online and offline into real time, we could see a major shift away from bank infrastructures such as Visa, MasterCard and SWIFT into new infrastructures, such as those provided by Bitcoin. This is a more significant threat to bank services because it is a crowdsourced bank.

Before I finish talking about social money, it's worth mentioning complementary currencies, which are also related to Bitcoin because these are often referred to as community currencies, and Bitcoin is the community currency of the mobile Internet generation. These currencies are on the rise as social money in the real world, and fuelled for broader acceptability through our networked world. For example, if I can exchange a London pound for a New York dollar of community effort via a trusted processor, then we could build a new, global complementary currency exchange. This is the idea behind Bitcoin, which acts as social money—a complementary currency—that would provide a global exchange for trade managed through Internet technologies.

In summary, social money is all about enabling the exchange of value between individuals and businesses through electronic channels. This exchange can be:

- **formal** through electronic money transfer systems such as PayPal or exchanges based on backing from valuable metals such as gold and silver
- **informal** through exchanging real money into other forms of value, including virtual money and complementary currencies

All of these are Internet-fuelled and managed to support the wider sphere of social finance, networking and media.

Social Lending and Saving

The earliest example of a new social finance model was launched by Zopa in the United Kingdom in 2005 and created a new form of lending. Since then, Zopa-style lending services have appeared everywhere, from smava in Germany to Ppdai in China to Prosper and Lending Club in the United States, as well as more and more UK domestic competitors, such as RateSetter and Folk2Folk.

The basic premise of most social lending is an eBay-style platform for savers and borrowers. The savers' savings fund the borrowers' borrowings, just like a bank, but the difference is that these businesses offer no financial management themselves. They are just a platform to connect savers who want a higher return on their savings, and borrowers who want a lower interest rate on their loans. These platforms just connect them and claim that there is no financial management taking place.

Zopa, smava, Ppdai and related firms are therefore like eBay. eBay does not offer a product but merely connects buyers and sellers. In the same way, these firms purely connect savers and borrowers. This is why Zopa falls outside the remit of the regulatory authorities, although this is changing as from 2014 when formal industry regulations will be introduced.

Social lenders also win out because they are small and nimble, with few employees or overheads, which mean that they can offer a service with minimal spread on the difference between borrowing and saving rates. As a result, they undercut bank rates significantly with a 0.5 per cent spread. This is why social lending works.

In terms of managing the risk on loans, most of this risk is managed by using traditional credit vetting services of banks, such as Equifax and Experian, and is the reason why the service has a minimal default ratio averaging 0.7 per cent. The ratio lowers to 0.1 per cent for the lowest risk lending operations, which is actually a better risk model than traditional banks achieve.

The ages of typical lenders range from 20 to 88 years, with an average age of 40. The amounts loaned range from £10 to £100,000, and the incentive for lenders and borrowers is to receive better interest rates than they would receive from traditional high street financial providers.

In the United Kingdom, Zopa and the other lending companies have been doing particularly well thanks to the credit crisis. For example, in 2013, Zopa's loan volumes ran at £20 million a month compared to just £6 million per month in 2010. The company anticipates processing over £400 million of loans in 2014, more than double the amount for 2013. This increase in business is also attributed to the issues of September 2008, as the credit crisis hit and UK banks HBOS and Lloyds merged whilst the other major bank, the Royal Bank of Scotland, had to be bailed out. This meant that the traditional sources of credit access shrank considerably post the credit crisis, and savings rates were also perfunctory as central banks followed a zero interest policy.

This UK success has therefore been replicated elsewhere, with firms such as the Lending Club in the United States taking over $10 million a month through their platform.

Nevertheless, this model has not succeeded in all countries, with Zopa's overseas ventures not working out for various reasons, most of them regulatory. Prosper also failed in the United States as the Securities and Exchange Commission (SEC) shut it down when it was generating around

$10 million a month and it's struggled to average more than $2 million a month ever since. There are no such systems in Africa, and the only other European success has been smava in Germany, but it needed a banking licence from BaFIN (the country's Federal Financial Supervisory Authority) before it could ramp up its business.

In other words, the financial protection rules of most countries have made it incredibly difficult to create successful social financing operations, even though the service they offer is not a financial one. Note again that Zopa does no lending itself, it just enables those who want to lend to connect with those who want to borrow at better rates than those offered by high street banks.

Another point is that these social financing operations do no marketing, but are trusted. This trust is generated by their community. For example, most of the social lending services have an open platform for discussions that are regulated by their customers. If one customer comes out and moans about bad services, there will normally be ten others who will shoot them down if they are wrong. Amazingly, some customers spend up to eight hours per day responding to community posts. Such customers are the biggest advocates of these websites and, as such, are unpaid marketing champions for the cause. As a result, the social community support the social offer, and having your customers as your community moderators not only means less staff dedicated to monitoring the conversation but also faster response times and more trust in the answers.

All in all, this is why these firms use social media for customer servicing extensively and state that Twitter is one of the best service tools they've ever seen. Why? Because complaints are short—under 140 characters—and therefore easy to deal with. Not just that, but their staff think it's cool to be using the latest technologies to deal with customers rather than some boring old call centre operation. Furthermore, it's in the public domain and that sends a powerful signal that they're not trying to hide anything.

The social tools have built a trust which, when the crisis hit, enabled them to compete effectively against traditional banks. In fact, traditional banks weren't particularly liked before the crisis but they were trusted because they were old, big, safe, secure and reliable. Now, that's not the case. Their image has been tarnished and the social lenders and financial firms have worked really hard on both the hard and soft things to ensure that they can compete. For example, most have a completely transparent business model aligned with their social community platform. They position themselves as being "available to talk" and pride themselves on being responsive and attentive.

But this has to be a complete commitment as you cannot be public some of the time, and private some of the time. Because it's in the public domain, you cannot follow that line and then ask the customer to take something offline.

Suffice to say, there is a world of direct social lending out there and it's now big business. For instance, Zopa recently gained over 2 per cent market share for all UK personal retail credit lending.

It is not without issues however, with the US government closely monitoring the way these sites operate and, in some cases, shutting them down. The problem with social lending services, as cited by the SEC, is that loans are not being repaid and this is the challenge for these sites—to get enough liquidity to be able to cover all the borrowings required, and to manage the risk of those borrowings. Many of the social lending sites cover these risks by using Experian, Equifax and other credit rating agencies, or through the offer of insurances, but any squeeze on funding strains the social lending business model.

As mentioned earlier, there is also social saving. Social saving builds on the themes of social lending but works towards savings targets. An example is called iWish from ICICI Bank. iWish provides a means for users to create a savings goal, such as saving for a car or a college education or to pay off a mortgage. As they save towards their goals, they can tell the world what they are saving for on their social network page, blog or website. As a result, their friends and family can contribute towards their savings goals and this is very friend- and family-oriented.

The leading company in this space, however, is the American innovator SmartyPig, which created one of the first social saving products in 2007. It now offers a direct online smart piggy bank in the United States, as well as partnerships with banks like BBVA for the Compass app in the United States, ICICI Bank for the iWish service in India and ANZ in Asia. In these instances, the overseas banks offer the SmartyPig service under their own brands.

Social Funding and Investing

Social funding and investing falls into a number of sub-categories, but the major areas are crowdfunding and social trading.

Crowdfunding differs from social lending in that it is investing for returns in new business start-ups and, like crowdsourcing, it pools the money of the masses into a nice venture fund to get things started. Much of the focus of crowdfunding has been around Kickstarter, the American leader in this space. Kickstarter provides a platform for funding by pre-selling your idea, rather than providing equity in the business. For example, you have a conceptual music idea, and you pre-sell the idea through Kickstarter with the hope of getting enough monies to fund the implementation of the idea (unlike other sites where you get an equity stake in the business).

Kickstarter kicked off in business in April 2009 and, three years later, had seeded $200 million in funds across 50,000 projects. Most of these projects are related to entertainment and the arts (about 60 per cent of all projects), although some are technology and related fields. For example, in its most recent success, Kickstarter generated $10 million in funding for a new venture called Pebble. Pebble is a smartwatch that will connect to a smartphone. According to the *Wall Street Journal*, the concept raised more than $1 million in its first day on Kickstarter—17 April 2012 to be precise—based on an offer to pledge $115 to pre-order the watch. By mid-May 2012, Pebble had achieved its goal of raising $10.27 million. The funds were gained from 68,929 people, making it the most crowdfunded start-up ever in dollar terms at that time. There is nothing like a cool gadget to get people excited.

Nevertheless, as mentioned, most of the projects are related to music, film, art, theatre, design and publishing, and these provide some interesting stats. For example, of the platform's 7,388 successful music projects in June 2012, 6,446 of them (87.3 per cent) raised $10,000 or less, 238 of them raised more than $20,000, 8 raised more than $100,000 and one (Amanda Palmer) raised more than $1 million.[26] Similarly, not all projects succeed in raising the funding required. In fact, about 41 per cent of the projects listed fail with only half getting the funding needed.

However, crowdfunding is big business—Kickstarter had $100 million of pledges by May 2011 and this increased to $250 million by May 2012—and now the service has expanded into other regions of the world. That's an important development, but it's not a clear space. There are other crowdfunding services like Indiegogo, crowdrise, razoo and more, and even specialist sites for vertical markets like MedStartr for start-ups in medicines. The United Kingdom has a number of crowdfunding sites, such as Funding Circle, CrowdCube, Seedrs and ThinCats, so it's a hot market space to watch right now. According to Massolution, a research firm specialising in crowdsourcing and crowdfunding solutions, crowdfunding platforms raised almost $1.5 billion worldwide in 2011, with a growth rate of 63 per cent CAGR. It forecasted that the funding figures would have doubled in 2012 to near $3 billion raised from 530 platforms, up from 452 in 2011. So this is already a serious alternative to bank credit for business and small start-ups.

Social trading is illustrated by two market leading developments: eToro and StockTwits. eToro launched in 2007 as a social network for foreign exchange trading and is now the largest social investment network worldwide. Over the years, it has expanded into full commodities, shares and currency trading, offering the ability to trade direct online as individuals or to follow "star investors" by copying their social profiles and investment portfolios. Based in Israel, the system uses real-time features to let users follow and trade based on other users' activities, and it has seen strong growth with

---

26   All statistics are taken from Billboard.

2.85 million accounts operating in June 2013, compared with 1.75 million in 2011.

The core of eToro is the ability to follow influential traders using a charting tool that shows every trader what all the other users are doing on the network at any point of time. eToro then takes this one step further so that, like Twitter, you can follow other traders on the network, watch what they do and copy their trading activities if you want. The traders who get followed, as a result, have a double revenue stream: one from their trades (if they're good) and one from those who copy their trades with top traders, known as gurus, commanding as many as 100,000 followers and 10,000 copiers.

According to eToro, gurus earn as much as $10,000 a month in commissions by attracting people to duplicate their trades and are motivated as much by their social peer status and influence as the money. eToro, like other investing sites, takes a commission on the trades made but otherwise does not charge for its service and therefore offers a compelling model, as does ZuluTrade, Tradency, StockTwits and similar social investment communities. For example, ZuluTrade, a social network focused on currencies, has seen its user base triple to 500,000 members between 2011 and 2013, with transaction volumes reaching about $40 billion a month.

StockTwits was launched in 2008 as a method of tracking tweets on Twitter about companies and markets that might influence trading strategies. The firm acts as a social, stock micro-blogging service, or a financial idea network if you prefer, and works by pulling in tweets from Twitter that have stock tickers marked with $ signs, such as $AAPL. It then mixes these with financial tools and analysis that's unique to the network so that anyone from investment professionals to beginners can share their thoughts about stocks through Twitter, Facebook and LinkedIn. By 2013, over 200,000 investors were sharing information and ideas about the market and individual stocks using StockTwits, producing streams viewed by an audience of around 40 million people across the financial web and social media platforms.

Between these examples, we are seeing more and more social funding and investing exploding into the financial mainstream.

WHAT DOES THIS MEAN FOR THE FUTURE?

It means that banks will be componentised, a point I've made several times already. The deconstruction of banks into component pieces is already happening and is being generated faster and faster, quicker and quicker, every day through apps and mobile Internet.

It is similar to the car servicing industry. In the 1970s, all cars were serviced by their manufacturers, who made fat margins from replacement parts and labour. The customer was forced to drive their car to the manufacturer, at the time of the manufacturer's choosing and would be forced to work to the manufacturer's agenda. Then a firm called Kwik-Fit came into the UK market, with the view that certain car parts—tyres and exhausts—were pretty much bulk standard and could be fitted without any real specialist knowledge or expertise. Result: cars could get these parts replaced at a fraction of the cost of the manufacturer, and whilst the customer waited.

This illustration shows how the industry was re-engineered from the supplier in control to the customer in control, and this is what social financial firms are trying to achieve—to take the parts of banking where margins are high for low value-add and make them accessible to all at low margins through high value-add based on direct connections enabled by today's technologies.

This attitude is driving into all aspects of banking from payments to loans, cards to deposit accounts and treasury to derivatives, and the result is that the banking industry is being componentised and commoditised through apps and new social business models and structures.

This raises a key question: what happens when your product is a username, your processing is an API and your customer engagement is just an app?

It's a question I've been playing with for a long time now, and recently realised that all the innovative and disruptive models of finance that are emerging are nibbling away at the traditional structure of banks:

- FIDOR is snibbling away at the core deposit model of banks, as are Moven, Simple, Alior et al.

- Zopa is nibbling away at the credit markets, as are smava, Prosper, Lending Circle et al.
- Currency Cloud is nibbling away at the cross-border activities of banks, as are Bitcoin, Azimo, KlickEx et al.
- Kickstarter is nibbling away at the commercial banking operations of banks, as are Receivables Exchange, Funding Circle et al.
- eToro is nibbling away at the investment operations of banks, as are ZuluTrade, StockTwits et al.

Every part of banking is being nibbled at by new start-ups. For instance, Zopa is a username, Currency Cloud is an API and Moven is an app. Each is targeting the product, processing and engagement that a customer has with their finance.

What does this mean for a bank? Historically, the bank would have owned them all. The bank owned the product, process and customer engagement. Most banks had this locked in to a vertical end-to-end structure that was tightly integrated and difficult to break. That is what is being broken apart by technology today.

So what does happen when your product is a username, your processing is an API and your customer engagement is just an app? Change. Banks need to start making strategic decisions before it's too late. This is not a new big thing, but it hit me squarely and clearly as I was thinking about the fact that banks are trying to evolve to keep up with EVERYTHING. They want to be the payments processors, the customer engagers, the mortgage providers and more. That is old world thinking. The old world is the one where, because the bank has the deposit account, the bank tries to leverage that relationship—which is proprietary, locked in and difficult to change— to get more share of wallet from insurances to loans. That is the old world.

As banks are being decomposed into constituent pieces, where customers will determine their relevancy, banks need to really refocus on where they're most differentiated and competent. Where is the bank really, really good? Banks are not good at everything. They are good at some things. Some banks are good at customer relationships, some are good at products and some are good at processing. Some are good at relationships and processing, some are good at products and processing and some are good at products and relationships, but I'm not sure I can think of any that are good at everything.

That's why there are so many new entrants and upstarts getting into banking and finance. The upstarts are trying to eat the margins from products, processing and relationships. Upstarts are focused on products (Zopa, Wonga, Kickstarter, etc.), processing (Currency Cloud, FIDOR, StockTwits, etc.) and relationships (Moven, Simple, Alior, etc.). Incumbents are hell-bent on preserving the status quo, ceterus parabus, caveat emptor and a whole lot more Latin stuff.

In fact, Latin is where the incumbents might belong, as the old language of integrated processes that deliver the product, process and service is just where that dialogue belongs. Customers will not live with that as the new world is one that breaks up everything, and then integrates it back together again. The new world is where banks offer APIs to process, usernames to access and apps to service.

Banks will not offer all of these. Some will focus on the process, some will focus on the product and some will focus on the relationship. To process, they will offer APIs to ensure they can get volumes on their wiki; to manufacture, banks will make sure their product is the most pervasive and ubiquitous on the net; and to relate, the bank will aggregate and integrate everything into simple apps that customers love.

That's the real challenge here: how to be the bank fit for the 21st century by focusing on what you're really, really, really, really, really good at. And you're not good at everything. You know that, I know that and your customers know that. So make a strategic decision to focus on what you're really, really, really, really, really good at, and then market the hell out of it to make sure everyone knows that's what you're really, really, really, really, really good at. Either that or let the new guys nibble at your best bits, leaving you with the bits you don't want.

DIGITAL BANKS FIGHT DATA WARS

Data is the future competitive battleground for banks. In fact, as stated much earlier in this book, data is the battleground of today but many banks are yet to realise this. Admittedly, some banks did acknowledge this years ago:

"Information about money has become almost as important as money itself."
—WALTER WRISTON, CEO/Chair, Citibank, 1967–1984

"Banking is just bits and bytes."
—JOHN REED, CEO/Chair, Citibank, 1984–1998

However, most banks have not, not even today.

When they do, banks will move towards data being their most critical asset—above capital and labour—and consequently will move into data wars with the heavyweight data managers of Google, Amazon, Facebook and more.

HOW VALUE CHANGES: BEFORE IT WAS DATA, IT WAS SALT

Data as a currency is nothing and this is why people try to rob banks online instead of in branches, because online is where the money is. The money is in the data. This is why data is the new money. This is nothing new as historically we have often migrated value and meaning from different objects as our means of trade.

In early civilisations, seashells and beads were key currencies, with the Yap Islands being a great example of such exchange. On these islands, large stones are viewed as the sign of wealth. But no substance was valued more than salt in olden times.

Salt is something we liberally sprinkle over food—because industrial processing allows us to have an abundance of salt today—but historically it was the most valued source of wealth. Greek slave traders often bartered salt for slaves, giving rise to the expression that someone was "not worth his salt", while Roman legionnaires were paid in salt rations known as solarium argentums, also known as a salarium, the Latin origin of the word *salary*.

Jesus said, "Ye are the salt of the earth" while trade routes such as the ancient Via Salaria, which led from northern Italy to the Adriatic Sea, were used to transport the valuable seasoning inland from the coast. This brought riches and prosperity to the bordering cities, which were often named after the white mineral. For instance, *Salz*, the German word for "salt", gave Salzburg and Salzgitter their names. The British monarchy supported itself with high salt taxes, with 10,000 people arrested for salt smuggling every year back in the 1700s, and the Erie Canal connecting the Great Lakes to New York's Hudson River was called "the ditch that salt built" in 1825 as salt tax revenues paid for half the cost of the canal's construction.

The only reason why the value of salt has been devalued is due to the industrial processing of salt, which allows all of us to enjoy the abundance of the 40 million tonnes we require each year.

The reason for discussing this is partly to think of money as being anything. It can be gold, beads, shells, salt or data, as any and all of these represent capabilities to exchange value. In economic terms, what has value is based on scarcity, and salt had scarcity historically, which is why it was more valued than gold. Today, it has abundance and hence is cheap.

Now data has abundance, and so is also cheap, but information is power, and so it's what you make of the data that has scarcity. In other words, turning data into knowledge is where the value lies today, just as turning rock and seawater into salt had value in ancient times.

As Georg Friedrich Knapp stated in 1924, "There are means of payment which are not yet money; then there those which are money; later still, those which have ceased to be money."

As data challenges grow, solutions will emerge. Just as salt was a currency, it was not the salt that was important but the quality of the salt extracted by the salt miners from different seas and rocks.

DATA AS A CURRENCY IS NOT NEW

In the previous chapter, we saw that data is a form of currency when we looked at online money like Bitcoin, virtual currencies like Linden dollars and gaming currencies like QQ coins. This made it clear that data is a currency. So yes, we might know and agree on that fact but, if data is a currency, we just haven't realised how much value this currency offers.

This was made clear by Craig Mundie, head of Research and Strategy at Microsoft, who said, "Data is the greatest raw material of business, on a par with capital and labour. What we are seeing is the ability to have economies form around the data and that, to me, is the big change at a societal and even macroeconomic level."[27]

Now this is where it gets interesting and brings data mining to the fore. The essence of data mining is to dig deep to find relationships between diverse and fragmented pieces of data. In banking, it honed in on the single customer view, with the idea of deeply mining customer transactions to

---

27   "Data, data everywhere," *Economist*, 25 February 2010

find out how to leverage sales. This was typified by Martha Rogers and Don Peppers' book on 1:1 marketing concepts, alongside others such as Friedrich Reichheld's views on customer loyalty. Now we all talk about the Experience Economy and Engagement Banking but I wonder whether any bank *really* understands these.

For example, the data mining days began in the 1990s with the whole focus being on data usage for sales. Get more cross-sell, get more relationship depth, get more profit, get rid of loss-making customers ... nothing was really focused on customer service in that era. It's similar to the days of business process re-engineering, where the push was for banks to reinvent the customer relationship from the external interaction viewpoint inwards ... instead, most banks opted for purely incremental improvements to internal processes to lower costs.

Now there is a big change.

That big change is the information economy and the ability of new players to use information as a competitive weapon. Deep data mining can now be used to leverage electronic relationships that deliver the depth, loyalty and sales that banks were seeking a decade ago, and it can all be done today without a human hand involved. We see this with Apple, Amazon, Google and other such companies.

On Apple, whenever you download an app or iTune, you suddenly get recommendations of a thousand others. Using its music network, every artist you listen to brings up five others you might like.

What Google does today is even more interesting. Google uses your IP address to send out local information and adverts that relate to your search history. Everything is sensed, analysed, algorithmically processed and then personalised so that the 1:1 marketing vision of a decade ago can be delivered cheaply and easily.

So what are banks doing with this? Not much. Most are not talking publicly about how they use customer transaction data as a competitive weapon because it is exactly that—a competitive weapon. Visa is one of the exceptions, saying that it can now analyse two years' worth of customer transaction records, or 73 billion transactions amounting to 36 terabytes of data, in 13 minutes using cloud computing. This would previously have taken a month with traditional methods of internal computer processing. What does this mean? It means that Visa can work with banks to sense customers' lifestyles, needs, relationships and desires. Banks can then target offers to those needs and desires automatically.

THE PREDICTIVE, PROACTIVE BANK

When Google knows my searches are ideas, it can predict what is relevant for me. If I searched for headache tablet side effects, it might recommend that I switch to paracetamol, and direct me straight to my nearest Boots or Walgreens. If I happened to be pricing TVs, it might offer me a special deal to get a discount from Best Buy or PC World. If you don't think that Google Analytics is the key to predictive, proactive marketing, Google predicts stock market movements pretty accurately as well as flu trends, election results and more.

In the same way, banks can use transaction data combined with search trends and other data to predict and then proactively offer a service in real time. That service might be offering car loans as you drive by the showroom of the BMW dealership you happened to be Googling the previous night or mortgages as you drive towards the estate agency of the agent you found.

Now that's all well and good, but it goes further than this as prediction marketing can now be embedded into the Internet of things. For example, a few years ago, Metro store in Germany built a prototype of the grocery outlet of the near future using NFC and RFID technologies. The concept store included the idea of dynamic pricing as you walked through the aisles based on your loyalty, shopping habits and more. Your smartphone would emanate your preferences and change prices dynamically for you based on sensing your presence through the mobile network and your smartphone.

As the Internet of things means that everything has Intel inside, intellisense becomes the competitive battleground using predictive, proactive marketing and deep data analysis of the holistic customer relationship for each and every individual customer. This will result in a likely combination of companies forming partnerships in which the Internet service provider, mobile carrier and bank create a partnership with each other. Retailers, manufacturers and more would then join these partnerships to incentivise bank customers to visit their stores. As a result, you would keep finding adverts, offers and deals all around you, as you were intellisensed for business in the virtual and physical worlds.

It is almost making the vision of Tom Cruise walking into the shopping centre in *Minority Report* a reality, with everything recognising everything based on embedded chips, biometrics and proximity search. In fact, forget the biometrics as we have intellisense thanks to mobile combined with RFID and NFC technologies.

This sensing of the presence of the payer and payee through the network can be seen in the use of mobile networks and apps, as demonstrated by Square Wallet and Check-In by PayPal apps where checkout is hands-free. The apps use the mobile network and software to enable payments to take place with no card, touch or transaction visibly made. It is all wireless and seamless, through the air.

We are already living in a world where the Internet of things intellisenses our buying habits and, if we're buying, we're paying for things. This means the bank that ties itself into the value chain of intellisense is the bank that will be at the heart of the next generation of retail payments. And that means being the bank that mines data to provide predictive, proactive, proximity based payments.

This also means that the augmented economy is already a reality.

THE AUGMENTED ECONOMY

"Any sufficiently advanced technology is indistinguishable from magic."

—Arthur C. Clarke, 1917–2008

The augmented economy, where everything is connected and communicating and transacting non-stop, became a reality in 2013 when Google launched Google Glass. Google Glass is a pair of WiFi glasses that allow you to see enhanced information about all that is around you in real time. Google and influential commentators such as Robert

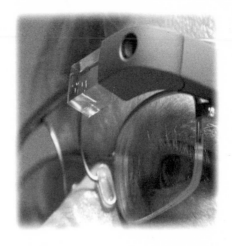

Scoble believe that this technology will change people's lives forever. The technology will have a profound impact on society, and therefore on customers and consumers. After all, if products and services can be offered at the customer's point of existence through an augmented delivery 24/7, then everything can be changed.

The example I normally use is Google's ability to understand our search and data usage needs. As we search, it can log our wants and desires, including those that we don't want anyone else to know about. These wants and desires can then be leveraged through partnerships. For example, if you searched for a Sony Ultra HD TV and found it at Best Buy online for $2,499, you might be driving past Best Buy the next day when Google Glass pops up an alert telling you that that particular TV is on offer for pickup for just $1,999 if you were to go in-store straightaway. This link-up may then be leveraged through extended partnership. As you pull into the store, Glass might advise that Citibank will approve a 36-month $2,000 loan at a 1 per cent discount on advertised credit rates. You don't need to do anything other than say "yes", "no" or "later", and all of this is stored in your personal cloud. The augmented economy therefore goes one step beyond the experiential economy.

There's even more happening than this though. In fact, Google's former CEO and now chairman, Eric Schmidt, recently published an interesting book titled *The New Digital Age* with colleague Jared Cohen that provides interesting visions for the digital future.

They anticipate that, a few decades from now, the average metropolitan couple will wake up to a massage from their bed as translucent screens follow them around the apartment and house robots perform all the domestic chores whilst they are out of the house. We will be using clothing machines that not only wash but also dry, fold, press and sort out our clothes for us (no more lost socks, yay!). Compute power around us will autocharge wirelessly and holograms will allow us to be in two places at once.[28]

So this world, where you continually get mobile adverts for loans as you pass the BMW car showroom, is very near. You get a mortgage offer five minutes before you walk past an estate agency because the bank knows that you were looking at mortgages online the previous night. You get a credit card balance transfer offer online as the bank has seen that you're making large direct debit payments monthly to a competitive provider. You are told about a new and improved account that would suit your lifestyle needs, thanks to comparisons with other customers and the accounts they use ... the bank has found customers like you and determined a better fit.

Although all of this is possible today, banks are struggling to leverage this opportunity because they are hamstrung by heritage. This is because banks do not analyse data on an enterprise basis but instead usually hold this data in divisional stores organised around products, channels and lines of business. And the politics internally are the greatest blockage for change and, without that change, banks are stuck with piecemeal data sets being analysed in pieces. That is not good enough today.

This is why banks need to completely re-architect their enterprise technologies to enable deep data mining across all data, and create semantic marketing programmes that sense customers' needs proactively and pre-emptively. Like algorithmic trading in capital markets where algorithmic

---

28   Schmidt, Eric and Jared Cohen. *The New Digital Age: Reshaping the Future of People, Nations and Business.* London: John Murray, 2013.

news feeds allow trading in equities to move in real-time high frequency blackbox strategies that maximise returns, we're talking about applying the same technologies to retail transaction services for customer loyalty and wallet share.

That's the battle about to begin as we move from managing data to using information as a competitive weapon, and at the core of predictive marketing is Big Data. If the battleground is augmented service, then Big Data is the weaponry to compete.

WHAT IS BIG DATA?

The term "Big Data" stems from World War II when the phrase "Big Science" was used to describe the rapid cycle of changes that occurred in scientific disciplines during and after the war. A good example of this rapid cycle of change during World War II was the invention of computing.

John W. Mauchly was a physicist working at the Moore School of Electrical Engineering at Pennsylvania University during the war, and he believed that an electronic computing device could be created to predict the weather. The idea was floated in August 1942 and, by June 1943, funds were allocated to the project. By the time the system was developed, the war was over. Nevertheless, the system that was developed, which was called the Electronic Numerical Integrator and Computer (ENIAC), led to the creation of the industry I have spent all my life working with—technology and information—as well as the weather forecasting service. You can't win them all.

Big Data was first used as a term in the late 1990s and no one can quite put their finger on how it came about. It appears to be through a combination of academic papers and META Group (now Gartner), all of which define Big Data as follows:

"Big Data are high-volume, high-velocity, and/or high-variety information assets that require new forms of processing to enable enhanced decision making, insight discovery and process optimization."

It may be simpler to say that Big Data is precisely the phenomenon that we have today, where every person on the planet is creating digital records such that we are drowning in data. For example, we are now creating exabytes of data every day. As mentioned earlier, an exabyte is a 1 with 18 zeroes after it, or 1,000,000,000,000,000,000 bytes—an incomprehensibly large number and illustrates well why we are drowning in data.

- There are 2.2 billion email users worldwide sending 144 billion emails every day, of which 61 per cent are considered non-essential and 68.8 per cent is spam.
- There are now almost 1 billion websites, with 87.8 million on Tumblr alone, and the average web page became 35 per cent bigger during 2012 (thanks to photos, videos, etc.).
- There are over a billion monthly *active* users on Facebook (posting monthly), with Brazil being the most dynamic country on Facebook, where the average user posts 85,962 items every month.
- Facebook adds 7 petabytes of data every month for photo content alone.
- There are over 200 million monthly *active* users on Twitter, posting 175 million tweets sent every day throughout 2012.
- There are 6.7 billion mobile subscriptions and around 5 billion mobile phone users generating 13 per cent of global Internet traffic, or around 1.3 exabytes of data each month (59 per cent of it is video).

The challenge of this ocean of data is to work out how to sieve and select relevant information from the data for marketing and sales, service and advice. This is the great opportunity of the new Digital Bank age: making knowledge out of disparate data because those who make sense of Big Data will win.

Data is the new source of competitive warfare, and data mining will be the weapon of mass destruction of the competition.

Many industries get this, particularly the new technology players like Amazon, Apple, Google and Facebook. It is the reason why banks fear these players because these players know how to sift the data and make sense of it. As one bank chief executive recently stated: "Our peers I can handle. We're in the same boat. But if Google opens a bank, with all their data—then we're in big trouble."[29]

Banks should fear Google as Eran Fiegenbaum, director of Security for Google Apps, has already made it clear that Google is "a bank for your data"[30] and this is a key point in my tenet of the future: banks need to be secure data vaults, and position themselves that way.

As discussed earlier, we are living in a world where the Internet of things is intelligently sensing our buying habits. This is the world of the very near future, and is driven by the unrivalled momentum and rapid worldwide adoption of devices. It will be a world where all hardware will be made smarter through not just the use of connected chipsets and next-generation parts but rather through the applications that add to their value.

The net:net of all of this is that banks and all firms will soon be focused on wireless transaction processing through the net. In other words, rather than mobile payments and mobile banking that we talk about today, we will be talking about augmented payments and augmented banking tomorrow and, in that world, money is meaningless.

MONEY IS MEANINGLESS

Money is meaningless because we no longer deal in money. We deal in data. The word *money* is usually associated with cash and, as most of us know, cash is no longer king, queen or even key as all banks and card processors have a war on cash. They have a war on cash because they want to replace it with electronic processing that is cheaper and easier, and electronic processing

---

29   "Technology take-off threatens bank foundations," *Euromoney*, September 2012

30   "Google: we're like a bank for your data," *Wired*, 29 May 2012

means that cash becomes data. Hence, money becomes meaningless because the data is what is important.

The problem with this view is that there is still a lot of cash around, with cash still representing over half of all payment volumes in most developed nations and still increasing in usage. For example, even with all of the advertising for mobile and contactless in the United Kingdom, the Cash and Cash Machines Report 2013 shows that cash usage increased by around 10 per cent for payments in the country in 2012, with the number of cash payments (by businesses and individuals) up from 20.6 billion transactions per annum to 20.8 billion, representing more than half (54 per cent) of all payments. Nevertheless, cash in the wider economy will decrease in importance over time because payment processors and financial institutions are all determined to replace cash with other forms of electronic payment.

This brings us to the core point that most people believe cash will decline over time and be replaced by electronic, digitised transactions. This is why money in the form of cash is less meaningful and demonstrates the importance of banks as secure data processors of money, rather than money transmissions processors. It means that the regularly quoted response from gangster Willie Sutton when asked why he robbed banks—"Because that's where the money is."—is very last century. Willie Sutton robbed banks physically, taking the cash out at gunpoint. Today, the gangsters take the money out byte by byte.

This is why money is meaningless because it's the data that is meaningful. It's the data that gangsters need to rob, not the money. Data is where it's at. That's why the majority of cyberattacks target financial institutions. According to the security company RSA, which produces an annual fraud report, 284 brands were targeted in phishing attacks during November 2012, marking a 6 per cent decrease from October 2012. Of the 284 brands attacked, 45 per cent endured 5 attacks or less. Banks continue to be the most targeted by phishing and experienced nearly 80 per cent of all attack volumes.

So when we talk about our wonderful new Internet age, the key is to realise that data is where the money is, not the bank, the branch or the cash machine.

This brings me to my core point: if data is valuable, what data is of most value and what role should banks take in this new model of value exchange?

BANKS ARE JUST DATA VAULTS

Banks need to think about how they reconstruct themselves for the 21st century as new data management firms from up-start payments processors to Internet service providers to mobile carriers all move towards the payments space. The war for all of these firms is to be the best at processing transaction data as people exchange information digitally online. As mentioned before, this means that banks are becoming pure managers of bits and bytes of data. It is the data that has the value today and it is the data that will be the basis of competitive battles in the future. Data is our greatest asset and raw material, not capital or people. That is what the technology has done for 21st-century society and for 21st-century banking.

Most people would be at far more of a loss if they lost access to their online accounts, had their usernames and passwords changed, had their identity copied and compromised online, or similar challenges, than if they were to lose their wallet or card. Some would feel their lives were lost if their Facebook or Twitter accounts were blocked or deleted whilst, for others, their World of Warcraft gold is more valuable to them than their total real-world asset base. The core of this is data and data leverage.

By the same token, data is where we have our greatest opportunity and threat. We talk about Apple, Amazon, Google and Facebook with admiration but the core of these companies is not music, books, search and social networking. It's data management. That is what Apple, Amazon, Google and Facebook have made of these businesses: massive data mining drones that allow us all to dump, tag, find, update and manage our online experience.

This brings us back to the core themes of data being more important than money, that the Internet of things will have us all drowning in even more data and that data access is our greatest vulnerability. These themes all have one core point for traditional banks and payments firms, and that point of opportunity is that the bank of the 21st century is not a bank as we would recognise it. It's just a secure data vault.

The vulnerability of data, and hence the secure management of data, is where banks and processors can truly leverage their capabilities. If data is more important than money, then the bank that securely manages data is the bank that will win. This is where the radical departure takes place from last century banking. Last century banking was predicated on money, paper and the physical transfer of goods. In contrast, 21st-century banking is predicated on data, context and the electronic transfer of goods and, most of all, 21st-century banking is based on data security.

The biggest fear of corporates and consumers is that transactions will not be processed properly, that their bank access details might be compromised and that their data and therefore their money may be stolen. That is why banks have to step up to a big challenge: guaranteeing data security. The banks of the 21st century need to be bold and guarantee that customer data is secure.

The issue with this is that it would make the processor or the bank a target for hackers, but that is the exact point. Banks should beat the hackers at their own game and make bold claims, such as "We guarantee your money and your data is 100 per cent safe with us." After all, if banks or their partners don't do this, who will? According to many in the industry, they do not believe that banks or even their payments processing partners are positioned to do this. In fact, some believe that banks should leave secure data management to people who know how to do this such as Google and PayPal.

This is where the biggest future weakness lies if this is the attitude of the financial community. If you give Google or PayPal the opportunity to become the secure financial data manager or the secure data vault of everything, then what is the role of the processor and the bank in that future? Surely this just gives the whole game away to someone else?

This is why the focus on data and data security is the key to the future. It is not a focus on money and financial security but data and information security that will differentiate the future winners and losers. In the meantime, banks will have to transition from the old world of physical monetary security to this new world of electronic data security. There is a transition time between the old world and the new, and the question is how long will this transition take? A decade? Or two? A year? Or two? Or will it be instant?

By way of illustration, if you look at the new world, many different models of payments and banking are already emerging. First, you have visionary financial services providers—Moven, Simple, GoBank, Bluebird, FIDOR, Jibun et al.—pushing the envelope of being vaults for secure data. Their premise is that the leverage of data and the knowledge they can gather from your data allows these firms to improve the value you receive from your shared electronic relationship. It's context, proximity, location-based proactive servicing of data value that these banks offer, and that is how they will flourish and grow.

Then there are other new models of finance emerging, such as Zopa, Friendsurance, eToro and more, that will change the game again. These providers are all seeking to connect people and money through social mechanisms, and base their business on seeing new niche opportunities for managing the exchange of data value.

Finally, a few hybrid banks are emerging, such as Alior and mBank in Poland, which offer the mixed old and new world capabilities to reach the broadest audience with the deepest relationships. Both of the examples are traditional banks with branches that have rebranded and relaunched as hybrid banks, incorporating social data security with bank data security.

In all of these models, the core financial offers focus on being the best at offering a remote, Digital Bank service that is fully secured and private. In other words, the best data vaults for money and more.

SHOULD BANKS ADVERTISE THAT THEY ARE SECURE DATA VAULTS?

Even though banks are becoming secure data vaults of digital information, to be truly regarded as such, you have to have trust in the safe keeper and trust in the guaranty that the safe keeper provides.

Traditionally in banking, the trust guaranty from banks has been in keeping your money, funds and investments safe and secure. In the future, the trust guaranty will be to keep your data safe and secure. Assuming a bank gets that licence to be the trusted holder of a client's information, the bank can then be viewed differently. For example, the bank can become a data miner, but not mining for financial data but data in any and all of its forms.

A bank may network businesses together to say that your business may benefit from a relationship with another particular business based on buying habits and supply chain and treasury similarities. A bank may network people together, and create human relationships, potentially even becoming a dating service for example. Just through these two examples, it is evident that banking is becoming less related to finance and more focused on being the best at utilising data and data analysis.

The challenge is that banks are not leveraging their data richness. After all, Apple, Amazon and Google are all data businesses that use the rich analysis of data as their key resource. In the same way that others use commodities or humans to create value, these businesses use data as their raw material to create value. That's what banks of the future will need to do.

Banks fear positioning themselves as data vaults however. Many do not see themselves as data advocates, data security experts or data managers. Why? Because the traditional bank has been a money manager and not a data manager and yet here is why banks should become data managers— Big Data.

Today, we produce exabytes of data every hour. So I'm going to take a pop at this mountain of data and say that data is increasing at around 2 zettabytes a year today, of which 65 per cent is redundant data, e.g. spam and transient. That leaves around 665 exabytes that has some value. Some of this is important but not critical, and some worthwhile but not that important. Using the third to two-thirds dynamic, this would mean that around 220 exabytes is important and 70 exabytes critical.

It is this last category that may be leaked by Wikileaks so that's the stuff that people want to secure. It is here that banks can make their data

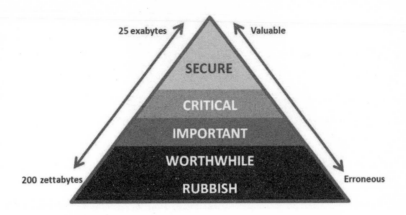

vault offer. Secure data with the bank and pay for that security. You would probably find that although people may feel their data needs to be secured because it's critical, only a third would pay for that security, so now we have our figure—20 to 25 exabytes of data per year is the sort of data that people would secure and pay for.

How much do, or would, people pay? Well, what is it worth to secure those photo albums you currently post on Facebook of your child being born and their early years? How much would you pay to back up your Twitter account? What is the value of those emails confirming your contracts over the last year? How much would you pay to keep your Bitcoin account secure? Currently, the organisation or the individual is responsible for securing this data. However, the bank could secure that data for a fee as much of the aforementioned has the same value as money for the individual or organisation concerned.

It would work by downloading a bank offered app that, once installed, allows you to tag any data with a padlock. That padlock tag would move that data into the bank vault, where it would be secured. If you were to ever lose that data—your disk was wiped, you accidently deleted it, your Facebook account was corrupted, your back-up was destroyed—you would be guaranteed to get it back from the bank vault. That is the bank's guarantee, and that has value.

How much for that service? That depends on how much the individual wants to pay. Like an insurance policy, if you value your data at £1 million, then you pay the bank an insurance premium for the bank vault's guarantee. Let's say it's around £250 ($400) a year for secure, backed up and defended or £100 a year for secure and backed up. That's £250 a year for a guarantee that the tweets, posts, updates, blogs and other stuff that you produce is guaranteed to be secure and backed up, or secure and defended. I imagine quite a few people would pay for that, especially as the volume of data is increasing every day:

- The volume of Internet traffic doubles every 18 months and is currently running at around 2 zettabytes, which is a trillion gigabytes, and most of it is video.
- The actual size of the Internet doubles every 5.32 years.
- By 2020, there will be 50 billion devices connected to the Internet, compared with 17 billion today.
- By 2020, there will be 6.58 devices per person using the Internet, compared with 2.5 today.
- Nanotech is already here, with computers and cameras at sub-1mm sizes.
- Over 100,000 telephone masts are being built every year.

- The number of WiFi units shipped has quadrupled in the last five years.
- Google averages 2 million searches per minute.
- Facebook users post 684,478 pieces of content per minute.
- Twitter users average over 100,000 tweets per minute.
- $272,070 is spent online every minute.

As can be seen, this volume of data is not just rising every day but is also increasing more rapidly over time. Some of this data will have value and it is that data that banks need to secure. Of course, a bank does not necessarily need to make this offer. If banks do not position themselves as secure data vaults, who will? Google or Facebook, of course. Google or Facebook could do this and, if either of them did, perhaps it could offer to look after money and other things of value too.

Meanwhile, the biggest issue for a bank is the silo structure of banking. This is because the traditional bank has organised itself around money in branches but now needs to organise itself around digital data. As I have already shown, the traditional bank has locked itself into products and channels, rather than customer and data, and the result has been a silo structure that is very difficult to manage unless the bank rebuilds itself from the ground up as a Digital Bank. This is what Google, Amazon and others had the luxury to achieve: being Digital Services and Digital Retailers, and this is what a bank has to re-engineer to become if it is to compete with these digitised providers.

What exactly would Amazon, Google and their brethren look like if they were organised like a bank?

IF AMAZON WERE A BANK

Imagine Amazon were a bank. What would it look like? How would it be organised? Well, let's do just that for a moment. Here's how I imagine Amazon would look like if it were organised along the lines of the banks I deal with.

Walking into the back offices of Amazon, one of the largest operations in the world, would be a shock. A place you would think would be a seamless operation of high technology would, in reality, be a bit of a mess. From an external view, it would appear to be like one great brand with multiple divisions, but if you were to dig away internally, it would look a little bit different. The book division wouldn't be talking to the music division. The music division wouldn't talk with the electronics division. The retail business wouldn't talk with the wholesale business. The wholesale business wouldn't talk with the cloud business. Oh, and the kindle division wouldn't even talk with the book division! None of them would share customer information with one another and, as a result, no one would know what customers were buying from Amazon as a group, when or with what sort of payment type. There would be no view on Amazon's share of wallet or who was cross-selling what to each customer.

The company would have tried to have improved this over the years, but the line of business heads for books, music, electronics, retail, wholesale, cloud and kindle have always been at each other's throats, motivated by their own line of business results. At one point, it was rumoured that Jeff Bezos thought about getting rid of all of the management and replacing it with a new organisational structure that would allow seamless integration of all divisions with a single platform for the company to see a single version of all the customer information in a single view … but no sooner was this mentioned, the board's management and chairman slapped Bezos around the face and he had to back down. This was due to a number of senior managers questioning his integrity with the chairman.

Oh, how easy it would be if Amazon were a brand new, fresh business that could change things ...

Ah, but Amazon *is* a brand new business and it has changed things! Of course, the company has divisions—and divisions are meant to do just that, divide—but Amazon's divisions don't divide the organisation by customer owners but by the logical structure of organisational delivery.

Ask yourself the following questions:

- What sort of business would divide customers across lines of business so that never the twain shall meet?
- What sort of business could have customers caught up in several areas of their business but dealt with as though they were all separate people rather than just one person?
- What sort of business could not recognise that a small business customer might be one and the same as their premium account holder?
- What sort of business could ignore the fact that this person is living with that person with two teenagers in the family?
- What sort of business would allow their loans business to stop their savings business from making contact with the customer, even though they work for one and the same company?
- What sort of business would allow their line of business owners to stake their turf for internal gain, at the customer's loss?

The answer to all of the above is simple: a bank. Yes, the silo divisions of banks mean that they ignore their greatest competitive weapon—data—and let others potentially gain this opportunity at their expense. This is not good enough in today's world of remote, digital engagement, especially when others can leverage this space.

THE FUTURE BASICS OF BANKING: DATA LEVERAGE

Banks need to focus on data and turn the data first into information and then into knowledge which, in turn, becomes wisdom, and wisdom is power. The more that humans add context and interpretation to raw data, the more powerful they become. Human interpretation can be programmed too, but it's the human spin on data that creates leverage and it is the silo structure of banks that stop them from gaining this leverage.

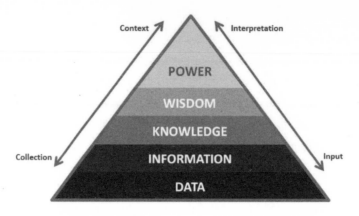

A diagram showing how data is power

For example, in the 1990s, I was working with one megabank on a re-engineering of processes project. We wanted to tackle the mortgage process as it was the easiest way to get quick wins. However, we ended up doing the money transmissions process. Why? Because mortgages cut across divisions and money transmissions did not. In other words, we were avoiding stepping on the toes of the baronial leaders of each silo of the bank.

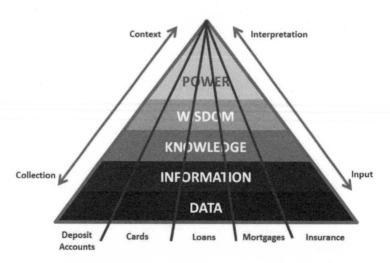

How bank divisions weaken the power of data

These silos of the bank cut the data cake into pieces and the more pieces, the less powerful the data becomes. The separation of information means that the information is a lot less meaningful than the picture you would gain from the whole. However, an enterprise view is not easy.

For example, back in the day, I used to market enterprise systems and the advantages they would provide of a single view of the customer. Back in the day, we would lament the issues of legacy systems and talk about overcoming the legacy through the development of modular, object-based systems.

Back in the day is today. It amazes me that over the twenty-year cycle of talking about these issues, we are still lamenting these issues. Today, we are still talking about the issues of legacy systems and the inability to create enterprise-based capabilities. And this is not down to a technology issue. Technologists have all the clever tricks to overcome legacy (middleware), enterprise (Enterprise Resource Planning, or ERP), single view of the customer (data warehouse) and modular, object-based systems design (Service Oriented Architecture, or SOA). No, the issue is the internal one of the bank itself. If a bank cannot get a single view of the customer at the enterprise level, then how is it ever going to effectively deal with knowing the customer?

And what about the ability to leverage the data for a single customer view? It is a wonderful idea but, again, the baronial silos stopped it: *I'm not sharing my data with Joe's division as I'm targeted on sales of my product, not his.* There's the rub of the issue. Each baronial head is protecting their turf and pay.

In delving deeper into this space, as the old saying goes, "What gets measured gets done and what gets measured and rewarded gets done first." If you measure a division on their sales performance, and they worry that they might underperform if another division had access to their customer, then they naturally block the sharing of knowledge and data with any other division. That's why banks have these silos.

Amazon and Apple do not allow these silos to hinder their business and their data leverage. If Amazon and Apple were run like a bank, they would separate customer data. They would organise themselves so that they had a book division, a music division, a film division and more, all competing against each other for share of the customer's wallet. This means they would separate customer data, and keep it protected. They would only know which books you buy and, separately, what music you buy and, separately, which films you buy and so on. For instance, they might know you downloaded the latest One Direction tune but would fail to grasp the sales leverage opportunities to also sell you the One Direction e-book and the One Direction video download. It just wouldn't happen.

As digital retailers, Apple and Amazon simply would not organise themselves this way, but it is the way that banks are organised even though they are becoming Digital Bank Retailers. For example, when I recently saw the bank that I had worked with in the 1990s on its re-engineering of processes project, I asked if they ever did tackle the mortgage process. The answer was no, for the same reason. Even if the bank were to create an enterprise customer view, could it use it? I'm not sure as the legal separation of some activities is always raised as a key barrier to achieving such a view.

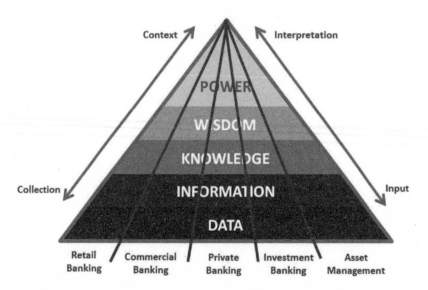

Another illustration of how divisions within a traditional bank undermine the bank's ability to leverage the overall data of individual customers

Like most areas of critique of banking, the easy answer is to fall back on the regulator as the issue. For example, "We cannot get a single customer view due to the Data Protection Act" is an easy way to say "Ah no, don't go there and try that." Alternatively, the rules about Chinese Walls across the bank are put forward as the challenge, with the insurance division unable to share information with the bank division which, in turn, cannot share data between the retail and commercial and investment divisions of the bank. Admittedly, with the Vickers and Volcker rules forcing the separation of bank activities, sharing information across divisions may be a real challenge but it's not the real barrier.

The real barrier is getting rid of the silos and re-engineering the legacy. The legacy that is not only the retail bank silos, but the bank silos overall. And this is where new banks have an opportunity. If you can create a new bank on a single data set, integrated with an enterprise view, then you really do have power because you can then start to create the predictive, proactive bank.

INFORMATION AS A COMPETITIVE WEAPON

A number of common themes are evident throughout this book:

- money being meaningless as data is key
- the battle over information, and how information warfare is the new game
- the fact that banks should move from being safe keepers of money to safe keepers of data

If banks are to grab the data mantle of being data vaults, then they need to think a little differently. This can be done by considering the following:

- Who are safe keepers of data today?
- What are their attributes?

- What does it mean for banks?
- What is information warfare all about?

It's all about viewing data as though it were capital or labour. A raw material for business.

Banks have long held the view that they are data managers. In fact, building on Walter Wriston's quotation that "Information about money has become almost as important as money itself", he expressed many other visionary views during an interview about the future of money in *Wired* magazine in 1996:[31]

> "Technology has overwhelmed public policy. People keep predicting this will lead to a crisis, but I don't think it will."

> "Money that can move. It's the opposite of patient money. But money really has no volition of its own. It all depends on the people who own it and use it."

> "The increased velocity of money gives you a difference in kind—not just degree. It's like a piece of lead: you put it on your desk, it's a paperweight; put it in a gun, it's a bullet. Same piece of lead. Big difference."

> "This is the first time in the history of the world that every major country has a flat currency that is not based on gold or silver or some commodity. Today, the value of money is hooked to nothing other than the information that flows through it."

> "Today, intellectual capital is at least as important as money capital and probably more so."

---

31   "The Future of Money," *Wired*, Issue 4, October 1996

"We originally said that land was wealth. Then we thought it was industrial production. Now we realize it's intellectual capital. The market is showing us that intellectual capital is far more important than money. This is a major change in the way the world works."

Admittedly, Wriston made these statements as we moved through the height of the information revolution discussions in the 1990s when Microsoft was rocking the world as mainframe moved to desktop, and Internet banking was bubbling on the horizon. Nevertheless, it should be noted that most of this banker's views that the basis for wealth has evolved from land to labour to information were formed back in the 1970s when technology first hit the banking system and moved everyone forward towards an information economy. Today, this vision is realised and businesses exist as information economies and they fight based on information.

Google is not a monopoly; there were and still are plenty of search engines around—Ask Jeeves, Lycos, the now-defunct AltaVista, Bing, etc. However, Google won this game early on by making algorithmic analysis of data more relevant and organised. It continues to do this today by making searches contextual and geographically localised.

The same applies to Facebook. Facebook had plenty of other players before it came onto the scene—Friendster, Friends Reunited, Bebo, Myspace, etc.—but we very quickly forget these other players when one wins out. However, Facebook is not a monopoly. It has competition and only maintains its leadership through continual innovation and enhancement of its information management capabilities.

Apple is another example. Apple was almost out of business when Steve Jobs returned. Through his leadership and vision of continually and elegantly innovating, the company bounced back, thanks to the MP3 player lifestyle revolution and the iPod. The iPod was the making of Apple over the last decade. It gave Apple back its heart and meant that the legion of Mac users, who loved the computer's simplicity and ease, could now use the Mac as a music machine. Then the vision of Apple was to introduce iTunes, and iTunes is the real engine as that is Apple's information advantage.

Yes, the iPod can easily be substituted, as can the iPhone, but iTunes has a unique hold over information and that's where real information warfare begins. Information warfare is all about continual evolution and leverage of data advantage over the potential and unrealised competition.

Which leads me to Amazon.

Amazon was all about books, or so we thought. Sure that's where it started, but it soon moved from books to music, films and more. The company then got really clever and started to make data mining its core art form. It began to data leverage by looking at dataprints—the unique way in which each of us searches, buys and consumes—and then relating these dataprints to one another to find relationships. By doing this, Amazon built its business by finding offers that you might buy, because people like you buy it, and the company can do this thanks to our unique dataprints.

Soon, Amazon became more of a behemoth of data, moving into selling anything from white goods to televisions, and it is easy to sell online when you know how to leverage data relationships. Even then, for Amazon, this was not enough. In recognising its information leadership, Amazon opened Amazon Web Services (AWS) to become the largest cloud-computing firm out there. Amazon now adds server systems to AWS every day that would have been the equivalent of the complete server architecture required to run the total retail business two years ago.

That's information warfare: leveraging systems expertise to get more share of wallet, expansion of market, growth of proposition and development of the offer into a range of services with no dependency on one particular area. If Amazon were still just an online bookshop, it would be dead. Amazon is, instead, an information guerrilla and gorilla. It clearly wins in the *information as capital* stakes.

Amazon also services banks through its cloud services. According to information provided by Amazon:

- Bankinter performs more than five million credit-risk simulations to evaluate the financial health of their clients on a continual basis. Through the use of AWS, Bankinter decreased the average time to identify a financial offer relevant to a client from 23 hours to 20 minutes
- A major bank in London is processing more than thirteen times more data since the risk team started using AWS for Monte Carlo simulations.

So banks are using Amazon for mining Big Data whilst, at the same time, worrying about Amazon, as well as Google, Apple and Facebook, and what they all might do to banking. The reason why banks worry so much about Amazon, Google, Facebook, Apple and others like them is because they all know how to use information as capital. They are all now pointing their information leadership at money and these guys know how to use information as ammunition.

- PayPal and Google invested $1.5 billion in mobile payment developments between 2009 and 2012.
- PayPal processed more than $20 billion in mobile payments in 2013, up from $14 billion in 2012 and just $200 million in 2008.

Can you name a bank that is investing in these areas of innovation with the same dedication and process?

MAKING DIGITAL BANKS SECURE

Over the past two decades, the world has changed dramatically because of an information revolution, a network revolution, a technology revolution. A revolution that connects everyone to anyone on the planet, and allows them to communicate and share. The last revolution of this scale was the Industrial Revolution.

Such transformations are called revolutions because they usually occur when there is progress, and progress creates riches for the few involved in the progression whilst the poor get poorer. The Industrial Revolution created the Peabodys, Carnegies, Rothschilds and Oppenheimers, among others, while the Information Revolution gives us the Gates, Ellisons, Zuckerbergs and Dorseys.

Revolutions also create revolts. There have been many instances throughout history in which the mass poor attacked the elite rich to rob them of their wealth. We can see the same today but the difference now is that data and the mobile Internet are making a big difference in allowing the oppressed or the poor to work together, speak out and be heard, increasingly by a worldwide audience.

Of course, banking has not escaped this global information revolution, nor the power of today's social Internet. Just look at Molly Katchpole, the young lady who posted a petition on Change.org, an online social pressure organisation, to get Bank of America to reverse policy and waive the $5 per month fees it was going to impose if people used their debit cards. The fee was to recoup losses due to the implementation of the Durbin Agreement, part of the Dodd-Frank regulatory changes in the United States. This agreement wiped out profits from interchange on debit card transactions and, as a result, many US banks decided to add a fee in order to recoup losses (*note:* Bank of America was not the only bank to do this, just the first to get the headlines).

The move proved so unpopular that Katchpole's petition rapidly gained traction, was promoted by Change.org and then was picked up by major national media like the *New York Times*. When the online petition reached 300,000 votes, Bank of America reversed policy. It resulted in the programme being voted the biggest PR gaffe of 2011 by most marketing magazines and Bank of America CEO Brian Moynihan admitting that it resulted in a surge of account closures. Note the speed of this change however, in that Katchpole posted the petition with 100 signatures on 1 October and over 200,000 signatures had been collected a week later.

100 signatures reached!

Awesome work, everyone! We reached our first milestone of 100 signatures... and now we're on to 200! Spread the word: stop Bank of America's debit card fee profiteering!

 Posted By Molly Katchpole Petition Organizer
October 01, 2011

 200,000 Signatures Reached! | October 07, 2011

Another Banking Giant to Adopt Debit Card Fees?

We made it on ABC's World News!

More at go.com

 Posted By Molly Katchpole Petition Organizer
October 05, 2011

There are many other examples of how the mobile, social Internet is impacting banks, such as the Wikileaks and Anonymous attacks on PayPal, Visa and MasterCard. At the time of the attacks, American firms such as MasterCard, Visa, PayPal and Amazon were blocking payments to Wikileaks, following the website's leaks of top-secret US government information. The leaks included footage of American bombings in Iraq that killed two Reuters journalists, something the US government had denied happening. Consequently, the government used its influence to get PayPal, Visa and MasterCard to stop processing funding for the Wikileaks services.

The real shock was the reaction of Wikileaks supporters to this action however. Supporters of Wikileaks, in the form of the hacking collective Anonymous, targeted MasterCard and brought its web services to a halt using a simple DDoS. The attack hit MasterCard's 3D Secure and broadband payments services, and went viral using the term Operation Payback ("an anonymous, decentralized movement which fights against censorship and copywrong").

As can be seen through these illustrations, the power of today's Internet must not be underestimated. This is why Josef Ackermann, former CEO of Deutsche Bank, stated in 2012: "We have a social responsibility, because if this inequality increases in income distribution or wealth distribution we may have a social time bomb ticking and no one wants to have that."

CYBERWARS: A FAR BIGGER THREAT THAN HACKTIVISTS

Whilst consumers are creating mobile social pressures and hacktivism, governments are creating global cyberattacks. This cyberwarfare is already rife, with a host of malware targeting Middle Eastern nations. McAfee Labs researchers recently debated the leading threats for the coming year and show that it's only going to get worse:

- "Hacking as a Service": Anonymous sellers and buyers in underground forums exchanging malware kits and development services for money

- The decline of online hacktivists Anonymous, to be replaced by more politically committed or extremist groups
- Nation states and armies to be more frequent sources and victims of cyberthreats
- Large-scale attacks like Stuxnet, an attack on Iranian nuclear plants, will increasingly attempt to destroy infrastructure, rather than make money.
- Mobile worms on victims' machines that buy malicious apps and steal via tap-and-pay NFC
- Malware that blocks security updates to mobile phones
- Mobile phone ransomware "kits" that allow criminals without programming skills to extort payments
- Covert and persistent attacks deep within and beneath Windows
- Rapid development of ways to attack Windows 8 and HTML5
- A further narrowing of Zeus-like targeted attacks using the Citadel Trojan, making it very difficult for security products to counter
- Malware that renews a connection even after a botnet has been taken down, allowing infections to grow again
- The "snowshoe" spamming of legitimate products from many IP addresses, spreading out the sources and keeping the unwelcome messages flowing
- SMS spam from infected phones. What's your mother trying to sell you now?

What is obvious from these developments is that cyberattacks are the new form of warfare that evades direct hand-to-hand or nuke-to-nuke combat. Like the classic 1983 film *War Games*, you don't need to have war with weapons anymore, just cyberweapons. And no nation is immune from attack.

For example, the United States came under attack from a cyberworm originating in China in 2010. Although China denied that this cyberworm was state-funded, the denial was slightly undermined by a news report on China Central Television a year later, which showed a military computer program selecting a target—in this case, a website based in Alabama—and hitting a button labelled "attack".

Maybe that's why Hillary Clinton now wants the United States and China to collaborate on cybersecurity for the future and why Barack Obama took time out to write the following in the *Wall Street Journal* in July 2012:[32]

> "It doesn't take much to imagine the consequences of a successful cyber attack. In a future conflict, an adversary unable to match our military supremacy on the battlefield might seek to exploit our computer vulnerabilities here at home. Taking down vital banking systems could trigger a financial crisis. The lack of clean water or functioning hospitals could spark a public health emergency. And as we've seen in past blackouts, the loss of electricity can bring businesses, cities and entire regions to a standstill. This is the future we have to avoid. That's why my administration has made cybersecurity a priority, including proposing legislation to strengthen our nation's digital defenses."

Obama is acutely aware of cyber vulnerabilities because he got hacked himself. In May 2009, he stated, "Between August and October (2009), hackers gained access to e-mails and a range of campaign files, from policy position papers to travel plans. It was a powerful reminder in this information age (that) one of your greatest strengths—in our case, our ability to communicate to a wide range of supporters through the Internet—could also be one of your greatest vulnerabilities."[33]

And there's the rub. We continually try to be one step ahead of hackers, hacktivists, cybercriminals and cyberthreats, but we are actually always one step behind.

---

32   Barack Obama, "Taking the Cyberattack Threat Seriously," *Wall Street Journal*, 19 July 2012

33   "Obama Outlines Coordinated Cyber-Security Plan," *New York Times*, 29 May 2009

Like the regulatory conundrum—you can only fix the system with regulation once you've seen it go wrong—the cyber conundrum is very similar—you can only block the attack once you've realised you're under attack. Sure, you can protect yourself against possible attacks, but knowing every nuance of every possibility of every attack? Can any company claim to be bulletproof?

No, but banks and payment service providers are the very ones who need to be bulletproof, especially when it is clear that the financial system manages the economic viability of nations and is therefore going to be one of the first lines of attack in national cyberwars. That was made clear to me when the chief information officer (CIO) of the New York Stock Exchange (NYSE) presented at a conference I chaired a couple of years ago, and said that the NYSE had been targeted in a cyberattack at the same time as the US Department of Defense. The US Department of Defense had a security breach, NYSE did not. This is why the banks can learn much from the cyberwarfare of governments.

In the latest developments in the Middle East for example, the latest systems attack bank accounts rather than nuclear plants. This is because the banking system is the heart of the economic health of a nation, with Gauss malware targeting multiple users in select countries to steal large amounts of data, with a specific focus on banking and financial information.

When governments engage in cyberwars that focus on the bank system first, there's going to be a meltdown at some point, and potentially these developments are far more threatening than those of the paltry hacktivists. For example, just as pure speculation, here is a short fiction about a cyberattack on Wall Street:

Shaiming Zheng had finally finished his masterpiece. He had created a worm that would infiltrate the heart of the American dream: Wall Street. Like the Israeli Stuxnet attack on the Iranian nuclear facilities in 2010, Shaiming had been hired to achieve the same result on the New York Stock Exchange.

NYSE claims that its servers are bulletproof and can survive attacks that are even more viral and malevolent than those that would target the US defence systems, but it was wrong and Shaiming had the means to prove it. His program would not only find its way into the NYSE system through the back door, via what would appear to be an official trade by Goldman Sachs on its high frequency trading platform, but it would also worm its way into the clearing system of the Depository Trust & Clearing Corporation (DTCC). Once in the clearing system, it would bring down America.

Shaiming was using a shadow trade to allow his worm to work its evil magic. First, the system would create a request for quote via Goldman Sachs. Once the order was filled by a reciprocal trade fill on the NYSE, the shadow trade would be passed through for clearing via the DTCC. At this point, the shadow would unleash the worm, which would then begin to infiltrate every settlement of trades on the DTCC systems thereafter.

It was something that was unthinkable as, until discovered, it would mean that all trading on the US stock exchange systems—not just the NYSE, but NASDAQ and more—would be disrupted and potentially forever flawed as the DTCC carries all the payments and settlement for all trading in US stocks and derivatives. The worm would bring down the system. That was the intention and that was what Shaiming believed he had built.

It had been so easy to achieve as he was not attacking the DTCC or the NYSE system but Goldman Sachs. Thanks to the powers that be, this had been easy to do when he found his ally, Sergey Alyenko. Sergey had been convicted of stealing proprietary information from Goldman Sachs about its trading platform in 2010. Although this conviction had been overturned in 2012, what the court didn't know was that Shaiming and his paymasters had paid Sergey $10 million to get the information they needed.

In actual fact, Sergey had not been stealing trade secrets about Goldman's trading platforms at all. What he had really been doing was creating the gateway on the platform to enable Shaiming to plant his worm on its system. Thank you, Sergey.

Shaiming pressed the button and held his breath. The worm was on its way. Would it reach its target?

SO HOW SHOULD A BANK PROTECT ITSELF FROM HACKTIVISTS AND CYBERCRIME?

The real challenge for the banking system is how to protect their firewalls from attack by hacktivists, goverworms and cybercriminals and, conversely, how to deliver easy access to online banking for their clients and customers. It's a real dilemma.

On the one hand, everyone wants mobile access to their account balances and to make payments. On the other, no one wants to consider the issue of haemorrhaging losses if they don't protect their account properly. This is also a challenge in terms of building business as many people do not use mobile banking for exactly this reason—they worry about haemorrhaging losses. There are two distinct focal points here for information security within a bank:

- protecting the bank's information from attack
- allowing the bank's customers to access the information they need when they need it

Looking at the first point, hacktivists are not really the issue here. A massive DDoS attack from the anonymous collective is concerning but bringing down a website does not bring down the system. MasterCard and Visa made this clear when they were attacked by Anonymous. Hacking a website is more of an inconvenience than a concern.

However, a targeted hack is a concern, and there are many instances of banks failing to deal with this properly. In 2011, for example, hackers got access to some of Citibank's customer data, with at least $2.7 million lost by 3,400 customers. That's small beans and is manageable, but shows the vulnerability.

The insider threat is even greater, with employees being able to gain millions by selling access to bank data. An instance of this also occurred in 2011, with Bank of America losing over $10 million thanks to a member of staff giving away account details to an identity theft ring. Again, it's small beans but when there's a crack in the firewall, it can soon grow into a fissure, chasm or canyon.

What happened to Sumitomo Bank is a perfect example of this. The bank nearly lost almost $350 million in a keylogger scam. You would think that this bank would have got its act together after such a close call but no. The very same bank was fined £3.5 million by the Financial Services Authority in May 2012 for serious IT governance failings.

Regardless, the banks are the data guardians, information providers and knowledge developers. Or they should be. This means that the way in which banks should guard against data failings from external attack is by having the obvious data protection: firewalls, secure sign-on, dual authentication with triangulation of access, real-time business events monitoring and so on. What I mean by this is that banks should be moving towards much-improved real-time tracking and business intelligence about their information flows, and this will alert them to any security breach. After all, most banks know that they will be breached. In fact, they know they cannot stop a breach. It will happen. The real issue here is how the bank deals with it and how fast. That's the key.

This is why complex event monitoring of business intelligence flows with real-time alerts is a key focal point. The ability for a bank to keep its finger on the pulse of every transaction across its global operations will be the key to protecting against internal and external threats. And if real-time business monitoring can solve the first issue—an external or internal security breach—what can be done about the second area? That is, ensuring ease of access securely. Again, it seems simple and yet so many fail at doing it.

I was astounded, for example, to read that a quarter of all mobile banking apps from world-leading banks like Wells Fargo, PayPal, CHASE and others were failing basic security tests.[34] Whether true or not, there are obvious flaws in mobile security right now, and yet there shouldn't be as

---

34   "Security Warning: 25% of Mobile Banking Apps Flunk Test," *American Banker*, 8 August 2011

mobile banking should be more secure than online banking. After all, the mobile phone is a useful authentication token, with its unique telephone number, the ability to use text messaging for one-time passwords (OTP) and even tracking the geolocation of the customer all being useful aspects of the system. Customers will always know where their mobile is and have it with them, unlike their wallet or credit card, and are far more likely to know when it is lost or stolen.

In fact, the more I think about mobile as an authentication tool, the more attractive it becomes. First, you can geolocate customers using mobile. Various solutions achieve this result using telecommunications masts, rather than mobile devices, as an independent verification mechanism can then be used to determine whether you really have your phone with you. This is the sort of tool that is already being used in some locations to determine if the customer at the ATM really is the customer by checking that they have their mobile with them.

Second, you can authenticate who the customer is interactively using OTP by text messaging. Again, used by some banks, an interactive text or app-based OTP process means that the mobile can offer a great second level authentication tool.

Third, you can check that it really is who you think it is by using mobile biometrics, and this is the biggest growth area. A while ago, Bank Intesa in Spain was using mobile apps for iris recognition. Nick Ogden, the founder of WorldPay, has created Voice Commerce to offer voice verification by mobile. Apple has launched the iPhone 5S and 5C with mobile fingerprint authentication. Meanwhile, my favourite authentication is Nymi by Bionym, a watchstrap that uses your heartbeat as verification.

The reason the latter is my favourite is that mobile is rapidly moving from devices to wearable, and so we will soon have mobile chips embedded in jewellery, watches, handbags, shoes and other fashion accessories. Yes, it's back to the Internet of things, but it goes beyond the Internet of things to the knowledge of everything.

Intellisensing and locating customers and verifying and authenticating them through the Internet of things will become the norm. It will be the case of knowing who is where doing what in real time, and being able to check it is who you think it is without forcing an action, such as a token or PIN being activated, but instead by sensing it's who you think it is through the network.

We are getting nearer and nearer to this eventuality every day, so let's stop worrying about fraud and risk with mobiles and start thinking far more about fraud and risk minimisation with mobiles. In this context, secure techniques mean that you can use the mobile telephone number and the geolocation proximity of the phone, text messages and apps, alongside a card and PIN, to make sure that the person who says they are trying to access the account is actually the person who should access the account.

The bottom line of securing banking is that banks will never be able to keep ahead of the criminal. That's the criminal's job: to continually test and try to break the security of the bank. This means that the bank must therefore always be one step behind those who want to create cracks in its firewalls. That means continual renewal of information security policies, systems and infrastructures, and making sure that the bank keeps up with the best practices in securing its customers' data.

In conclusion, banks should place themselves firmly at the heart of information security and offer customers a secure data vault. This is the real opportunity for now and the future for financial organisations—to guarantee security of mobile transaction and mobile data. Unfortunately, most bankers react to this by saying, "Doesn't that make us a target for hackers?" Yes, that's the exact point. Banks should beat the hackers at their own game and make bold claims like 'We guarantee your money and your data is 100 per cent safe with us". After all, if banks don't do this, who will?

Again, the reaction of banks to this is often negative. Banks believe they are not positioned to do this, and that secure data management should be left to people who know how to do this, like Google, Facebook and PayPal.

The problem with this is that we're just giving the game away to someone else. It's a very short-sighted banker who wants others to securely manage data while they just focus on managing money.

What can banks do about it and what are the solutions to insecurity? Security. Certainty. Confidence. These are the three things that banks must provide and guarantee.

BECOMING A DIGITAL BANK

At regular meetings, I talk to banks about how they are handling the changes demanded by customers thanks to mobile and tablet computing, the implications of app-based banking and what a future app-based bank might look like, i.e. how it would work and what it would mean for the customer connection.

It is already very clear that there are fundamental challenges with app-based banking. For instance:

- It has meant that some banks have had to replace their core Internet banking systems within five years of implementation.
- Some banks deployed apps for the Apple iPhone but within eighteen months, their customers switched to Samsung Galaxy.

Many banks feel overwhelmed with the speed of these changes, and the fact that this makes it very hard to work out where to place bets for the future.

WHERE TO INVEST?

One of the biggest challenges that banks face is how to ensure that any investments in technology provide a return in the time frames given, particularly as things may change again so quickly. For example, many banks currently delineate and differentiate between mobiles and tablets, but that will change as mobiles get bigger and tablets get smaller. In other words, mobiles will become tablets and tablets will become mobiles. Then, following quickly on from that, there will be unlimited bandwidth and unlimited storage available 24/7 on a device that's always in the customer's hand or handbag.

The problem therefore is how you view the business and how you invest. Much of this comes down to a long-term view, but most banks don't have long-term views. Banks live in the short term and short-term investments take precedence over the long term.

This is also a reflection of the lack of competition amongst banks and the ease of copying. If you look at the Big Five banks in the United Kingdom for example—HSBC, Barclays, Lloyds, the Royal Bank of Scotland and Santander—when one moves and does something different, the others will do the same if it makes sense. If one bank makes waves, the others will have copied it within a few months. That's why something like Barclays' Pingit app stands out because Barclays launched peer-to-peer payments by mobile two years before most of the other banks even considered it.

At the other end of the spectrum, there are some things that the banks should be copying, like PayPal or Square, but many of those at the top running the banks are simply not aware of them. This is where the mismatch occurs.

When asked whether the changes we are seeing today will force a fundamental restructuring of banking, most banks believe it will. And that's why a wise understanding of and investment in social technology is crucial.

Historically, banks were arrogant and had the view that once you got a customer, you could keep them for life. The banks believed that it would have to take something extremely serious to mess up the client relationship and prompt the client to leave. Thus, banks developed their new channels through the years with this mindset firmly in place.

However, the introduction of the mobile tablet into everyday life has brought about a more rapid cycle change. Given that most people own at least one such device, they now have at their fingertips an alternative way of banking. Thus, customers will ultimately change the way banks will operate in future. Already they can use alternative payments mechanisms. They can get apps to do things their way, as they want. Banks need to wake up to this change—because what has been sacrosanct historically has gone forever—and start investing accordingly.

THE IMPLICATIONS OF FAST CYCLE TECHNOLOGY CHANGE

What does all of this fast cycle change with consumer use of technologies mean? It means that when a customer is at home applying for a financial product—which could be anything from a credit card to a mortgage—the minimum customer experience will need to be at least as good as the experience with, for example, Amazon or the user will just shut down the application and go somewhere else. This is a result of the attention deficit disorder of today's modern world. If you cannot engage the customer within seconds, they will leave. If anything is difficult in the process of dealing with you, they will leave. If there is any challenge to check out, they will leave.

This means that you will have to rethink everything to be completely customer centric. That's an opportunity but it is also a threat. In fact, such changes have the potential to threaten the industry establishment if they continue going forward. A good example is in payments, which is already transforming into a direct, P2P operation thanks to mobile and is sometimes run by non-bank providers. Non-bank providers now handle over 15 per cent of all payments worldwide, up from virtually zero 10 years ago, and this trend is accelerating.

Whether the rest of banking goes the same way remains to be seen, but it will fundamentally change the way the customer interfaces with their bank. You only need to look at children to realise that they have moved to consumer-based touchscreen intuitive technologies. If you show them a computer, they don't know how to use it. That's the speed at which change is occurring here, and banks must keep up with that change or be sidelined by the digital revolution.

This drive to keep up with change is not coming from one division or another but across the whole bank group, even the corporations are interested. It is recognised across the board that the bank must embrace mobile and tablet computing. The big issues though are about how paradigms are inverted.

Mobile means that everything is turned around. It's not about how much you can put into the app, but how much you can take out of it. It's not what needs to be locked down and only opened when it needs to be opened; it's all about opening everything, which is only locked down when it needs to be locked down.

In other words, a whole range of the fundamentals of financial services are being challenged by the digital revolution. These fundamentals are being knocked on the head. Things are now 180 degrees different to what they were, and it's very hard for a traditional player to deal with this. After all, the existing players and incumbents are super tankers that are difficult to change. To get a super tanker to turn takes fourteen turns of the wheel for every degree of change, and you cannot turn any faster or the tanker will capsize and sink. It's dangerous. It's the same with the incumbents and traditional players. They cannot turn 180 degrees quickly as they will flip over and sink.

This does not mean that the incumbent banks will be unable to meet these challenges. Rather, it's more to do with mapping the new world onto the old world and how the banks go about it. If banks think about it that way, then the question is about how to evolve the company to keep up. It all takes time, however, and is the reason why most banks will end up in partnerships and co-opetition with new players and telcos.

NOT APP-BASED BANKING BUT OPEN BANKING

This leads to a debate as to whether apps or APIs will make the difference in future. Most bankers believe that new companies will appear that will drive the need for the next big things like the next Google, the next Facebook and the next Apple. The banks won't do it. Banks cannot turn the tanker around to do such things for a start.

So what banks need to focus on is making sure that they are included in the next big things by opening the bank functionality to be included in the start-ups that build these new capabilities. In other words, get the bank included through API functionality in the apps of those who are cool. As part of that, banks need to ensure that they are working in real time and working the way people want.

There is a potential sacrifice issue here, especially if you start to talk about opening banking to the world. This is because banks trade in security and, as people become more comfortable using technology and specifically portable devices, they won't trade with security anymore. They will start to use apps that aggregate services and payments for them, and will transact freely without the bank's security controls.

What this really means is that the customer may feel more in control but they will, in fact, be less in control. This brings it back to the point of how to keep it customer centric. The focus must be on the customer, keeping the customer secure and looking after their needs. Doing so then shifts the focus onto the core of banking, and people want two things from their bank:

- access to their money when they want it
- advice about money when they need it

A lot of companies—banks and non-traditional banks—have done a lot of work in the first area. They can give you access to your money when it's needed. The latter leaves a lot to be desired though and app-based banking gives a major advantage here in terms of giving people financial education and direction. That's a great opportunity, as you have to remember that there's still a person at one end trying to help a person at the other end.

This is an essential part of the debate because there is a lot of talk about apps, branding and being cool, but if you look at social media, how many banks could commit to social media and be credible in this space? It's about the relevancy to the customer and being part of the customer's life, and that part of the discussion is as challenging as the technology part.

THE CORPORATE VERSUS CONSUMER SPACE

Moving the discussion further, we need to talk about corporate versus consumer needs. It is quite clear that app-based banking and open-API banking is not just a consumer thing. Many banks think that mobile is only relevant in the retail context, but mobiles and tablet computers are being used everywhere from corporates for treasury management, to wealth for portfolio management and to retail for general payments and banking.

This is where it gets confusing. The best illustration of such confusion is a colleague's experience in dealing with a corporate treasurer who was moving

£20 million of funds and was told it would cost quite a high percentage of the amount for moving the funds. The treasurer turned around and said, "But I bank with you as a personal customer and just moved £2,000 to Spain and it didn't cost me anything. Do you just add costs based on the number of zeros on the transaction?" This is the dilemma because that is exactly the way banks used to work—separating the corporate experience from the consumer experience—but you cannot work that way anymore as banks are dealing with the same person: a consumer and a treasurer. This new generation of corporate client does not understand the old way of banks.

Banks charged per transaction based on the amount, the urgency and the correspondent banks in the process, especially with regard to the corporate client. Customers don't get that anymore. Customers expect real-time transactions globally, and to pay the same whether they are transferring £1 or £1 million. A little like a telephone call, they think it should be easy and immediate.

It's also worth bearing in mind that some corporate users are becoming more sophisticated in their use of digital than the banks. For example, there is a new generation of treasurers emerging who expect real-time payments in their hands 24/7. They have an iPhone or iPad app at home for their consumer banking, and they expect the same ease of process and responsiveness for their corporate banking. They do not want to deal with old cash processes as they see everything as digital now. They believe that the days of moving money around a large retail operation are numbered, as they want the process automated. They don't want to be moving cash around, and dealing with cash management and cash security. That's the old world of retailing and the faster everything moves to digital for these guys the better.

That's an opportunity for the bank but it also poses a dilemma. While banks are trying to make things easier for corporate customers so that they can make a payment without having to call into a central system to get a password or whatever, in so doing, it might be encouraging behaviours that banks do not want to encourage in a corporate user context. The priority has to be security for the client, and it takes time for a bank to get to the level where that can be provided, particularly for high-value corporate transactions.

CHANGING THE BANK CULTURE

App-based banking is bigger than the corporate versus consumer discussion, as it's not just one market area that has caught the mobile bug. It's the whole world. This is mainstream change, and that makes it a cultural change.

This was illustrated by an anecdote from one bank friend who said that, back in the 1960s, the bank had a Head of Electricity. When it was new, it needed management. Therefore, in a parallel with this old world of electricity, there is now a Head of Digital. This means that the bank is organised with a digital team, who sit in a silo to understand the needs of the digital customer. The result is that the bank has a few hundred people out of several thousands of people in the company who are focused on managing customers' digital needs.

You cannot allocate the understanding of this new world to a small team, separated from the rest of the organisation, when your customers have changed fundamentally. Everyone in the bank needs to understand them. The very fact that banks create a digital or mobile team within the bank makes everyone else in the company feel that they do not have to do digital or mobile. They can ignore this space as someone else has taken responsibility. When something is changing so fundamentally and so fast amongst your customer base, that is unacceptable.

GEOGRAPHICALLY HOMOGENOUS OR DIFFERENT?

Are mobile and app-based changes homogeneous or different in different parts of the world? Obviously, geographically, there are nuances about how rapidly markets have digitised and you cannot stereotype. In some markets, like Kenya, the governments have actively encouraged the technology into the country because they can see its opportunity to change things. In other markets, like Turkey, the regulations have forced the banks to focus on innovation. That is why there are so many new models of banking and technology coming out of Turkey. Hence, it's clear to see that regulation has a really strong play here in terms of what happens and how fast.

It's not just regulations though, as countries and continents are changing fast. If you take Africa for example, give it five or ten years and their infrastructure for banking will be light years beyond Europe and the United States. This is because they have no heritage or legacy to overcome and can deploy the fastest new capabilities almost overnight.

This is somewhat frustrating when you consider countries like Spain and Italy. Italy, with 25,000 bank branches, and Spain with 33,000 have been slow to change, and it is easy for the banks' management to say that this is because of the culture of the customer. The customer wants to continue to do business that way, when this is clearly not true. It's the culture of the bank and the bank wanting to continue to do business that way.

So it really comes down to competitive and market forces. For example, if you compare the United Kingdom and France, France is far more advanced today as several of its leading banks have been competing to get customers to move to new channels and services. In contrast, in the United Kingdom, it takes someone to move, otherwise everyone will just stay where they are.

Innovation is not a set process however as, with all things new, banks will want to compete and keep up, especially if their competitors move in this direction. There will be different business models for different banks in the future though. The business model may even be different for every consumer. Some banks will offer face-to-face branch servicing, some won't. Some banks will open up all of their processes as APIs, some won't. Some banks will aim to bring partnering with telcos, IT companies, retailers and more to the table while some banks won't. This means that there will never be a single structure, but many hybrid structures to suit different customers and markets.

Some new, free banks that are mobile only might even emerge. Could Barclays become Pingit Bank for example? A little like HSBC had to create First Direct for call centres, and Cooperative had to spin off Smile for the Internet. Equally, all banks will be looking for partnerships. Any bank that is not looking at the changes we are seeing today, without taking a view about who could help them to compete in this space, would become an anachronism.

It is important to remember that while a bank might have all of these changes and innovations, there is still the fundamental need to provide the basics of banking services underlying all of this: processing a transaction, clearing a cheque, making an international transfer happen smoothly and more. Some banks cannot even handle these basics effectively, such as changing an address. So how can a bank expect to roll out a shiny new app or an API if it cannot even get the fundamentals right? Real-time balances and payments will be a big challenge in the future for a bank that cannot cope with the basics today.

All of this brings up another big question: how does mobile change the branch experience? You will never take away the branch, but you can change it. For example, many banks have in-branch digital screens and advertising, and are changing their in-branch experience. They offer customers a coffee when they arrive, and many are taking that on board. The point then is to rethink the conversation and process of the branch—what are you going to do or say to engage the customer more or better? That is a critical point for as much as we talk about systems, the core of banking comes down to people. How is the customer experience improving? This then justifies investments in branch and mobile, as both can engage the customer experience better.

THE FUTURE

Around five years from now, there will be a radical change from where we are today. We may have all our banking services in the device or it may even be a chip under the skin or something. Who knows? The challenge in all of this is to know what to invest in. Which areas are going to take off and work? If you get that wrong, you could lose out big time in terms of not just money, but reputation and competitiveness.

Incumbent banks that I talk to feel that this would not change their banks' operations radically however, as the biggest factor that will not change is customer apathy. Most customers do not leave the bank unless they are forced to, and customers will still be apathetic about banking five years from now. They do not care about banking that much and so, as long as it works, they are happy to stay with the bank. This was demonstrated by the LIBOR-fixing scandal, after which people did not leave Barclays, and the 2012 payments glitch at the Royal Bank of Scotland, after which people did leave. The former may not have been something customers condoned but it did not affect them personally. The latter affected some people personally, in terms of not being able to make payments, and that was a prompt for change.

What is obvious overall is that banks will rethink their business models around assessing risks, processing transactions, manufacturing products and retailing services, and they will reinvent the front and back of the bank. Furthermore, partnerships with Google, Vodafone, Amazon and others could become the norm rather than the exception. These partnerships will change the model for CRM and processing, and banks will find that their knowledge of the customer will actually be richer and deeper as a result. As long as banks accept that they can partner better with businesses that do the parts of the process better than they can, then they could survive and thrive.

Banks know that they are not good at everything but are good at some things, and so they must focus on what they are good at. Then the challenge is how banks embrace culture change. Culturally, can banks adapt and evolve to partner and process, and what are banks offering in the partnership and process? Do banks own the data or should the partner? Do banks provide the core processing or are banks sitting on top of someone else's core processing?

The culture of the bank is actually more important than the technology and, at the core of the culture, is this question: does the bank understand the customer and their needs in this new digital age?

DIGITAL BANKS ARE STILL BANKS

Ever since the Internet first appeared, we have believed that new forms of commerce would emerge and take over from the old way of doing things. They have, of course, only not in banking. Yes, the banking system has changed over the last three decades—just look at how we are all now running around with mobile banking apps—but the competitive landscape has not.

That is a controversial statement in itself, but it is a fundamental one as, when I look at today's landscape of banking, it is not dramatically different from the market of the 1980s. It has new channels—call centre, Internet and mobile—and it has new structures—nearshore, offshore and cloud—but the point I am really getting at is that the core competitors in the markets are pretty much the same as they were back in 1980.

Here are a couple of proof points. According to a 2012 study by Yale University,[35] the average lifespan of a company listed in the Standard and Poor (S&P) 500 Index of leading US companies has decreased by more than 50 years in the last century, from 67 years in the 1920s to just 15 years today. Yet, in most countries, banks have been established for over a century yet rarely does a new competitor enter into those markets. For example, when Metro Bank opened in the United Kingdom in 2010, it was widely

---

35   "Can a company live forever?" *BBC Business News,* 19 January 2012

remarked that this was the first new retail bank in the country for over a century.

And, when you review the largest banks in the world, the list remains fairly consistent. For example, according to the *Banker* magazine, the top five banks in the world in 1999 were:

1. Citigroup
2. Bank of America
3. HSBC
4. Crédit Agricole
5. Chase Manhattan

In 2010, the list had changed but not much:

1. Bank of America
2. JP Morgan Chase
3. Citigroup
4. Royal Bank of Scotland
5. HSBC

This is because banks are integral to commerce and the economies of countries. This has been demonstrated time and time again, no better than in the most recent financial crisis. Banks can cripple economies or enable growth and progress, and their role is obviously to support the latter than create the former. While this recent crisis has damaged that position, it has not changed it. Banks need banking licences to offer banking and, without that core requirement, the economic system would fall into anarchy.

Just look at what happened in the virtual world of Second Life, as illustrated in the chapter "Digital Banks Are Social Banks", when its virtual banking system collapsed and Linden Lab, the company behind Second Life, refused to take any responsibility and rejected calls for compensation. After much protest, the firm eventually backtracked and changed its policy to state that, in future, in order to be a bank in virtual life, you had to be a bank in real life. In other words, even in these new worlds of commerce, you need to have a licence to operate the fundamentals of banking: deposit holding.

That does not mean that new banks and new forms of commerce will not build on the banking system, but it does mean that the core of banking has to remain with banks. Banks that are licensed, comply with state laws and are subject to auditing and supervisory interference.

These unique capabilities of the industry—an industry that in many ways is almost a nationalised service, but just not run in a nationalised way as that would give governments too much incline to corrupt—make it the foundation of all commerce, including new forms of commerce. However, things around that core are changing, and changing fast.

NEW FORMS OF COMMERCE

Taking into account that the world needs banks to be licensed as a fundamental provides some view towards the future based on the PayPal model. PayPal began as a pure person-to-person viral payment mechanism and, over time, has matured into an established player in banking. Although the firm has a banking licence, it prefers to work with banks to build its business as a pure payments processing focused organisation.

This does not mean that PayPal will not change this premise and become a bank one day but, right now, it is the only new non-bank play of any note to have made inroads into the financial system and has achieved it all on top of the system. PayPal's play being to make banking and payment easier by wrapping the process into an easy way to get the thing you want, rather than having to think about paying for the thing you want.

Amazon has done the same with click-to-pay, as has Apple with its aggregation of microtransactions through iTunes and apps. However, in the case of Apple, the company could change the world if its Passbook wallet included a monetary exchange capability. Apple's Passbook is a virtual wallet that, once activated, will provide integrated coupons, loyalty programmes and other offers. Google introduced such a wallet in partnership with MasterCard and Citibank in the United States in late 2011 but it has not taken off yet. The reason being attributed to the lack of critical mass is Google's decision to limit its virtual wallet to only one type of handset. Conversely, Apple with its smartphone dominance globally will see 100 million handsets automatically activated with virtual wallets linked to 400 million iTunes accounts. That is critical mass. Again, like PayPal and Google however, the model is one that leverages the bank's system rather than replaces it.

This is also true of other new entrants, such as Moven, which launched in the United States in 2013. Moven aims to create a truly social mobile financial service, where gamification, personal financial management, social media, social networking, payments processing and traditional banking all come together in a simply integrated form.

An example of one of Moven's new forms of commerce is illustrated by its patented CREDScore, which takes a person's social influence from various online social services, such as Facebook, Twitter and/or LinkedIn, to change their credit rating. The more influence the person has online, the better their credit rating; the less influence, the lower the rating. In part, this is also leveraging the data from social scores to assess people's trustworthiness, with the view being that the more trustworthy they are socially, the more they can be trusted financially. The core processing for bank services within Moven's operations is still a bank partner however, which is similar to other new players in the United States like Simple and SmartyPig.

SOME THINGS ARE CHANGING HOWEVER

Although much of the financial ecosystem remains within the bank realm, there are some signs of change in this new world, particularly where people are connected 1:1 via the mobile Internet.

M-PESA is an example of a near-bank system that transacts 20 per cent of Kenya's GDP outside the banking system. Since M-PESA was launched in March 2007, the number of people who now have bank accounts with the country's traditional banks has almost quadrupled. The reason? As mobile money provides inclusion for the unbanked and underbanked, they become recognised as financially viable citizens and therefore for financial inclusion by being banked. *See* the interview with John Maynard from M-PESA for more on this.

Similarly, when banks find they can no longer offer customers services that they could before the credit crisis, such as credit, other services gain traction. This is clear from the rise of crowdfunding platforms like Kickstarter and social lending services like Zopa, smava and Prosper.

For example, Zopa, launched in 2005, was the first social lending platform in the United Kingdom. Its mission was to provide an eBay-style platform for loans where those with money could invest it across many borrowers, with the risk being managed by the platform. The company struggled for its first three years of existence because no one really understood its model of operation and, on top of this, it had limited funds for advertising.

That all changed when the credit crisis hit and consumers suddenly found that their funding drug—low interest borrowing—was withdrawn by the traditional banks. Without access to funds, people sought alternative fund sources and found Zopa. Similarly, savers who were receiving poor interest rates sought alternative investment avenues, and they too found Zopa, which offers interest on savings that is typically higher than with a traditional bank.

A perfect storm has led to Zopa now controlling 2 per cent of the UK personal credit market today, managing around £200 million of funds. Not bad for an Internet start-up that has no bank or banking licence involved.

Hence, when we discuss alternative forms of commerce, we are potentially seeing the fledgling growth of new financial models that are being fuelled by the flames of the banking system's failure to keep up with changes in demand and service.

FIDOR BANK: THE NEW FORM OF BANK

It may surprise you to hear that one bank is already managing virtual and real currencies in one place. It is a new bank in Germany called FIDOR Bank. Launched in 2009 with a full banking licence, FIDOR Bank aims to bring together all of the elements of new forms of commerce and provide them as a full banking service in one place.

The bank takes value from World of Warcraft and Diablo, storing this as a valid exchange currency alongside precious metals—real gold and silver—and euro funds. The bank offers crowdfunding and social lending services but does this through partnerships with specialists, such as smava. Similarly, it offers global payments processing on a mobile smartphone wallet, but again through a partnership with hyperWALLET. The bank also brings in gamification with money, as well as social media integration. For example, customers can log on to their bank through Facebook Connect and can play spread betting games on its partner website (https://brokertain.fidor.de/de).

In fact, the really fun thing that the bank does is increase its interest rates based on its Facebook Likes. The more Likes FIDOR Bank's Facebook page receives, the higher the interest it pays to its customers on their deposit accounts.

Maybe this is why the bank has spent just €100,000 on its marketing efforts for the past three years, to gain over 75,000 users at a cost of just €1.33 per user registration.

HOW BANKS ARE ENABLING NEW FORMS OF COMMERCE

In this landscape of change, there are several examples of bank models that are encouraging new forms of commerce from partnering with new entrants—PayPal, Moven, Simple, SmartyPig—to innovating with new services (*see*, for instance, the interview with Mike Walters from Barclays Bank). However, interestingly, most of my clients still believe that they can fast follow these players downstream rather than innovating as first mover. This may be true but if new forms of money—bitcoins or Zynga credits—are managed by new forms of bank, such as FIDOR Bank and its expected followers, then potentially the new form of commerce will be purely managed by a new form of player.

That is not a disaster but it will change the financial ecosystem as the virtual wallets will be hybrid with the real wallet, just as the virtual world is becoming hybrid with the real world. And that is where my real focal point comes into play, in that this hybrid world in which we live is enhanced by a digitised augmented reality, meaning that we really need to stop thinking of the world as channels—branch, call centre, Internet and mobile—and just think of it as a digitally enhanced, augmented financial experience.

That is what the new players have fundamentally realised and if banks and traditional players ignore this fundamental, then they will not only lose out on the new forms of commerce, but on the old ones too.

THE NEW ECONOMICS OF DIGITAL BANKING

Back in the 1990s, Kevin Kelly, senior maverick and launch editor of *Wired* magazine, told me that everything would become free thanks to the Internet. I thought he was nuts at the time, but how wrong was I? In his article "New Rules for the New Economy", which appeared in *Wired* in 1997, Kelly devised twelve lessons about how to think about the Internet. Those lessons were difficult to absorb at the time as he was far too ahead of his time.

I went back to these lessons recently and realised rather quickly that banking will soon cost nothing. In other words, loans and payments will be provided for free. To explain where I am coming from, it's necessary to understand Kelly's lessons, which I've summarised here:

1. **The Law of Connection—Embrace dumb power:** With everything having an inbuilt computer chip connected to a network, start thinking about how to use those inbuilt chips.
2. **The Law of Plentitude—More gives more:** In the network economy, there's loads of everything and little of nothing. There is no scarcity because it costs nothing to churn out more. This means the more you give for nothing, the more you get of everything.

3. **The Law of Exponential Value—Success is nonlinear:** Because everything is connected, small changes can explode into global and seismic movements overnight. Just look at Facebook and Twitter if you want to see this one in action.

4. **The Law of Tipping Points—Significance precedes momentum:** The tipping point is the point at which something goes from being a micromarket to the stage of critical mass where everyone has got one, like the iPod. It occurs at a much faster rate and a much lower point of mass in the network economy.

5. **The Law of Increasing Returns—Make virtuous circles:** The more people in the network, the more value the network has. As a result, every additional member increases value exponentially.

6. **The Law of Inverse Pricing—Anticipate the cheap:** It used to be that quality improved with higher prices in the industrial age; in the Internet age, quality improves with lower prices over time. The law of price:quality has flipped.

7. **The Law of Generosity—Follow the free:** Because value increases with abundance, and the cost of production is virtually nothing to create more copies, flood the market with copies of your product for free because the more people who have it, the more valuable it becomes and the easier it becomes to sell product adjuncts.

8. **The Law of the Allegiance—Feed the web first:** Networks have no clear centre or boundaries and therefore no clear organisation. You cannot feed a network top-down so feed it first as the only "inside" now is whether you're on or off the network.

9. **The Law of Devolution—Let go at the top:** Everything is dispensable. A network market domination can be replaced just as quickly by a new one. Just look at Friends Reunited, which was displaced by Facebook, or at AOL, which was replaced by broadband general accessibility. Sell when you have reached the peak, not after.

10. **The Law of Displacement—The net wins:** The question, how big will Internet commerce be? is irrelevant as everything will be on the net.

11. **The Law of Churn—Seek sustainable disequilibrium:** Instead of leaving businesses, people will just continually morph businesses and improve them in a never-ending rebirth process through the net.

12. **The Law of Inefficiencies—Don't solve problems:** Create ideas and put them out there unformed, as the net will finish them. You don't need to solve problems, just start ideas. Linux is a great example.

I do not intend to discuss all of these twelve lessons but the one that really stands out is #7—follow the free. Follow the free? What? Give everything away for nothing? You must be mad. That's precisely what everyone thought about Kelly back then, but he persevered.

What he was really getting at is that the more you build a following, the more valuable you become. The more valuable you become, the more you can charge a premium. Today, this train of thought is far more obvious but, back in 1997, Google, Facebook, Android and all the other good things of today's web were not around. We were in the Microsoft Windows 95, AOL and fax era. Today, it is obvious that if you have a million or more daily users, you can sell advertising and other nice "add-ons" to those users. But remember that these are not locked-in users; they are fans. And fans of Google, Facebook and Android could dump these products overnight for a better version, just as Yahoo! search fans, Friends Reunited fans and Apple's fans have done (although only a small number in the last case).

So what does "follow the free" really mean? I guess this can be answered by the fact that I blog for free. Why do I blog for free? I blog for free because I enjoy it and it brings me business because people see value in my insights. If I charged for those insights on a daily feed business, I don't think I would get many supported but, by offering those thoughts for free, I get invited by banks, conference organisers and vendors to advise them worldwide.

It's a bit like newspapers. I get free newspapers these days, but they are paid for by the advertising in the paper and propped up by website services linked to the paper. Nowadays, the *Guardian, Telegraph, Sun* and *Evening Standard* get far more web traffic than any newspaper revenues or sales ... and their web traffic is provided for free because each click generates advertising revenues. This is what those in the newspaper industry misunderstood to start with, but now they get it big time.

It is also what the music industry misunderstood but is now starting to get. These days, you don't sign music artists to write songs and sell records, you sign them to write songs and give them away for nothing so that people will follow their website, buy the t-shirts, come to the gigs and download the odd track. This is why entertainment firms now sign their artists up for 360-degree contracts—all the music sales and the rest—rather than for a recording contract.

Which brings me round to banking. We have already talked about the future model of banking and its pricing model which, as I say, will cost nothing. Just like newspapers, blogs, music and even books and live streaming rock concerts, banking will be free. My payments will be processed for nothing. My loans will be charged at zero margin, as will my savings. PayPal, Zopa and SmartyPig are offering various structures around these models of banking, but it is still early days.

So here's my vision of the new world order. Banks will offer all of their administrative and transactional services for no charge. There will be no charge for being in the red and yet I will still get good rates when I'm in the black. So how will the bank make money?

First, by having millions of us in their community. Second, by partnering with firms that advertise and provide services to their millions of financial community members. Third, by selling ancillary products and services such as hats, t-shirts, umbrellas and nice leather binders and folders. If you don't believe me on this point, take a look at ING Direct in the United States as this bank was doing precisely this ten years ago because it built fans rather than customers. That is a key. Finally, by providing me and the corporate customer with some real value, such as aggregation services, lifestyle financing advice, real-time risk management, identification of missing tricks and so on.

This final point relates to providing far more information to the consumer about their financial lifestyle or, as it is commonly known today, personal financial management (PFM). PFM is already a mature market that started with firms like Mint and is now crowded with too many players, most of them backed by software developed by Yodlee. It is a space I've tracked for a while as, back in the late 1990s and early 2000s, Yodlee was making aggressive noises in the retail online world as the aggregation engine. Unfortunately, aggregation didn't work a decade ago as it was just too early. Customers didn't like the idea of giving their bank details and passwords to a strange, untested, third-party engine and, on top of this, banks told them that, if they did and had their funds swiped, it would be their tough justice. So aggregation stuttered and stagnated. But you have to hand it to Yodlee as it's still around today and is successful, partnering with many of the key innovation providers of PFM.

So why is Yodlee working today when it didn't a decade ago, and is PFM the same as aggregation? By answering the second question first, we'll also get the answer to the first. No, PFM isn't the same as aggregation. PFM is a functionally rich set of financial tools that help consumers—and businesses for that matter—aggregate their financial transactions services across multiple providers into an advisory engine, often Yodlee, that can help them get better returns from their money.

PFM links you with other users who have financial behaviours like yours, and shows you how to improve your financial returns based on what people like you do. PFM might link to your mobile and social networks, allowing you to do a lot more intelligent financial structuring and operations. PFM can alert you to budgetary and balance issues, payments and billing notices, and interest saving or gaining opportunities. In fact, depending on which

PFM provider you go with, PFM can pretty much do anything you want with your banking service ... and PFM providers are popping up all over the place to show different capabilities in what is an increasingly crowded space.

Some want to focus on the social aspects of finance whilst others on the financial management aspects; some want to provide offers and coupons whilst others want to provide advice and analysis of your financial behaviours; some want to provide PFM online—on the mobile and on the tablet PC— whilst others only care about functionality rather than interface. In other words, all of these PFM systems are slightly different with some easier to use than others, some more functionally rich than others and some clearly in the lead over others. It goes further than this, however, as PFM combined with mobile provides real-time financial analytics and management for every individual and company being serviced by the bank.

REAL TIME AND PERSONAL

Another game changer for banking is real-time payments and real-time services. Mobile money in real-time changes the game and here's how.

Roll back a few decades to the pre-Internet age. This was the age of the first screen: the television. You would only get to notice things through the screen in your living room, and that would be in the form of a screaming advert. You could get reactivity by going to the branch and talking to the bank, based on the screaming advert that got your attention.

Then we entered the second age of the screen: the desktop. The desktop screen gave us interactivity but you had to go to the desk to get onto the screen. You could interact with your bank, but it would again only be on a reactive rather than proactive basis.

Now we have entered the age of the third screen: the smartphone. The smartphone is with us 24/7, in our pockets and handbags. The screen never leaves us, and we can be contacted at any time of day or night.

Here's where the light bulb switched on. With a mobile financial service we can have real-time PFM rather than PFM about our past—or passed—

financial transactions. That's really powerful. For a while, there was talk about PFM being the new era of banking, with alerts and budgeting apps giving us all we would need to know about our money. Well, it's not. PFM is interesting and important but it only gives you a reverse view of your finances. It does not plan ahead, it just summarises what has gone before in a pictorial way. In other words, it is an Internet-based second screen era application.

Source: My Bank Tracker

PFM may be good and helpful but the mobile gives us PFM^2—Proactive Personal Financial Management—the third screen era financial solution. The example that switched on my light bulb is walking into a shop and looking to buy something. Anything. Let's say a panini and cappuccino in Starbucks for the sake of illustration. So I get my phone out to pay and the phone not only tells me the PFM piece about how many cappuccinos and paninis I've bought in Starbucks over the past month, week or year, but also whether I can afford it. That may sound redundant to some of you but if your phone can show you proactively your behaviours and habits financially and, in real time, alerts about whether this next transaction will take you overdrawn, then that's really something. Think back to when you were a student, hard up or broke (you might still be for all I know). Every penny counts and every transaction can be a moment that sends you into the overdraft zone. All those nasty fees and charges, and the shame of it.

But now you can have that cappuccino and panini, not only knowing that you have spent £50 in Starbucks so far this month and have far too many paninis and cappuccinos, but also knowing that you can afford it. That is real individual 1:1 servicing. It also means that you receive highly personalised attention automatically through alerts that say "Do you know your pension will only pay you half of what you earn? Top up your pension premiums now ... you can afford it. Look ..." and then show you graphically and visually why it makes sense. The same could be true for investments, loans and other products. For the corporate customer, for instance, it might be real-time portfolio and cash management positions for treasurers to improve allocation of resources, real-time analysis of market and credit movements to ensure minimisation of exposures, real-time tracking of products and finances through global windows to financial services and supply chain systems, and more.

The fact is that it is the information value the bank adds in advising me on my financial behaviours that will really lock customers like me in because the bank can then get under my skin and into my brain. This will be the new bank model, and the new bank order post this crisis will weed out the banks that get the follow-the-free model and provide real value as opposed to those transactional banks that are just processors.

BANKING-AS-A-SERVICE

Banking-as-a-Service (BaaS) is a new model of banking based on cloud computing structures of digital banking. Bearing in mind that the bank has moved from integrated to modular, this is the new way of working where bank processes are apps and bank processing are APIs.

As this is a slightly confusing as well as technical discussion, let's start with the idea of cloud computing in banking. Cloud computing is a wide and diverse operation that has gained a panacea status of being all things to all people. It's Salesforce.com, Azure, Exalogic, Amazon and more. Key in "Cloud Computing" on Google, which also provides clouds, and you will get sponsored adverts from HP, Intel, Siemens and others all talking about clouds. It's Software as a Service, Platform as a Service and Infrastructure as a Service. It's public clouds, private clouds, hybrid clouds. It's every and any darned thing you want and, as a result, it's lost its meaning.

As a result, bank CIOs have heard about cloud computing but have no idea how to articulate what it is to their board and CEO, how to justify it, how to present it as meaningful and how to get a decision. The board and CEO have heard of cloud, but hear it's dangerous. They think it's the reason why Sony and Citi got hacked and why Amazon servers were out for days causing businesses to lose money. They consider it risky and a loss of control.

The experts know that this is not the case as, in its simplest form, if you run your bank on anyone's technology you might as well think of it as a cloud. But the risk of losing scale, resilience, security and control is the core issue at a bank's heart, and no bank is willing to take that risk with cloud, especially if no one can define it. Talk to anyone and they will define "cloud" in different ways and, in all of this confusion, the decision maker is left bewildered.

Nevertheless, we are moving from a world of finance where technology was core to efficiency in its first wave, and differentiation was core in its second. Initially, mainframe computer power and then business process outsourcing (BPO) and virtualisation created efficient computing capabilities for financial firms. Then the ease of modular computing, service-oriented architectures and Ajax Web 2.0 made computing applications the differentiating factor between a winning bank and an also-ran bank. Now we are moving to an age where computing and applications just don't matter.

Everything will be utility computing through the cloud. Just like the iTunes app store and Google's Gmail for consumers—few really care how it's done and who does it as long it's there—banks will gradually move to clouds. The art will then be in how the banks put their apps and resilience together through the cloud rather than how they build and manage their internal fortress.

This shift involves three stages and is a journey that most banks have begun to embark on or soon will. First, banks are already moving towards clouds for shared service applications such as marketing databases (Salesforce.com). In the second wave, banks will move core infrastructure onto private clouds and then, in the third wave, towards hybrid and public clouds. It will just be a natural evolution over time and the concerns of managerial teams will gradually disappear. Before you know it, all banks will be in the clouds. By that time, computing and applications for banks will be just like Gmail and iTunes for consumers—just stuff you plug and play and pick and choose from.

Like a smorgasbord of utilities, the trick for banks will be to make their plate of edibles the most attractive to the target audience they are trying to reach. By that time, we will all think of technology, software and infrastructure along the same lines as we do the Internet—just something we plug into without caring how it works. This then leads on to the component-based bank.

THE COMPONENT-BASED BANK

Banks have traditionally been vertically integrated businesses where the end-to-end process is offered to the customer as a complete package. Deposit accounts, trade finance, payments processing, loans, credit, mortgages, savings, investment and so on are wrapped together as pieces of business. Within each separate product stream, banks also integrate the end-to-end so corporates run their payables and receivables, electronic and paper, domestic and foreign exchange all through the one bank. The same applies to consumers who run their entire everything through the bank when it comes to money, payments and transactions.

This vertically integrated structure is the piece that is changing most through digitisation, as new entrants attack each part of banking. These new entrants include Currency Cloud, which offers foreign exchange processing, eToro, which offers portfolio management in investor services through social trading, and Moven and Simple, which offer bank front-end user experiences that are exceptional but do not focus on any of the back-end functions.

Essentially, what is happening is that bank functionality is being broken apart, divided into its lowest common denominators and then reconstructed into new forms. The best way to illustrate this is by looking at a specific piece of banking, such as payment processing.

Traditionally, payment processing has been viewed as its own specific product silo, but it's not an individual product line. For most banks, it's an integral part of the bank operations. It's the glue that hooks the customer to the bank. It's the core of their offer. This is why banks find it so hard to think of payments neutrally, objectively, dispassionately. Payments are not objective, they are emotional. For most banks, they are very emotional. Ask a banker to outsource core payments processing and they'll give you a look like you're the devil's spawn. It's just not done. And yet, payments is no longer the glue for a bank, but more like the foundation, and even builders don't always drill the foundations. They bring in specialists.

That's what banks need today—to bring in common component providers and develop value on top of their services. Now this is where it gets interesting. As I've just stated, banking has historically been a vertically integrated industry, providing an end-to-end service that is wrapped around the customer and is incredibly difficult to unlock. And yet it will be unlocked as banking is driven into a componentised industry where you have a payment app, a balance app, a cashflow app, a budgeting app, a fraud app and so on and so forth.

That's Banking-as-a-Service and Banking-as-a-Service is coming around faster than many might believe if you check out all of the new players in banking:

- Social money and payments: iZettle, Payatrader, mPowa, SumUp, payleven, Inuit GoPayment, Square
- Social lending and saving: Zopa, RateSetter, smava, Prosper, Lending Club, Cashare
- Social insurance: Friendsurance
- Social investing and trading: StockTwits, eToro, Myfxbook, Fxstat, MetaTrader Trade Signals, Collective2, Tradeo, ZuluTrade, Nutmeg
- Social trade financing: MarketInvoice, Platform Black, the Receivables Exchange, Urica
- Payday Lending: Wonga, Cash America, Advance America
- Goal setting and gamification: SmartyPig, Moven, Simple
- Crowdfunding: Funding Circle, Kickstarter, Indiegogo, crowdrise, Razoo

The list goes on in each and every area of banking. There are hundreds of these start-ups, as well as some companies that have long been established as disruptive, out there and to think that I've not even mentioned what Facebook, Google, Amazon, Apple, Bitcoin, Ven Currency and others are doing.

Each and every area of banking is being broken down, componentised and reconstructed into new forms and new business models by the new Digital Bank regime of cloud-based mobile-social data analytics. Suffice to say that the componentisation of banking and shift from vertical integration to horizontal components that can be put together however you like is happening and happening fast.

BANKING BECOMES PLUG-AND-PLAY

As these developments move forward, banking simply becomes a smorgasbord of plug-and-play apps that the customer stitches together to suit their business or lifestyle needs. There's no logical reason why banking shouldn't be delivered *as-a-Service*. In fact, it is already just that for some people. For example, here's an illustration of banking with no bank involved. Using prepaid cards, you can load and use a MasterCard and just keep topping up without ever using a bank. Equally, some cards provide prepaid capabilities that have no limits.

Alternatively, some people might use PayPal or other services for payments. Although PayPal needs a bank account to open your account—it runs its on-boarding check through the banking system— once the account is up and running, the user could close their bank account and purely exist within PayPal via revolving credit. For savings and investments, Zopa would work well, offering the most competitive rates on saving and lending in the United Kingdom for most savers and borrowers.

All in all, it would be an interesting experiment to load up on these services and try living on prepaid cards, revolving balances on PayPal and savings and borrowing through Zopa, just to see how long you could survive off the banking network.

Even corporates could do this, and some do by running their own bank internally. Using Banking-as-a-Service, corporates would build a full financial service using providers such as First Data, the Barter Network, PayPal, Funding Circle and related services. I'm not sure they should do this, but it would be interesting to see how far they could push the boat.

What I'm really getting at here is that the old model of banking, where everything is packaged together around a deposit account with a cheque book, is bust. That's why some banks are starting to white label and break apart their traditional services so that corporates can just buy the bits they need. That might be a SWIFT Gateway here, Internet payment service there, international money transfer here, cheque processing there ... all bits of banking, all priced and packaged as a plug-and-play service.

For corporates and consumers, there will also be niche operators who use Banking-as-a-Service to offer new banking models as integrators and aggregators. These integrators bring the pieces together—Mint and Yodlee are already not far off the mark—and provide them in a far more competitively priced model than traditional banks. This is the future bank, and traditional banks will need to reconsider their services to compete with this zero margin model.

Banking-as-a-Service. Think about it. Banking ... as a Service. Now that would be nice, wouldn't it?

WIDGETS IN THE COMPONENT-BASED BANK

The component-based bank is the core of Banking-as-a-Service, a method of taking complex applications and offering them as web services where you pay for what you use. In other words, banks offer their capabilities for anyone to plug into their services from payments processing to balance checks. The components themselves are widgets. Wikipedia defines a software widget as "a generic type of software application comprising portable code intended for one or more different software platforms".

For banks, these widgets are offered as simple pick up and drop code for anyone to incorporate financial functionality into their service. A great example of a financial widget is the one that can be generated easily by PayPal users to take credit and debit card payments online. The process takes about five minutes and then can be plugged into any website to receive money and, for small merchants, is a major bonus.

These widgets are plug-and-play for anyone wanting that piece of bank functionality or, if the firm that wants this functionality is more sophisticated, they might pick up the code as an API. An API is slightly more complicated and Wikipedia defines this as the software code that instructs "how some software components should interact with each other. In addition to accessing databases or computer hardware, such as hard disk drives or video cards, an API can be used to ease the work of programming graphical user interface components." In other words, an API allows a programmer to incorporate the financial functionality without working out how to program it themselves as that component is prebuilt by the bank and ready to drop into anyone else's software.

So now we're banking on a widget, what's the point? The point is that Banking-as-a-Service allows banks to be decoupled into their constituent components and offered as widget-based functionality through the net. It's radical but obvious, and applies to all aspects of retail, wholesale, investment and payments functionality.

HSBC was one of the first banks to adopt this approach with then chief operating officer (COO) Ken Harvey stating in 2009 that he could launch the bank into any country simply and easily thanks to the bank's technology structure. All the IT is free, he claimed, because HSBC build it once and then deploy it globally through the network so that it can be used by thousands of staff and customers in almost 200 countries. That is the cloud component-based bank in action, with one program built for thousands of users in hundreds of countries.

Once you have network-enabled components, you can add any branch, product or even country onto the network at no extra cost. That's the power of Banking-as-a-Service. Banking-as-a-Service means that any module, component or function of a bank can be application packaged and network enabled. The balance statement widget, the payments transaction widget, the loan application widget and so on.

Spanish bank BBVA realised this as a first mover when it launched the *Tú Cuentas* (Spanish for "You Count!") service in 2008. Tú Cuentas was the first bank service to really push the boundaries of mobile Internet with:

- customisable budgeting tools and alerts, personal financial management with usage comparisons so that you could be advised of financial deals that people like you take advantage of
- aggregation capabilities to act as a trusted portal to all your financial accounts
- the ability to break down its service into functionality that suits your lifestyle via widgets
- all tools being available on a range of iPhone, Blackberry, Nokia and other mobile services

This was and still is groundbreaking innovation, and BBVA continue to provide such service today through its innovation centre in Madrid. However, most banks do not get it, making it easier for new players such as PayPal, Zopa, SmartyPig and Wonga to step in and deploy widgets for loans, savings and payments.

Using such widgets within Banking-as-a-Service allows a bank or new entrant to gain customers with no extra work as, once built and deployed, there is no extra cost for having more users on the network. This is clearly demonstrated by the experience I have in running my own business: the Financial Services Club.

Ten years ago, the Financial Services Club would have cost around $800,000 per year in mailing, printing and telephone costs alone. On top of this, about another $150,000 would have been spent on the cost of physical meetings. Today, the only costs incurred are for those physical meetings. The digital network—blogging, mailing, website services, etc.—is almost free, excluding my own time and effort to create the content.

This is the challenge for banks. A decade ago, 70 per cent of costs were wrapped up in materials that are now free. Ten years ago, the biggest barrier of entry to banking was building the bricks-and-mortar branch network. Today, you do not need that bricks and mortar, just a mobile app and website. That's what HSBC's former COO made clear when he redesigned its technology. HSBC can now enter any country with a mortgage, credit card or deposit account product and the only costs are the physical investments in buildings. The rest is on the network.

This is not limited to retail banking either, as the new European equities exchanges are demonstrating. BATS Chi-X and NASDAQ, among others, are each launching radical new trading systems using leading-edge technologies at a tenth or more of the cost of the traditional exchanges. They also have a tenth or less of the staff. This is precisely why these new trading venues can charge 10 basis points per side to clear and execute trades in under 2 milliseconds compared to seven times the cost and many times the time taken by the incumbents. No matter which area of financial services you want to point to, you can see new entrants and innovative incumbents changing the model using the concepts of Banking-as-a-Service.

Combining these thoughts, Banking-as-a-Service delivers:

- the ability to grow without any additional costs by simply adding more traffic onto the network
- the componentisation of the bank into widgets which can be picked up and dropped by staff and customers as they choose
- the opportunity for staff and customers to create banking home pages that are completely personalised to them

- the integration of banking functionality from one bank with others in a completely flexible aggregated manner
- future-proofing for the semantic relational networking of the next generation web
- totally flexible, totally comprehensive, low-cost, high tailorability for every part of the banking organisation

The bottom line is that anyone can now launch a widget for a banking app and make it available anywhere for free and, as a result, rapidly build market and mindshare.

HOW DOES THE PRICING AND ECONOMICS OF BANKING-AS-A-SERVICE WORK?

If the bank recognises that most activities outside direct servicing of the customer are commoditised and all processing and technology is priced at near zero, how does it make money?

Commodity processing being made freely available is a radical departure from bank histories, where margin is made through customer lock-in. Such a transformation will therefore be a radical culture shock for many bankers and, yet, the pricing and economics is relatively obvious.

Let's start with the cost of building Banking-as-a-Service. The cost can be however much you want it to be. In HSBC's case, the cost of building its global Internet service was around $250 million, but that's fairly cheap considering it was building a global bespoke service. Most banks, however, will not be looking at $250 million developments, but more likely a few thousand dollars to deploy a piece of functionality. The key point is that whatever the cost is, once it's built, it's built. That's it. You have sunk the cost and built the widget.

Now, the critical point is not to protect the widget but to get everyone to use it. What's the point of investing in a development if you can't get volume? That's the point of Banking-as-a-Service. Once you've built your widget, then the focus has to be to build up the volume and volume increases fast these days. That's how BATS Chi-X garnered over 10 per cent of the traditional European exchanges equities trading within a year and, having built the system, it is why BATS Chi-X fought a volume war with other players, such as Turquoise and NASDAQ OMX. It is why Zopa, SmartyPig and PayPal are leveraging volume.

That's how any bank-building components should be thinking today. Volume. Because additional volume adds zero cost and purely feeds return on investment. Another way to look at this is to think of it in terms of making a movie. Once the movie is made, and the budget has been spent, the point it to get as many people as possible to see the film to make the return so that is why you market the hell out of it. The same applies to banking widgets in Banking-as-a-Service. Market the widget heavily, build up the volumes fast and focus on the service delivery—the human interfaces—as your critical value-add differentiation. Your value-add is how you package the widgets and present them, not the widgets themselves.

That's why Citigroup has been marketing its APIs, apps and other services heavily. It wants volume on its widget, and Citi is one of the few banks that have been white labelling their systems to other banks. It clearly understands the Banking-as-a-Service components.

The same idea is also illustrated by telecommunications companies that understand networking. For example, I once worked for NCR when it was owned by AT&T. I always remember the AT&T management talking about "minutes on the network, it's all about minutes on the network", and that's the key. Once you've built the infrastructure, it's all about getting volume because it costs you no more to process a billion calls than it does to process one. Which brings us back to the economics of banking in the future under the Banking-as-a-Service model and the culture shock this creates.

I was recently with a head of payments at one bank who said, "Our technology guys asked me why we charge more for a $50 million payment than we do for a $5 payment when the infrastructure costs to process are the same. Are they mad?" No, sir. They are asking an obvious question at the heart of the change that needs to be made within banking cultures as they realise the change that technology now delivers. This payments executive was from that old school of banking waking up to the realities of the new world.

Thirty years ago, when many senior bankers were starting out in banking, they were told that technology was expensive, inflexible and had to be used forever, or at least until the systems crashed. That's why every project was massive, time-consuming and demanded huge cost.

When SWIFT, MasterCard, Visa and the key networks for transaction processing were built, for example, they had to be built by an industry consortium. No individual bank could afford such a huge project or cost, thus the cooperative groups across all banks back in the 1970s. Back in 1975, the bank technology economic model involved massive cost that could be recouped slowly over time through usage. Cost was depreciated slowly, and could only be covered by high prices and margins. Hence, banks, SWIFT and the card companies all worked hard to create the infrastructure and cover the costs of that infrastructure through high transaction processing and interchange fees. That was back then. This model had changed a little by 2000.

Then the industry was hit by a thing called the Millennium Bug or, as most remember it, the "Year 2000" fiasco. Leading up to the millennium, there was immense pressure to refresh all systems to deal with the fact that, up until then, they had been designed to represent the year using only the last two digits of the year, rather than all four digits. As a result, everyone believed rightly or wrongly that their systems would fail on 1 January 2000 and so renewed such systems at extremely high cost.

Once the Year 2000 fiasco was over, many systems had been renovated and rationalised and the costs of building new systems had reduced somewhat thanks to HTML and component-based modelling. Therefore, banks found that while the time frame and cost of building new systems had been fundamentally reduced, they were still faced with a technology challenge as the costs for usage and pricing had not come down as fast.

For example, when the then CEO of SWIFT, Leonard Schrank, was interviewed in 2003, he made a number of statements about how SWIFT was well underway to using IP-based messaging and that costs for a typical SWIFT message had come down 70 per cent in the last ten years whilst volume had increased four-fold to 8 million messages per day. SWIFT gave those savings back to its banking members because it is bank-owned. However, banks have not yet passed all these cost reductions on to their customers but, thanks to today's competitive forces, they will. Today, competitive forces recognise how the network has changed these pricing models even further.

Today, the cost to build has become virtually irrelevant if you are using the right tools but, once built, the volume can be increased really quickly, thanks to openness, standards, ease of networking and communicating. In other words, the economics of banking has fundamentally changed. This is because banking is based on technology, and the economics of technology has fundamentally changed.

The new economics of banking—technology and systems, processing and functionality—are virtually free; anything that is commodity activity should be brought in as a service; and all pricing is for value-add, not commodities.

Today, it is a no-brainer to build new functionality, or even micro-functionality, and then deploy it openly, transparently and easily across the network. That's why banking should be free. That's why it will be free because banks can build micro-functionality in their widgets and make money out of volume.

If I can get a thousand banks to serve a million companies processing a billion transactions through my widget of commoditised functionality, then I make money, and that process is far better than one bank working with a hundred firms to transact a thousand times through my very expensive and out-of-date legacy infrastructure. The latter is the old way. Banking on the network is the new and better way.

How do banks make money in this new world? By being the lowest cost integrator of the best white-labelled banking widgets, and then charging for advice and superior services to add value to the commodity services offered by others. This final part is where the culture shock will really hit. In a world where every bank is offering transactions and processing for nothing, how can you make me feel you're so worthy as to be worth a fee? The answer to that one is to focus on the customer experience. The customer experience, service, dialogue and advice will become the critical differentiation and profit point.

COLLABORATIVE COMPETITION

Bearing in mind that banks are now offering components and customers will integrate and incorporate those components as they see fit, another change will occur. Banks will collaboratively compete. Sometimes they will be partners and, at other times, they will be competitors. This will not just occur between banks but between banks and telecommunications firms, technology vendors, information providers and so on.

It seems like an oxymoron to talk about collaborative competition and yet for years we talked about co-opetition, which is almost the same thing. Cooperate or collaborate to compete implies both cartels and price fixing but, in today's reality, has nothing to do with either of these. Today, it's the idea of collaborating to improve business models through robust and reliable open-source architectures whilst identifying the differentiating components internally within these collaborative models for competitive purposes.

Let's illustrate with an example that's top of the list today—risk. When Lehman Brothers collapsed in September 2008, it happened during the week of one of the biggest banking conferences in the world—SIBOS—in Vienna. SIBOS had various themes and finished on the Thursday with a great presentation by Don Tapscott, one of the authors of *Wikinomics*.

Tapscott talked about his whole approach to the social network and the new age of the Internet, and illustrated the power of such thinking with a story related to the writing of his latest book. Apparently he finished the book just before Christmas and asked his son what he thought of it. His son said that it didn't matter what he thought personally; what was more important was the collective view. Consequently, he offered to create a Facebook group to critique the book. "Sure," said Dad and son dutifully created the group on Christmas Eve. By the end of the day, 300 teenagers were actively reading, digesting, dissecting and critiquing the book such that, by Christmas Day, it had pretty much been re-written and was far better for it. That's the power of the collective, the collaborative cohesion of the whole rather than the fragmented view of the one.

Tapscott then made this appeal at the end of his presentation: "The risks in the financial system must be better managed in the future so why don't we create an open-source group for risk managers? A Facebook for Risk Professionals if you like. This group could then share and discuss risks in the financial systems and have contributions from all. Effectively, risk management becomes an open-source arena so that everyone can build a more robust, reliable and resilient future."

Since he proposed such a system, what's happened? Not much, or not much in the risk management space that I can identify anyway. It seems we're all waiting for the regulators to come up with their plans before implementing ours, but isn't that wrong? Which brings it back to the theme of collaborative competition, which is another dimension of the new economics of banking.

Collaborative competition says that things that are not offering differentiation, that have been commoditised or that are general industry-wide issues and infrastructures should just be widgetised and made to be plug-and-play. This processing capability and knowledge should then be made available to all. These pieces add little value, they are commoditised and they should be free or virtually free.

That's the nature of collaboration. For example, Google ads gather a great deal of knowledge and processing power, so why not have Google ads pay for banks' commodity processes and transactions. Then, as a bank, you focus on the areas where you differentiate. These are the customer-centric parts of engagement, acquisition, delivery and fulfilment. The result is that banks could outsource compliance and create common shared components for the AML and KYC regulatory requirements for account opening. AML and KYC then just become a cheap widget of functionality that you plug and play. Banks could drop a widget into their system for payments processing too—just use a white-labelled processor—and even find a widget for a bit of credit risk management based on an open-source structure. Then provide a little bit of service improvement by offering their savings vehicle for children, through a partnership with SmartyPig for example, whilst focusing on their own deployment of service around high-end wealth management for the children's mums and dads.

The only part of the banking operation that has been developed and deployed in this model is wealth management servicing. The rest—all the processing, compliance, risk and ancillary products—has been dropped in as widgets of functionality into the banking structure. And those bits are all the bits of collaborative competition therefore. Banks can then compete with the providers of their widgets, and can also collaborate with them to use their processing where it makes sense or where it makes their own infrastructures more robust and reliable.

In conclusion, the banking industry is quickly starting to operate more like the car industry. A quarter of a century ago, car manufacturers prided themselves on having the best manufacturing. They produced all of the car's components, and the manufacturer with the best components offered the most expensive cars. Today, nearly all cars are based on standardised and commoditised manufacturing of the pieces. The manufacturer no longer manufactures; it just assembles the pieces into the whole and adds its own unique recipe of chassis and engine to differentiate. Take BMW. In 1980, the car company manufactured thousands of unique components for its cars; today it just assembles them. But it's still BMW and the final product is still an aspirational brand. BMW may use commodity components that VW, Ford and others use but it assembles them into a brilliant car that swishes, swooshes and whizzes far more sleekly and smoothly than many others.

That's how banks will compete. All the components will come from the assembly line of banking functionality, but unquestionably the banks that assemble them to address a specific target audience in the most appropriate way will win that audience's business.

LAUNCHING THE DIGITAL BANK

If we were creating a bank today, how would we create it? This is a question that comes up regularly, especially as the focus is moving increasingly towards the Digital Bank concept where everything is built around the mobile Internet rather than bricks and mortar. Now, let's be clear, building a bank today requires many things. The first issue that we would need to address is what sort of feeling we would want the bank to convey. For instance:

- Are we a technobank or a human bank?
- Do we want to encourage human interactivity or remote interactivity?
- How do we believe we are different and what can we deliver to customers to show that we are different?
- Where are the weak points in the current bank offer, and how do we exploit those?

These questions cannot be answered with a simple yes or no, but need to be pondered individually so that they do not become imponderables. So our first point of focus would be how to deliver something the current banks do not. What is that?

Current banks deliver secure deposit taking, transaction processing, branch access, an ATM network, facilities for loans, credit and mortgages and more. They deliver such capabilities primarily through branches, with call centre and mobile Internet as adjuncts. The only banks that differ from this are the online-only banks and banks without branches like First Direct. However, these banks are owned by traditional branch-based banks and use the parent's capabilities to offer the branch and ATM services they themselves lack.

So, if I were opening a new bank, the first thing I would focus on is opening a bank without branches whilst doing a deal to get access to the ATM network, which is easy to do in the United Kingdom thanks to Vocalink.

The second thing I would think about is how to create a bank that was cool. The Apple of banking. If we wanted to create a new bank that was cool like Apple, we would start with an amazing online user experience designed for mobile and tablet computers. A snazzy app store financial offer. Admittedly, some already exist, but they are not mainstream or designed for core banking. Most new apps for banking from new entrants have purely been to dance around the edges of deposit taking, but not going for the core.

If we designed a Digital Bank, a bank based on Internet protocol, a bank wholly focused on today's mobile Internet, what would that mean for the deposit taking area? It would be a challenge, as a cool Apple-store style app bank would be too weird and funky for some. So it would need some gravitas somehow. Does that mean investing in branches? No. By way of example, Britain's best-loved banks today are Smile, an Internet bank, and First Direct, a bank without branches. Branches are irrelevant when launching a cool new bank.

What's key to a cool new bank is to be 21st century and heavily into mobile, social and online. So my first tenet of my new bank would be to launch a differentiated Digital Bank brand that is cool.

What does "cool" mean in banking? Offering apps that are PFM capable and simple to use online and on mobile. Making it securely cool by authenticating me using my geolocation and signal. Making it simply cool by never asking me for names, account numbers and passwords but simply giving me a personal space where my voice activates the services. Making it truly cool by offering me gifts and goods for loyalty, such as flights and iTunes based on account usage. Making it way cool by offering me those gifts and goods as I Google to buy them or walk past the store. And making it cool by relating to me based on how I want to relate to you. This means talking to me as a human when I call, and making me feel that I am really understood because my data has been understood.

Then, to give it gravitas, I would invest heavily in a marketing campaign—both viral and mainstream—with a personality or personalities whom everyone would find believable. Someone they could trust. Someone who is not easily bought but needs to be impressed. Someone like a leading celebrity consumer champion—an Oprah Winfrey—whom I would convince of our cause. Having a leading advisor on board in the advertising would be a coup, and it would only be an endorsement Oprah would give if she really believed the bank was different and better.

With that as my start point—a cool Apple-style bank offer that is mobile app-centric and celebrity endorsed by a trustworthy figure—I would then start thinking about how to organise the bank and its cultural approach.

CREATING A COOL AND FAIR BANK

The next question my new bank needs to answer is around customer focus, which strongly relates to culture. The first thing my bank has to achieve, once it has its vision of operation, is to clearly define the customer.

My customer would not be a demographic. My customers will cover any bases they want. And here is an important point to make, I will not predefine those bases, they will. After all, I would have no target client base except one: those who want to deal with a cool and fair bank through the mobile Internet. That would attract its own client profile.

You may say that I'm wrong, and need to be far more marketing savvy, but the people who want to deal with a cool and fair bank through the mobile Internet have no predefined definitions. They may be young or old, black or white, Catholic or Jewish, ABC1 or unemployed (there are plenty of unemployed clever people out there with money!), male or female, the list goes on. I would then build very specific areas in the bank's mobile Internet channels of service that cater for diversity, and specifically target the needs of ethnicity, religion and gender in a cool and fair way.

So what would my bank's customer be like? My bank's customer would want to deal with a 21st-century bank in a cool and fair way, and to be treated like a human. My marketing programme would therefore focus on using social interaction online to attract viral amplification. It would make it clear what cool and fair banking over the mobile Internet means, and how to engage with the bank. It would Twitter, LinkedIn, Facebook and YouTube its services to build a fan base. It would dialogue online in a hugely human way. And it would be transparent in fees and approach.

It would build its processes based on the customer outside-in view of the interactions and user experience people desire, and it would target to overcome the things that piss off most people, such as lock-in fees, hidden charges, balloon payments on overdrafts and so on and so forth.

It would make it clear what "fair" means by defining this and making sure it is practised in everything the bank preached. A bit like Google's "don't be evil"—even though it sometimes appears to be—my new bank's motto would be "don't screw the customer", and I'd make it clear how I would avoid doing that. My bank would support customers joining a "screw loose lounge" where they could rant and rave and discuss and debate, and there would be a "live and unscrewed" section for staff and management to air their hang-ups and thumbs ups.

All of this would mean that my hiring policy would have to be to hire cool and fair people who get the mobile Internet, so my hiring would be based on a tweet: "Do you want to work for a cool and fair bank?" Respondents would then be interviewed if they replied to my tweet, and would be vetted based on whether they smiled when they came through the door. They would also be vetted to see whether they picked up the £20 note that I left on the floor in the corner as they came through the door and, if they did, did they give it back?

The culture of the bank would be defined this way, with the aim to create a happy culture of cool and fair people who get the mobile Internet. This happy culture would create happy customers. Customers who like cool and fair banking from a bank that gets the mobile Internet.

I would also define "cool" in my own way. A cool bank is a bank that people want to be with, either as a customer or as a member of staff. Like Apple is thought of as cool, this bank would differentiate its brand based on being clearly interested in the customer, and by being responsive, modern, transparent and honest. In other words, a fair bank that gets the mobile Internet.

Don't get me wrong. None of the above is easy, simple or can happen that fast, but it would be worth a try, wouldn't it?

CREATING A BANK THAT MAKES MONEY

So how are we going to make money from this brand new bank? This is the toughest question as it's quite easy to make money in finance by focusing on rate churn. Just offer lower interest rates on loans and credit cards, and higher interest rates on savings and investments. This is the approach that many have taken in the past, and it works.

Take the approach of Citi for example. I always remember one of its strategies revolving around the notion that to enter a new country it would always start with credit cards. Credit cards is easy as it gets business on board that makes good money at low risk if you do it right, but it's purely a rate tart business and inspires zero loyalty or stickiness. The issue is that you can have great service but if you fall into the trap of competing on interest rates, then you undermine that service. Sure, you have to get a customer … but the important thing is to keep them and get share of wallet. This is well understood by some.

For example, if Tesco gets you, it's going to get you for everything. This was made clear by the then CEO of Tesco PLC, Terry Leahy, who spoke at a conference at which I keynoted in 2009. Leahy stated that: "In our move from retailing products to bank retailing, it amazes me that the current incumbents reward the new customer rather than the existing one. That encourages promiscuity and commoditisation. If you can reward the existing customer more than the new one, by learning more about them, then you can price your products better."

It's also an approach that is being taken by the newest retail bank to launch in the United Kingdom, Metro Bank. Metro Bank promises no more stupid rules. For instance, when it launched its Individual Savings Account (ISA) product, the press release made clear that it would be the "first ISA aimed at savers who are fed up with confusing bonus rates which disappear after a year. The Instant Access Cash Isa has a rate of 2.35 per cent and is guaranteed to increase in line with the base rate until 2013. Metro says this means customers won't be left feeling cheated after being tempted by an initial high rate, as they would when a bonus rate drops off."

First Direct also gets nearer the mark with its approach that gives a new customer £100 to join its bank and another £100 if that customer leaves within the first six months. That sounds risky, but it knows its service is so great that customers will stay. That's why the bank offers this guarantee.

So my approach would focus on upfront in fairness, transparent in fees and clear in my offer. I would then make sure that people were incentivised to join, making it more beneficial to stay than to leave and avoiding the rate churn by being a bank that people want to be with, i.e. cool.

That will make money, believe me, although it will take time and will not be easy. First Direct took seven years to deliver a profit and Metro Bank has not made a profit since its launch, so none of this is easy. However, if you can attract business based on a culture of being the fair and cool bank that gets the mobile Internet, then it will at least ensure longevity of relationship and retention of the customer.

HOW THE NEW BANK WILL WIN

Now there's that word again—cool. I've used it deliberately throughout this chapter to describe a bank that people want to be with. That's what "cool" is all about.

I once jokingly referred to it as the bank where the staff do not wear suits, which was actually more pertinent than I originally thought. After all, UBS has a dress code for its staff that is very exacting.[36] Mine wouldn't. It would be smart casual every day. It would define a brand around cool values of fairness with transparency through the mobile Internet. It would have branches, but only a few Apple store style branches where the Genius Bar would be run by people who really get the numbers of finance. And they wouldn't have to wear suits; they could wear whatever they wanted as long as it was designer label.

Maybe I am just being dreamy, but the bank that is cool has to be one that people aspire to be with. It is an aspirational brand, and I cannot name any bank right now that is aspirational for the masses. For the general populous, I cannot think of one, aspirational, cool bank brand out there.

Don't get me wrong, there are cool brands out there. Dependent on your age, Harley-Davidson is a cool brand and, as everyone says every few minutes, Apple's cool. Apple always has been. It has a fan base. Yet Microsoft is nerdy. Why? Because Microsoft is for suits; Apple is for consumers. Microsoft is business; Apple is design. Microsoft is for workers; Apple is for creators.

So to be a cool retail bank, you have to be different, creative, aspirational, accessible, very consumer focused and, in this century of mobile broadband, hi-tech. Maybe it is for these reasons that there is no "cool" bank out there because banks are handcuffed to legacy.

To sum up, the new bank will differentiate by being in the customers' interest whilst making money by gaining their loyalty and advocacy. It will

---

36   For men, shirt collars must be wide enough to pass a finger inside and shirt cuffs must show between 1.5 and 2.5 centimetres beyond the jacket sleeve. Female staff who wear skirts must ensure their skirts descend to mid-knee and no more than 5 cm below the knee. For more UBS rules on what to wear, check out "Bank tells women what to wear and men to shave" at http://thefinanser.co.uk/fsclub/2010/12/bank-tell-women-what-bras-to-wear-and-men-must-shave.html

appeal to a demographic that is not defined, apart from its psychology. Thus, it will be defined by a psychographic rather than a demographic. The psychographic is to appeal to those who love Apple and technology. The customers want to be with the bank. They think the bank is working with their interests at heart. They don't want branch-based banking, where mobile Internet is an adjunct. Instead, they want a bank built just for them based on a mobile Internet focus, where branch is an adjunct.

So my bank would be built from the ground up, with a customer view based on the mobile generation and how they behave and interact. Once that outside-in view is defined, I would build the infrastructure to deliver apps of functionality across mobile Internet devices.

The bank would be a Digital Bank first and foremost, with humanity augmenting that reality. Humanity would pervade the bank through the fun and cool approach to interactivity via the mobile Internet and, as the bank grew into branches, the branches would be Genius Bars for finance with a cool and fun approach that breathes humanity and fairness into the pores of all human operations. Something like that anyway. Either way, it would be better than living on a century-old system of branch centricity that handcuffs us to that past.

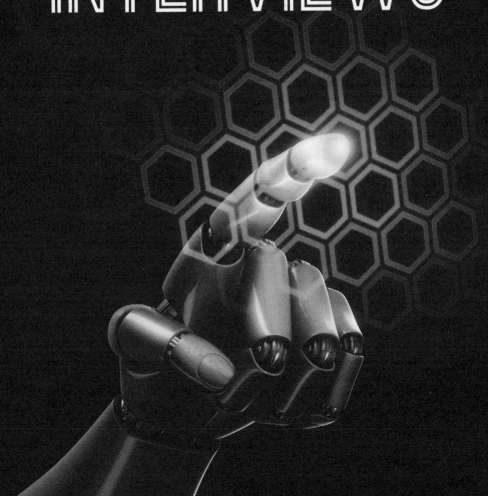

PART 2

INTERVIEWS

BANCO SABADELL
(Spain)

with Pol Navarro
head of Direct Channels and Innovation

Although many of us hear about problems in Spain and issues with the capitalisation of some of the banks there, few of us may realise that Spanish banking is a hotbed of innovation. Bank Inter created an iris recognition app for the smartphone as a secure device and BBVA was one of the first banks to implement a full personal financial management system for the mobile Internet anywhere in the world. Banco Sabadell is the sixth Spanish financial institution by assets and also demonstrates thought leadership through social media and smartphone innovations.

What does innovation mean to you?

We believe innovation is a need to adapt to an environment, which changes faster and faster. If companies do not change at least as fast as their environment, they will not survive. The digital revolution arising from the convergence of communications and media, along with social changes derived from the use of social media, has brought about a new model of social relations. Thus, if consumers are changing, companies need to find a new model for servicing and establishing new relations.

Many banks are introducing new services and improving their channels to better interact and communicate with customers. However, in our opinion, we face a new paradigm. Customers have gained power and freedom in their relationship with companies and with banks. Thus, a new way of doing banking should emerge; one that will allow customers to experience what they are already enjoying in other areas of their day-to-day activities. It is a banking relationship with a seamless multichannel approach, but with a human touch.

We think that banks need to focus on innovation in three main areas:

1. Improving your operations: "Make things cheaper and more efficient", such as creating the paperless branch
2. Improving your customer experience: "Make things easier and simple", an example being mobile banking
3. Developing new areas of business: "Make things different and generate new areas of revenue", for example with social media banking or P2P payments

How does the bank incorporate innovation into its operations?
At Banco Sabadell, management is highly conscious and supportive about innovation. We have built a pioneer image in the use of new channels to serve customers and are a reference point in innovation. We truly believe that this image brings value to our franchise.

We approach innovation through three levers: technology, processes and customer service model. For example, before incorporating social media tools into our client relations, we incorporated social media into our internal innovation and improvement process. We created BS Idea, a social network where employees can collaborate and present their ideas to be enriched, criticised and voted for by other colleagues. In 2010, employees generated more than 3000 ideas.

Recently we launched a campaign that claimed "This isn't remote banking, it's taking the bank with you." With this campaign, we wanted to show all the servicing capabilities that the bank can offer customers from a very dynamic, versatile and modern perspective. Therefore, customers can enjoy the advantages of service—24/7 access from home, immediacy, etc.— without losing the proximity and the service that are inherent to our values. "Taking the bank with you" implies that we will be close to our customers when they need it, wherever they are.

Our aim is to have multichannel branches. We need to involve our employees in this multichannel approach and extract the potential of their implication in social media. This means we have to decide about the role that employees need to play, which is not a straightforward question.

In the current climate, is innovation important or should banks just focus on survival?

We think that survival is linked to innovation. If companies are not able to adapt to the new digital environment, they will not survive. And if they do not do it fast enough, they will not survive either, because other companies will do it faster or better.

Another thing is that, in the current context, innovation should be more productive than ever. This means that we need to invest in the things that show off our capabilities and which fit with our project. We are not saying that we only need to invest in initiatives that will generate revenues in the very short term. If we thought that way, we would not be investing in social media since that is not a huge source of revenues at present.

What are the things that you see as being innovative out there?

What we think is more innovative is what banks are doing to change the customer service and relationship model. When Internet banking emerged in the 1990s, we thought it would change the banking industry. It has added transactions and convenience for customers, as ATMs did earlier, but it did not change the essence of customer-bank relations. These relations did not change because trust is built in the branch, and trust requires the human touch.

So what we see as truly innovative is going from Internet banking to Facebook or Twitter banking. Customers can interact with people at the bank but gain flexibility in time and space. There is still a long way to go to gain the full potential of this opportunity.

Some banks, including Banco Sabadell, are taking steps to incorporate social media as a service channel, and this is not only for communications but also for service and, in the future, we will incorporate it into the branch. For us, this is what we see as truly innovative since it is transformational. Of course, to be successful, this should come along with simpler and easier banking.

On the other side, we think that mobile banking will be at the heart of our service platform, from daily transactions to payments everywhere: person-to-person, retail chains, online payments, etc. At the end of the day, it's about building an easy, simple and friendly bank.

I know you've been active in launching early apps for the bank on the iPad and other devices. Have these been successful or are they just gimmicks? In 2010, we were the first financial institution in Europe with an iPad application. It has been well accepted by our customers and we keep improving it. For example, we recently integrated social media into the application. Other institutions have followed suit. We were also the first institution in Spain to have an application for all mobile devices—the iPhone, Windows Phone, Android, Blackberry. We were also the first to offer the remote deposit capture for cheques in Europe.

We do these things because innovation is one of our values and is very much related to service, with our figures showing that customers are taking advantage of this effort.

Currently, more than 17 per cent of our online customers are active mobile banking users. This means that nearly one out of five individuals who access our online banking platform does it from a mobile phone. In companies, this ratio is one out of ten. Moreover, 80 per cent of service transactions are now performed through remote channels. This is very significant in a country like Spain, which is not at the forefront of Internet penetration in Europe.

The previous figures only refer to our mobile banking platform by the way. In addition, we have approximately 700,000 users of our SMS alert service, which is approximately 30 per cent of our customer base.

Your social media usage is something that you talk about a lot. Does it cost much to do this?
Management at Banco Sabadell understood from the beginning that we needed to be present in social media. We think that the web is like the high street and social media is like the pub where people go to chat. We saw quickly that people talked about us and that we could talk to our customers and potential customers, as well as provide service. At the end of the day, markets are conversations, and we want to be part of these conversations.

We started in 2010 by listening to what people were saying about us. Then we evolved from listening to using social media as an integrated service channel, and later as a video content viralisation platform. We saw that, in some ways, it was more powerful than traditional communication tools since it allowed us to have conversations with our clients.

We see social media as a new service channel. Many of the conversations that we have with our customers are about services and products that the bank offers. The point here is that these conversations often take place without being initiated by us.

For example, a taxi driver praised Banco Sabadell's service and the point of sale terminal that was installed in his cab. After reading his comments, we had requests for this service from other cab drivers who also wanted the product. The magic is that we didn't start the sales process directly for that offer. A satisfied customer did, and the virality of social media did the rest.

Our social media efforts are fully integrated with our organisation so all of our service interactions are managed by our multichannel service team while all viral content is generated by our communications and marketing team. From our experience, we have learnt that the best approach is to engage every department from traditional media to social media and from strategy and marketing to operations and customer services.

And what innovations do you foresee for the mid- and long-term future?
For the mid term, we are watching different trends. Regarding social media, we think the future will be about integrating Big Data on your CRM to increase the knowledge about your customers and provide a more personalised experience. This Big Data will come from different sources: conversations on social networks, credit card transactions, social reputations like Klout, etc. Another trend will be the evolution of loyalty programmes based on mobile, location and gamification, like the Foursquare of banking.

For the long term, the concept of "smart cities" and "the Internet of things" will allow us to attach financial services everywhere because everything will be connected in all metropolitan areas, making transactions easier for customers, merchants and city services.

ABOUT POL NAVARRO

Pol Navarro is a highly qualified digital business, customer service and e-commerce strategist. He is a recognised thought leader, speaking internationally at several banking, mobile and Internet conferences. Navarro's main role at Banco Sabadell is as head of Direct Channels and Innovation, where he leads all activity related to new channel development, new customer services and innovation. He received a graduate degree in Computer Science at Universidad Autónoma de Barcelona, an MBA at Universitat Oberta de Cataluña and Harvard School, and an executive degree at IESE Business School.

ABOUT BANCO SABADELL

Banco Sabadell is the sixth Spanish financial institution by assets. Founded in 1881 by a group of local businesspeople from Sabadell, the bank has transformed itself into one of the country's biggest national banking groups with a strong international presence. Its main business is retail banking, where it is viewed as a leader in affluent banking, SME and international commercial banking. The bank also has an important private banking division.

Banco Sabadell has strengthened its position within the banking industry with domestic and international acquisitions over recent years. It has integrated banks with NatWest, Herrero, Atlántico, Urquijo and, recently, Guipuzcoano in Spain; in the United States, Transatlantic Bank, BBVA Miami, Mellon United Bank and Lydian Private Bank. Its capabilities to assimilate new institutions in an orderly and efficient manner and in record integration time has made Banco Sabadell a reference case in these operations.

BARCLAYS BANK (UK)

with Mike Walters
head of Corporate Payments

Barclays Bank has recently been gaining plaudits for innovation around payments. It started with a major push around contactless payments as the first issuer in the United Kingdom to move towards NFC, and followed up on this success with the launch of a new peer-to-peer and consumer-to-corporate payments app for smartphones called Pingit.

Perhaps you can tell us a little bit about Barclays' strategy as the bank is seen as an innovator today, thanks to much of what you are doing in payments. What's changed?

The key focus for us is around an understanding and recognition that it is increasingly important to consumers to find it easy to transact and that is changing very quickly, particularly as a result of the rise of mobile technologies. And the infrastructures that the banks have provided to facilitate transactions for consumers has been a relatively stable platform for the past few years, but that has also changed due to the introduction of things like Faster Payments in the United Kingdom, which allows near real-time transactions.

The combination of these two factors—new national infrastructures and changing consumer needs—has given us a toolkit to think differently. We then asked: how will consumers change as a result of these developments, and how will corporates change in their delivery to those consumers?

And in Barclays' case, we decided to innovate by bringing together the fact that we have a large retail consumer bank footprint in the United Kingdom, combined with a large cards business in the form of Barclaycard and a major corporate banking capability. The aim has been to show that Barclays is a leading payments brand and one that is committed to making the consumer's ability to transact faster and more efficient. That is why we have been pushing the contactless payments process through Barclaycard to target the lower value cash transactions. This has been promoted strongly with the launch of PayTag, a contactless sticker that you can place on any phone, and contactless wristbands.

Another key thing we did is to create an app for consumers called Pingit. That was developed in the second half of last year [2011] and then launched and released in February this year [2012]. Pingit allows consumers to send payments person-to-person, using just mobile telephone numbers. You do not even need to be a Barclays customer to use this.

The release of this created a market of consumers which then attracted corporate interest, and so we have since been launching several services for corporates to work with that consumer app, such as paying with QR codes via Pingit for utility bills.

And what sort of results have you found since moving into the mobile payments space?

The speed of growth of the consumer population who are downloading and using our mobile app has been very rapid—over 700,000 people downloaded the app in its first three months. Since we launched the Corporate Solution, we have spoken to hundreds of clients who are keen to work with us and we have been signing them up quickly.

Who is a typical Pingit user?

The majority are iPhone users under the age of fifty. Interestingly, the demographic is well distributed across that age range and geographically across the United Kingdom, which really shows the broad appeal to both Barclays and non-Barclays customers.

What about your commercial customers? Are corporates interested in this too?

Yes. As already mentioned, we offer various ways of processing company bills via Pingit. One way is to register your business with us, then customers can pay a company just by typing in the company's registered name and amount to pay. We then introduced the ability to pay by QR code. QR stands for "Quick Response" and is a barcode of black dots that can be used on mobile telephones by reading them on a smartphone camera. It is incredibly easy to store a lot of information on these codes, including the company name, account details as well as the customer's name and account details.

Similarly, firms can send out a bill to a customer with a QR code embedded that includes all of the payment details and the payment amount. All the customer needs to do then is hold their phone over the code, check that the payment amount is correct and approve the payment. That's it.

For the corporate customer, not only do they get all the customer data that they need—account number, payment details, etc.—but it's now enriched with the customer's mobile telephone number for further verification and potential marketing. Fast, simple and easy for the consumer and, for the corporate, it makes reconciliation and tracking of payments far easier than ever before. In fact, corporates could eradicate reconciliations and exception management through this.

This technology is hugely flexible and provides us with a range of new and exciting opportunities to work with for both consumers and our corporate customers.

It sounds like a win-win situation?
Absolutely, and I think it will change the face of commerce over time. In fact, the ability to bring together faster payments, mobile technologies, apps and innovation is already changing business processes.

For example, think of a real-time refund. Imagine that an angry customer calls your call centre about an over payment or something like that, and the call centre representative could just reply, "Well, here's your money back with an extra £5 to say 'sorry'." That payment could be made in real time to the customer's mobile telephone as they talk to the agent. A real-time faster payment refund via mobile. Not only will that transform customer service but business too.

You imply that the end customer is now in the driving seat of commerce thanks to mobile technologies. Is that right?
Yes. We deal with corporates who work with customers, and consumers are the key focal point of change right now. If consumers have the willingness and interest to adopt new services, like NFC contactless and mobile, then that is the direction that our corporate customers will take and we have to support that.

ABOUT MIKE WALTERS

Mike Walters is head of UK Corporate Payments at Barclays Bank in London. He is responsible for the product management, performance and profitability of Barclays' suite of corporate payments products ranging from physical cash to complex integrated electronic payment solutions.

Walters joined Barclays on its Business Leadership Graduate Programme in 2002, having read Law at Warwick University and achieving a Masters degree in Management at Nottingham University. Since joining the bank, he has worked in a number of relationship teams managing large UK and Multinational Corporate Relationships for the group, securing successful migration of a number of FTSE 100 clients to Barclays. In early 2007, he was appointed Sales Director for Multinational Corporates headquartered in the United Kingdom, Scandinavia and the Netherlands. Walters moved to become Regional Director for North American Financial Institutions following the formation of Global Transactional Sales in January 2009 before moving to his current role in July 2010.

ABOUT BARCLAYS BANK

Barclays Bank is a UK mainstream bank that leads the pack with regard to innovation on the high street, notably in its card operations and mainstream banking services. Indeed, it has been an innovative bank for many years. It launched the first credit card in the United Kingdom back in 1966 and the first loyalty scheme in 1986. It was also the first bank to bill payments via the Internet in 1997 as well as introduce contactless payments in Europe in 2011.

BITCOIN
(global)

with Donald Norman
co-founder of Bitcoin Consultancy Ltd

Bitcoin is one of the first implementations of a concept called crypto-currency, a secure digital currency for exchange by anyone, anywhere globally. Bitcoin is designed around the idea of using cryptography to control the creation and transfer of money, rather than relying on central authorities, and it is the first time that such a system has been launched. Although it is stumbling through its early evolution, many believe it could become the currency of the future. If this is the case, then what does it mean for banks?

Let's start with something that some people find confusing, what is Bitcoin?

It's cash, digital cash. It can be used to buy and sell goods and services. What makes it unique? There is no central location or place that mints or prints the coins. It's just cryptographic data, meaning you need no central bank or issuer as everyone on the system has their own ledger of accounts.

The network assesses the transaction history and monetary amounts in circulation democratically. There's no reliance on human honesty or worry of human error. This, in turn, means cheaper commerce.

A great deal of the press coverage has dismissed Bitcoin as something that is subversive. Do you agree?
When Philip Zimmerman created PGP encryption, the concern was that if such technology got into the hands of terrorists or others, they would be able to encrypt their communication. But actually encryption in all formats has made society inarguably safer. So the press talking about Bitcoin being subversive is a bit like saying the Internet is only being used by drug runners and pornographers. Yes, it may be used illegally but it has a much wider social benefit. Bitcoin is a neutral technology. Just like the Internet, there will be a long progression before it becomes mainstream. The Internet started as just a bunch of protocols and was used by developers and techheads. Now it's mainstream. That's what we see happening with Bitcoin. Adoption is a by-product of infrastructure and end-user friendliness.

How are governments reacting to Bitcoin as it's difficult to tax and control?
The head economist at Harvard, Ben Friedman, has focused on e-currencies for a long time and predicted an e-currency would be uncontrollable by governments, as money moved to become a form of digital cash back in the late 1990s. Ten years down the road and his prediction has come true. Since then, he's written more about how governments will adapt to such a currency and how the world will change. What is his main point? Liberalising the transfer of money need not be feared. It's simply a case of currency coming in a form that can be zipped around the world, rather than just being localised. Sadly, I think there will always be misinformed modern Luddites. What they don't realise is that, short of shutting down the Internet, laws restricting the usage of this new technology are unenforceable and will only be followed

by those who will use Bitcoin for legal purposes and social good. Hence, restrictions or even a social stigma will only slow positive progress.

But money laundering is a concern here.

This system is not designed for money laundering as everyone has a ledger of all of the transactions that have ever taken place. It's like BitTorrent, a file-sharing program. The file it shares keeps track of every transaction through the economy's history. So anyone participating with the Bitcoin economy can see what money moves from which account to which, not who owns the accounts, but the fact that the transaction took place. It's not hard then to trace the flow of money and, if people try to spend from a suspect wallet, you can investigate the trail of funds. In other words, it's all traceable. Those who come out against Bitcoin pontificating that it's a tool for money laundering are highly misinformed or wilfully ignorant. It was not designed for that purpose and while people may be successfully laundering relatively tiny amounts of capital, their success is a result of law enforcement not conducting proper investigations because they do not understand the technology or, and more likely, because not enough money is traded currently to be taken seriously. Two million dollars a week can't compare with the money laundering estimations and history we see in the regulated sectors.

And what about taxation issues? Is Bitcoin a tax avoidance mechanism?

I'm not sure how that will develop. If a decentralised currency takes off, we'll just see other forms of taxation arise. Everyone can become a legal tax avoider through their online wallets, which I think is great. Right now only the rich can afford to practise tax avoidance, loopholing our ideals of democracy and equality into a game. This is a legal process of tax avoidance based on a global, digital currency, just like the rich currently use offshore companies to do the same with traditional currency.

Surely it would be better for governments to adapt a new system of taxation to be fairer to all, rather than focus on this? Avoidance only for the rich is discriminatory. Perhaps sales tax will go up.

One of the controversial things about Bitcoin is the limit of issuance, as only 21 million bitcoins are being issued. So there's a limitation there that's false and people don't like it.

Well, any law is changeable in the Bitcoin system. If we see more than half of the network determining that the protocol needs to change, then they can democratically vote by altering the code or downloading a patch and, if enough of the network does this, it will change. But that's not easy. Already potentially hundreds of thousands of people are using Bitcoin, so to get a majority to sponsor a change in the protocol, there would have to be a good reason.

What about the limit and its finite amount? Is that good or bad?

It's not a problem. Right now, you talk about a bitcoin and quote prices in bitcoins as their valuation is a few dollars. But you can divide bitcoins into such small amounts. If one bitcoin is worth $1,000 in the future, then people will start talking about millicoins. If it's worth $1,000,000, you can send a nanocoin. You see this in countries with hyperinflation. In Brazil (real/cruzeiro), Iran (rial/toman) and other countries, they just rename the currency officially or unofficially when it becomes less valuable. The same thing can be practised for a currency that becomes more valuable.

But finite currency levels undermine monetary control of days of old as central banks won't be able to issue more currency to ease economic issues, such as the quantitative easing of Europe and America in recent times.

Well, if there's no central issuing authority to issue more or less money for monetary control, then that's the real issue. You can't address the issues in economies with money, but I would argue that ordinary fiat currencies are actually less of a benefit to societies and economies if those currencies can be manipulated. We know corruption in all forms at all levels in all countries is rife. If fiat currencies are corruptible, and by definition all are, then they can do more harm than good. Perhaps there needs to be an evolution of currencies, and there will be a natural selection by the people of the strongest. That might be the dollar or, in the future, bitcoin. I can send a bitcoin from anyone to anyone else in the world without impediment, without regulation, without fear that the transfer is going to be stopped or that my account is going to be frozen or that the person I am sending to is going to have problems with their account. I can send money to anyone in the world as long as they can connect to the Internet.

This sounds radically new.

It is revolutionary. Now, we have had the technology for a long time to send money cheaply. The telegram a hundred years ago fulfilled the same function but Western Union had a monopoly on it. Digital currencies themselves raged in the early 2000s, but the difference is that any centralised digital money is the same as money. This is what PayPal did, but a lot of merchants have no recourse in the arbitration of funds as there is a central agent. You need that agent to manage disputes, chargebacks and resolutions between buyers and sellers and act as an arbitrator. Even video games like Second Life have the government coming in regulating nuances of their economy. Bitcoin said, "No, thanks." The biggest strength of this currency is that you can send it for next to nothing and there is no control or added cost to the sending of a bitcoin. There are no chargebacks. When the money is sent, the money is sent. Just like cash. The merchant knows they have the money when the money is received. So where this will first be taken up is by businesses that will depend on Bitcoin, like microtransaction businesses. These businesses can't use traditional currencies, but if you can send a penny around the world easily and cheaply, then these firms will thrive. The other business will be from firms that want to access international markets from one country and have issues with chargebacks and structures. They may be shipping under $35 goods or services, or shipping a digital service rather than physical goods, and these firms may find that Bitcoin, relying solely on code and mathematics, is the only currency they can use.

It's a bit technical however, isn't it?

That's the biggest barrier to Bitcoin. It's not end-user friendly. Every client is working off the first codebase. Satoshi Nakamoto solved the last logic problem to create a decentralised currency. He's an academic, incredibly smart, but not a computer engineer. The code was not written in the most efficient way therefore, but every client today has built off this code. Now, for the first time, we are rewriting the code from the ground up to be more efficient and effective. The new code is being built from scratch in a modular fashion so merchants can take it and change it and it will be much faster and end-user friendly. That's going to really spark the adoption of Bitcoin, a bit like the web browser sparked the uptake of the Internet. It made the Internet intuitive and usable by non-specialists.

You mentioned PayPal, and there were many e-money operators back then. What will make Bitcoin mainstream as there are other services like Ven Currency and Flattr?

Well, most others are more like Facebook Credits. It's just a digital parallel to Disney Dollars. The usage is restricted to merchants who accept the control of that currency by the issuer. That stifles commerce rather than liberating it. It also brings with it overhead, lots of overhead. As mentioned, Bitcoin has no central controller or issuer. It's decentralised and all the advantages that we talk about build off that decentralised nature. It's the first time we've been able to use a decentralised currency. It's a very young technology therefore, and because it is young, it is not end-user friendly. It's hard to use, because you need to be tech savvy, but this will change. The outside infrastructure is still being built and much of this is, therefore, analogous to the early days of the Internet. In the longer term, an ecosystem will develop and the coinage will be at least as easy to exchange as making any other online payment.

But one of the things about Bitcoin is that its price fluctuates rapidly. For example, a bitcoin was worth about $2 in February [2011], $30 by June and is now worth $2 again. That's not creating reliability or trust, is it?

The price fluctuation has to do with media attention, adoption and speculation rather than the currency itself. Supply and demand, the market sets the price. In the past few months, we've seen much less volatility than ever before with Bitcoin whilst liquidity is increasing. The more it's adopted, the less volatile it'll be. About $2 million a week is exchanged between traditional fiat currencies and bitcoins compared to trillions of dollars per day with FX in traditional markets. As Bitcoin gets more adoption therefore, the fluctuation and volatility will reduce.

So we will have to live with price volatility until Bitcoin becomes mainstream?

Yes and no. The price fluctuation is attributable to some very specific activities. For example, Bitcoin reached a value of about $31 when one user's system was hacked and all of their coins were stolen. The person who was hacked had $500,000 of bitcoins and admitted to using a Windows machine with known viruses. The money was dumped on the markets and the value of bitcoins halved overnight. Since then, we have developed software to protect users from themselves without having to rely on us, a bank or any third party. Users can now generate a transaction file on their offline device, transfer the file to an online device and make a transfer even on insecure devices.

There are also a lot of speculators out there who are buying bitcoins and holding them on exchanges. Others are arbitrageurs, playing the bitcoin price markets. Whilst the coinage is in early adoption, these activities will make the price volatile, but that will change as adoption increases.

And what will create adoption?

Intuitiveness, end-user friendliness and awareness. Bitcoin is a new technology and akin to the Internet in two ways. Remember the late 1990s when everyone was saying, "Don't use credit cards online. You'll be compromised?" That's what Bitcoin is going through. Luckily, every day, more legitimate merchants accept bitcoins. The website https://en.bitcoin.it/wiki/Trade lists just some of those offering goods and services via Bitcoin. The page has grown massively in just a few months. It started with small eBay-style businesses. One-man firms offering tech stuff like servers and server space. Now, the merchants are more mainstream and unrelated to Bitcoin, offering music, shopping and even financial services. These firms have no relationship with Bitcoin, except that they now also accept payment in bitcoins.

Finally, what's the long-term view of Bitcoin?
Many have big ambitions for it. They say look at Zimbabwe. Look at the wars in former Yugoslavia where citizens had no choice but to fund a genocidal war through the hyperinflation of their currency. I don't know if any of that will stop. I'll be happy though when people, especially those less well off, will be able to send money internationally without having to pay outrageous and inexcusable transfer costs.

ABOUT DONALD NORMAN

Donald Norman is the co-founder of Bitcoin Consultancy. The group works on software development for core bitcoin code as well as building the road map to bring the advantages of Bitcoin to a scalable and enterprise level. Norman has appeared as an advocate of Bitcoin in publications like *Reuters, Newsweek,* the *Wall Street Journal* (SmartMoney) and the *Independent* as well as on CNBC and others.

ABOUT BITCOIN

Bitcoin is a peer-to-peer payment system and digital currency introduced as open-source software in 2009 by a visionary developer called Satoshi Nakamoto. It is a crypto-currency, so-called because it uses cryptography to control the creation and transfer of money.

Bitcoins are created by a process called mining, in which participants solve a complex mathematical code to create a bitcoin and, in exchange, they receive a payment for the newly minted coin. As more coins are minted, the more complex the codes become and therefore the slower the production of a new coin. In this way, Bitcoin ensures that the production of the currency is limited. Users send and receive bitcoins using wallet software on a personal computer, mobile device or a web application.

Commercial use of Bitcoin, illicit or otherwise, is currently small compared to its use by speculators, which has fuelled price volatility. Nevertheless, there has been growth in the use of bitcoins as a form of payment for products and services, and merchants have an incentive to accept the currency because transaction fees are lower than the fees typically imposed by credit card processors.

FIDOR BANK
(Germany)

with Matthias Kröner

chief executive at FIDOR Bank

Can you tell me a little about FIDOR Bank and how you got started?
Back in 2005, we were looking at innovations in social media and related areas. We saw that there was a lot of movement going on that was changing the world of retailing, publishing, distribution and so on, and felt that we could do the same in banking. We realised that you could not pretend that there was nothing happening in this space and felt that this was actually a great opportunity to open a new form of retail bank. Therefore, we applied for a banking licence in 2007 and received the licence in 2009, just after the credit crisis had started in Germany. We had to wait eighteen months to get the banking licence and, in that time, we had a look at how financial institutions were reacting to the crisis, how they communicated, what problems they faced and the reaction of the public. We saw that the loss of trust in these institutions was a big issue and, coming out of that scenario, we felt there was a completely new way of running a bank. We could combine the social aspects of banking that we wanted to launch

with the opportunity created by the loss of trust in banks, and this is where FIDOR Bank started.

How are you different from traditional banks?

We think banks are very much black box and not customer centric on the one hand, and that banks do not cope with the new way of living the digital lifestyle on the other. This is what we have tried to improve and this is how we differ to traditional banks by combining the developments of Web 2.0 and the Internet on one side and trust on the other. FIDOR stems from the Latin word *fides* meaning "trust", and we create and encourage trust through our community-building focus.

How would you summarise your approach to technology?

We have concentrated on the parts that we believe to be key differentiators for the bank, and then we partner or buy off the shelf the areas we view as commodity. Core banking, for example, is something that has to run and be reliable but it is a commodity area we can buy off the shelf for this reason. On the other hand, building a financial community on a social platform is a key USP [unique selling point] for FIDOR and so we needed to develop that ourselves. We also wanted to provide other key enablers like mobile money, and for these areas we operate partnerships with firms like hyperWALLET to provide best-of-breed servicing. So we combine commodity, best-of-breed partnerships and our own bespoke developments to deliver the ultimate Web 2.0 experience for our customers and community.

Do you have many partnerships?

We very much rely on partnerships. We identify these partners by constantly discussing what is and what isn't a core competency for our bank. This is important as the total number of staff at FIDOR Bank is 27 people, including the board, and this staff is serving something like 145,000 registered customers in our community. Half of these customers connect with our payment services and one in five are full banking customers, so there is a lot of work for a small number of staff. This means we are very dependent upon cooperating with partners, and it makes us very willing to look at partnerships.

How do you choose these partners?

We cannot be the sole drivers of quality and innovations so we like to team up with customer-centric innovators and services. The platform example I would use to illustrate this is the FIDORPay Account, which is a very open ecosystem. The ecosystem incorporates and adopts offers from partners in what we call "apps", as in the Apple app style. The customer can then set up the way in which their payments account works for them, in the same way you would set up your iPhone. It's totally flexible and unique to them. This can only be achieved through collaboration and partnership however and we, as a company, develop these capabilities and then ensure that they conform to the rules, which are the regulations to maintain our banking licence.

Within these partnerships, do you use cloud computing?

Our technology people philosophically think cloud is potentially relevant but, in fact, we do not use cloud computing today for four main reasons. First of all, we feel that it is not that secure for financial servicing and we are careful about, and possibly distrust, the use of cloud. We prefer to know where the data is stored and security is crucial to a bank, so this is why we stay out of any discussions about cloud today. Second, we do not feel it is necessary to use such services. We are too small to require this sort of scale of service right now, but when we scale, we may consider it then. Third, what would happen if you were in the cloud as a company and suddenly your cloud partner had a security problem and cut you off? I would not want to see that situation occur and have a customer caught in a position where they cannot get hold of their bank data in the cloud. Finally, for our back-office operations, we focus on resilience and security and we need it to be approved by our auditors. I am not sure they would be happy if I came up with a cloud offer today.

But you have a lot of partner relationships where you let your partners' processes on your behalf, such as The Currency Cloud for cross-border payments. Is that not the same as using cloud?

But in the context of those relationships, we are the cloud. It's not as though we are putting our bank services in a cloud-computing operation like Amazon.

So it depends how you define cloud?

Yes. There are very many ways of talking about cloud, and I am referring here to placing my operating systems and bank data in the cloud. I would never place my bank data in the cloud but outsourcing is different.

Do you not think cloud is just like outsourcing?

We are using outsourced services, but the difference between outsourced relationships and cloud is that we use outsourcing for very specific reasons. For example, if I outsource the running of my machines, I know who the companies are, I know where they are, my auditors have approved them and they are working according to the requirements of a German banking regulator. We don't have that today with cloud computing. The quality and security standards are not there yet, and a typical cloud provider is not able to give those to us.

So you don't believe cloud is appropriate for a bank?

I can see some positive aspects of cloud, but problems arise if you have other people's money, as we do as a bank. Then there are dangers. For example, if you are running your systems with a third-party cloud service, then there could be an issue one day where they cut off the service to the customer. That is a threat and a fear for us and is why we do not want to go down this route.

I always try to think about the direction of our customers and am cautious about using cloud unless our customers need it. I really know that our customers want to have a relationship with the bank and social media offers that capability for example. However, they are concerned about security, and even if it is just a feeling of insecurity, it is not a good thing. So the customer has to feel 100 per cent secure using our bank.

Yet you open source a lot of your community building to the crowd?
Technology wise, we are more like an open-source development of services for our customers and this facility provides a philosophical bridge between crowd and cloud. We are thinking about how to set up a structure of more and more community services that are open-sourced. We would not provide this open-source structure without security however.

I like the open-source analogy, as it puts cloud in context. What this means is that we won't be talking about cloud in the future per se, just about how to provide improvements to the customer experience.
Absolutely. I get fed up with people going to conferences and coming back with the latest buzzwords like cloud. We need to be thinking far more about how to improve customer service first and foremost. That should be the one guiding light. It should always be how to lighten the work of our back office and improve the experience in the front office, not about the latest buzzwords.

Finally Matthias, looking at the bigger picture, how do you see FIDOR Bank developing in the future?
We recently launched a separate IT company, which totally underlines the importance of IT and technology for our business. This will provide the technology related to the bank and to our customers to other organisations that are looking for similar capabilities. We are also in progress talks with partners to franchise and white label the FIDOR Bank offer into other markets. This provides a huge chance to leverage our capabilities. On the other side, we are focusing our efforts on integrating services from our partners into a much more seamless integrated offer for our customers. These are the two technology areas we are focusing on for the near term.

ABOUT MATTHIAS KRÖNER

Matthias Kröner has been CEO of FIDOR AG since 2006 and is responsible for investor relations, corporate communications, strategic development and communities. Prior to founding FIDOR AG, he built DAB Bank, the first continental European online broker, and in 1997, at the age of 32, he became the youngest director of a German bank at Direkt Anlage Bank AG.

ABOUT FIDOR BANK

FIDOR Bank was launched in Germany in 2009, with a full banking licence to offer a new style of banking. Completely different from any traditional bank, FIDOR Bank is purely online and tightly integrated with social media to enable customers to merge their social lives online with their financial well-being. The number of Facebook Likes the bank receives, for example, sets interest rates and value can be stored in the form of money, commodities and even World of Warcraft Gold. Lending takes place in both traditional form and via peer-to-peer capabilities whilst money is moved by mobile transactions globally.

FIRST DIRECT (UK)

with Paul Say
chief marketing officer at First Direct

According to Paul Volcker, the last great innovation in banking was the ATM, but do you think being a bank without branches is innovative?
When we launched back in 1989, it was absolutely revolutionary. We suddenly launched onto a market that was used to going to a branch Monday to Friday, a branch that was not open at weekends, that only opened around certain hours—9 to 5 if you were lucky—and you had to queue up for your money. If you needed to see your manager, you had to make an appointment. Suddenly, we launched this telephone banking service that was available 24/7, 365. You could phone us on Christmas Day and New Year's Day. That was absolutely revolutionary at the time. Today, it is a hygiene factor. A lot of the things that First Direct does or started out doing are now hygiene factors for banks, but certainly when we started out it was absolutely revolutionary.

What is it that makes you different if it's just a hygiene factor today?

I believe it's the magical rapport we create with our customers, and that comes down to the people. That's not just the person who deals with your basic banking calls, it's also the person who deals with your digital problems if you have issues with Internet or mobile banking. It's fundamentally born out of respect for the customer, and putting the customer in control. It's giving the customer banking on their terms, helping them to do what they need to do with their money when they need to do it. I fundamentally believe that's the magic that we create. You can't bottle it. That's why it's not been replicated. Over time, people have hired people from First Direct. We see some of our people join other organisations, but fundamentally they cannot replicate it on the scale we have achieved here.

So is your innovation your culture?

Absolutely. We totally believe that people matter more. It's interesting that in the digital age, people are more important now than they've ever been before. For example, I was talking with a colleague the other day about a business problem we are trying to solve so we went back to some papers we wrote five years ago. Back then, we said we are neither a telephone bank nor an Internet bank, but that we are a Digital Bank, with the people to prove it. Digital is so much wider now as a term, and so much more meaningful. It embraces telephony, it embraces mobility, it embraces the Internet, but it also embraces all the new platforms that are emerging, such as the iPhone and Android. I totally agree with that cultural point therefore, and also believe in the human element of this as well. There is a movement towards authenticity and, in this technical age, that's really tough to create and particularly on digital platforms. Creating that emotional chemistry that you get as the takeaway from the experience of our call centre for example. You cannot just create that magic. On reflection, that's the single biggest revolution that we created in the banking industry. It's also the single biggest puzzle we try and solve day in, day out.

How do you keep that culture to be different though? For example, a lot of the banks measure call centre staff using metrics such as the number of calls they get through in a day with satisfactory closure within x minutes, and so on and so forth. How do you measure staff effectiveness?

Regarding those environments where you are asked to hit certain average handling times, queues on the boards and so on, we have a similar sort of philosophy but we try to make it more playful and fun for people to achieve those standards. That comes through doing odd things. For example, it is appraisal time at the moment, and so we have wigwams dotted around the building because we want people to go for a huddle with their Big Chief, so to speak. We just try to lighten the mood and make it less pressurised. We also empower our people so that if a customer conversation is getting complicated on the phone, we say that this is OK. That's because the customer is the centre of everything we are trying to achieve here. So we have those standards and measures, but we take an adult approach to those metrics and standards and also try to make it fun.

Do you think technology is the main driver of innovation?

No, it's an enabler but not a driver. For example, we recently started to use social media type technologies—community forums and that sort of thing—which is by no means radical, but nevertheless a technology innovation. We knew that customers had great experiences with us, and that was because they had real conversations with us and those conversations are two-way, and that is what we wanted to provide in our social media delivery. So the way we look at innovation is that there is a brand dynamic that is key as part of that innovation. The brand dynamic for First Direct is that we create a magical rapport with our customers through great conversations. Equally, there is a cultural dynamic. So the technology must be married with the brand and cultural dynamics if it is to be appropriate and effective. For example, we have a campaign at the moment called Talking Point (www.interactive. firstdirect.com/enthuse.html). Talking Point allows our customers to talk live and unedited about money and much more, including First Direct. The cultural dynamic driving that idea is that there is an element of mistrust generally in the banking world right now, and we wanted to take our brand dynamics of magical rapport of great conversations, and marry it with this cultural dynamic of mistrust. The result is that we created Talking Point to allow people to search for authentic experiences with a financial institution they can engage with. That is giving us a position in the marketplace of transparency and authenticity. So I'm a big believer that technology is an enabler of innovation, rather than the single driver, as there are other factors such as brand and cultural dynamics. I also believe this because you can sometimes try too hard to apply technology to your brands, and customers can reject you if you try too hard. That is why it took us at least eighteen months to find a place for the whole world of social media, and it is because we wanted it to feel natural. We were not going to force the technology and that experience on our customers if it didn't make sense in the context of our brand and the experiences they were having with us. Does that make sense?

Yes, although it raises some questions too. For example, most banks apply technology for cost savings but you seem to be looking for technology to enhance customer experiences.
That's right. When we launched text message banking, for example, we knew there was something in SMS messaging on phones, which was about alerting customers and keeping them up to date. We actually positioned text message banking as being like a sixth sense when we launched it. The fact that we would send you a text alert when you're about to go overdrawn, for example. Isn't that great, to have a bank that alerts you before you go overdrawn?

But other banks would see that as bad as they can make money out of customers being overdrawn. That's why they won't do social media or twittering or blogging because it's just marketing froth. It doesn't make money.
It depends what you see as being of value. If value is pounds and pence, then does it really shift the dial on its own? No, it wouldn't. But if you see

it in the context of contribution in terms of brand equity and the company credentials that you create around doing this sort of thing, then there's inherent value in that. There's also value in terms of word of mouth. People start talking about you when you do things like this on their terms, not the bank's terms. On the back of this, business comes. A key thing here is that recommendation is as good as writing the business, as people do work on word of mouth, particularly in this age. So don't look at this just in terms of bottom line contribution, look at it in terms of your brand credentials, customer service experience credentials and how customers will talk about you outside of the bank, in terms of word of mouth and recommendations. First Direct really benefits from that. We are the UK's most recommended bank and have been for a very long time. We do benefit from that because we know that when people join us, they are joining us because they've heard great things about us or somebody has personally recommended them.

That raises two things however. One is that if you are that successful, how come you are not Britain's biggest bank? And second, if you have that expectation when customers join you, does it set the bar too high so that customers might be disappointed?

On the latter point, we have a satisfaction guarantee. The first thing is that when people join us, we give them £100 as a warm welcome to thank them for switching, as it's a bit of a hassle to change your bank. But we also put our money where our mouth is as we promise that if they don't like the switch, then we'll move everything to wherever they want to go afterwards and give them another £100 to say sorry. We're absolutely confident that we can offer a satisfaction guarantee when you join us because we know we are that good and we are willing to put our money where our mouth is to prove it. That's not arrogant. It's just that we are confident in the experiences that our people are creating with customers.

So why aren't you the biggest bank in Britain?

I can best answer that by saying that, when we started out, we really played to a part of the community who were completely disenfranchised by their banking experience. So therefore, we grew very quickly because a lot of people said, "I'm going to switch, and it's worth going through the pain of switching." We continue to occupy that place in the marketplace, the switchers. In fact, our target market is affluent, professional people, which is a very niche marketplace of the total switcher market. So we're not growing by ten market share percentage points every year. What you find is that we deliver small organic growth, but when we bring people in, we build the relationship and deepen the relationship with them. Therefore, we grow their product holdings, and that is our real focus. Rather than just acquiring new customers for one single product, we would rather acquire one customer for many products. The result is that we have a group of very profitable customers banking with us, who have extremely high levels of satisfaction and therefore recommend our services to their peers.

Finally Paul, back to technology and innovation. What do you think will be the key technologies for changing the customer experience in the future?

Well, we bought some iPads for the team here to trial, and when I took the iPad home my three-year-old daughter picked it up. Watching her interact with it made me realise that the whole principle of keyboards will be redundant soon. It certainly will be for my daughter as she's already using touch screen; she's using her fingers; she's interacting directly with the screen, rather than through a keyboard. So creating touchscreen interfaces and experiences for our customers is going to be a really interesting area and a critical one to explore. The other area is any technologies that help to create a human engagement. The fact that you're touching the screen is a human engagement, as it's creating chemistry between you and the experience of the brand that you might be interacting with via the device. That humanness, and bringing that humanity into the digital world, is going to be the next space.

What about video as a channel, as I know you've trialled that?

We're pondering that right now at two levels. Absolutely, the idea of talking to a screen is going to be a place that we're going to have to embrace and confront in the future, but there's one thing about First Direct that is key here, and that is the mystique about that voice you hear on the end of the phone. As a brand, creating a visual representation of First Direct on the phone does raise this question: is that a good thing? In particular, as people create pictures and have a visualisation of the person they are talking with on the telephone, and where they are. That's all part of the experience of First Direct, and I wonder if we might erode the mystique and some of that magical rapport as technology moves forward.]

ABOUT PAUL SAY

Paul Say was head of Marketing for First Direct from 2009 to 2011, after being head of Marketing and Communications for HSBC Bank International in Jersey. Say initially joined HSBC in 1999 as an e-marketing manager and helped to launch its television and Internet banking offering. He is currently director of Marketing for Sage UK and Ireland.

ABOUT FIRST DIRECT

Since its inception and launch as the first branchless bank in the world in 1989, First Direct has succeeded in creating a completely different bank business model. A telephone and Internet-based retail bank, it is regularly voted the best bank in Britain for customer service, for example. First Direct is a fully owned subsidiary of HSBC UK.

mBANK
(Poland)

with Michal Panowicz
CEO and co-founder of mBank

Since the launch of the new mBank in the spring of 2013, the service has been recognised globally through various accolades and awards for innovation and service. This is probably because the bank is not only a revolutionary renewal of a traditional bank, but one that cannibalised and ate its parent. BRE Bank, the main bank, opted to rebrand completely as mBank at the end of 2013 in order to capitalise on the innovative bank's success. What is happening and can a traditional bank truly compete with the new entrants? It appears to be that the answer is a resounding yes.

What is the background to mBank and your role there?
mBank was one of the first online banks to launch in Poland in 2000. At that time, the concept of running a successful bank without branches was considered to be bizarre. It succeeded in leaps and bounds though, gaining 2 million customers within a few years and changing the traditional

banking model by offering a service with no fees on checking accounts and higher interest on savings and deposits. It also drove the adoption of payment cards which was, at this point in time, a novelty. There was therefore a lot of process and legal innovation that mBank introduced. This was to allow these direct and digital processes to be introduced to the industry and prove acceptable to the authorities and then with the consumer. Everything we do is done with the purpose of being online digital and direct while some of the other banks cannot even do the basic online services because their approach is intertwined with their branches. For these banks to compete with mBank was difficult therefore, as it involved massive restructuring of systems and processes which was costly and hard to achieve.

After a decade, everyone had pretty much caught up with what we were delivering. The branch-based banks had competitive web services, not that they were committed to such services in the same way, but the functionality was there. The gap that had been there in the beginning had diminished, and competitors now offered free online banking services in a similar way.

The concern then was that, going forward, mBank might lose its edge. This is when I joined the bank. I was hired in 2011 with the mandate to introduce a fresh perspective and identify the next project for mBank to set its strategic platform going forward. In other words, to find a new vision for the bank to compete effectively in the future.

We began by having a number of creative strategic workshops, with people from all over the bank generating ideas about what we could do in retail banking in the future. We generated 120 ideas and implemented 20. That was the scope of reduction of what could be done versus what was feasible to do, even though we ended up implementing one of the biggest innovation portfolios in banking that many have seen.

The issue is not one of generating ideas therefore, but of being able to realise them. How to organise the process from a cultural view and create a willingness to change internally. That is a big challenge: the internal disruption and ability to accept that change.

Was the focus on simplifying the customer experience?

That was not the premise of how we started but simplification did move to the top of the list in the process. The challenge is the human-to-computer interaction model, which has not been resolved yet but has evolved massively in the past decade. In the 1990s, a game changer was graphical user interface, invented in the 1950s, but by replacing DOS shell, it opened the world of computing to mass audiences, first to information workers, then to consumers. Still early browsers were not able to recreate it, so for a long time Internet interactions were far inferior to PC ones. That is when table-based banking was born, based on early browsers, and it hasn't changed much since. Meanwhile the Internet and browsers made tremendous progress and now Internet applications are almost as interactive and graphical as native PC ones. That is when the notion of interactive modern Internet user interface began. Then we added touch to the screens to make it far easier for people to interact with machines, and that is where we are today.

Now we need to apply that to finance, and how engineers design the digital experience to be more consumer oriented or consumable. That is why we now see people using TVs and magazines and trying to push buttons rather than pointing and clicking.

So that is what creative start-ups like Simple or Moven are doing?

Yes, I think so, but only to a limited extent. When you compare the start-ups in the industry—Simple, Moven and others—versus the incumbents, then I think you start to see that they simplify user interface beautifully, but through very limited product ranges create a rather simplistic version of banking. For example, think about the concept of giving someone just a checking account and debit card and then they try to call the bank. It's true that these are the most essential products that you use most frequently but even mass customers need more from a banking service. There is frequent need for credit cards, cash or a car loan and, at one point, also investments or a mortgage. We are not just talking here about affluent and wealthy customers but also the mass-market consumer who needs a broader range of services. When you enter the world of the mass-market consumer, you see that the new start-ups do not offer all of those services however. Simple and Moven do not offer loans for example and it may be even structurally challenging for them to get to this point.

The key is to give people choice with easy access. Our loans process is fully online and has an easy check-out experience. We will approve and disburse you a loan straight to your checking account within three to five minutes if you are a customer who deposits a salary into our account. And we will have a 30-second version by the end of January 2014! That is a guarantee we provide because we have systems in the back office that support these things. As you apply for loan, a fully automated process verifies credit checks and salary confirmation, and so you get the loan there and then. In our new mobile application, it will be virtually "one tap" while you're there in a store heading to the checkout. No waiting. We don't wait for a banking teller to do things; we just get these things done by an automated and online process.

Then there is a space for things that are not simplistic. We call this complexity on demand. An example is when you get your checking account or card statement. Most banks will give separate statements for each of these, as you get these services from different divisions and you need separate logins for each of these services. We put these services all in one, like a Mint-style service. Only at mBank it is fully actionable— you do not need to log on again to a banking service to act on your statement review.

This means that the first thing you see is a simplified view of your money. All of your money. You then have complexity on demand, meaning that you can click through and see more accounts combined as a picture. You can change things to reflect more detail, and get into a granularity of finance which you may not have experienced before. It is not something everyone would use, but we put this together with the same customer experience look and feel as something like Google or Facebook. This means that if our customers want complexity, they can have this on demand but with a feeling that is familiar. The aim is to make it simple to manage money and make it fast and easy to use.

The last piece of building the new mBank was to make it a single-page application, where we have a modern front end with JavaScript and HMTL and then, by using AJAX, you can get more information. What this means is that you might have alerts and requests that you use today with the bank, such as "Remind me about paying my tax" or "Remind me of the date for making payments against a card so I don't get charges". You would usually only see those requests and alerts when you go to the page that relates to those payments. That would usually not be on the home page, but several layers down against that specific card or account set-up. We don't do this. Thanks to the technology design, these alerts and requests are part of the home page and appear dynamically through the technology architectures we have deployed.

When these appear, you can click or touch on the alert and then it takes you straight there. So our design is very simple but it does not take away depth. You get all you need, using the latest design and technology architectures of today. It is simplicity with depth and offers complexity on demand.

What has been the customer reaction to this?

All 2.7 million of our customers have access to the new service of mBank, and adoption is steadily progressing. Nearly 40 per cent of the entire logins to mBank services are now with the new mBank. That is a standard scenario in which we provide the new and old mBank service in parallel and gradually people move across. Bear in mind that most people have been using the old mBank for over a decade so this new service is very different for them. If you go back to Geoffrey Moore's *Crossing the Chasm*, only 15 per cent of people want something new while 85 per cent do not want things to change. That is because people have to unlearn what they know and learn something new. That is tough, and so we were amazed to find that we got 15 per cent of mBank customers switching to the new services within the first two-and-a-half weeks. By the end of June, the early adopters and innovators were all there. And now, five months later, we have 450,000 people not just logging in but using the service. We are now 25 per cent above the chasm, with 40 per cent who have switched to the new service.

And this is not like Moven or Simple. These new entrants are focused on the innovators and leading-edge users in a market of 314 million consumers and, so far, have gained around 10,000 users in total. We are converting millions of mass-market consumers who were already with the bank in a country of 38 million. This is the fastest product growth we have ever had. We had 450,000 customers using the service within a few months. That is phenomenal growth.

We also have some offers that are specific to these customers, such as merchant-funded rebates targeted against customers' transactional behaviour. A total of 390,000 people signed up for this service and some of our best users have already earned €250 in rebates, which is three times the interest the average banking customer would get from their deposits in a year. And that is just within the first five months of the service.

We are permanently over 1,000 contacts a day in our digital branch service: video, voice, chat and real-time collaboration in a communicator-like browser window. So far most of that usage is in chat. We had 10 to 12 per cent of the entire volume of the contact centre represented in our digital bank within five months! Sales results are even more encouraging. On 11 per cent share of traffic in October [2013], the digital branch was able to sell 38 per cent of investment products. And all that while, our regular call centre service was eight to ten times more effective in direct sales than an average bank in our region, as demonstrated by separate studies by ZED and Finalta in 2012.

It will take some time before the service becomes ubiquitous but to be where we are in just five months is a great thing, and we are very happy with how this has progressed.

And how is the competition reacting?

It is not easy for them. They will probably take one to two years to get their heads around what to do and how to react, and then another two to three years to deploy a competitive service. They will have to make some tough decisions too, such as whether they add this to their current core banking offers or build a completely new de novo service. Obviously, it is easier if you launch a new bank but then they will lose the benefits that come from the network effect, scale, ability to do real-time credit scoring and more.

Equally, if they don't do this, they will find it hard to adapt the internal technologies and culture to deal with the mobile Internet revolution and services that we have deployed. This means that it will take them longer, maybe three or more years, to adapt.

And it means that the management of traditional banks will have to think differently, as most executives came through branches and naturally put less stake in digital. Creating and implementing digitally enabled processes that remove the need for branch-based services is going to be a big deal. Unwinding the structure that was not built for digital will be hard.

This does not mean that we have no competition, but it does mean that the existing incumbent competition will find it hard to adapt, change and compete in the way that we have achieved.

ABOUT MICHAL PANOWICZ

Michal Panowicz is the managing director of mBank, and managed the project of New mBank (BRE Bank) as well as being its co-creator. Employed at BRE Bank since 2011 to oversee this project, he previously worked in Poland and the United States. From 2006 to 2011, Panowicz was employed in the Business Management Office at Microsoft headquarters in Redmond, WA, where he was responsible for creating complex directions of the company's development, such as the natural user interface strategy, the strategy of the company in competition against Apple and its business effectiveness improvement. Prior to this, while at eBay, he was involved in working on the acquisition of Skype and while at Boston Consulting Group's office in Warsaw, he created the development directions for the major Polish banks and financial institutions.

ABOUT mBANK

mBank is a key player in the Polish banking sector, being the leader of Internet banking. Although mBank's business model is under constant development and differs fundamentally from traditional banking models, the main features remain unchanged: mBank does not offer everything invented in the financial world. The bank instead focuses on a limited number of innovative products and financial services required by customers, and believes that banking should be simple and user-friendly. These elements are fundamental to its business model and have not changed since the launch of the bank in 2000, as a subsidiary of BRE Bank.

BRE Bank SA is an entity dependent on Commerzbank, the second-largest private-sector bank in Germany and one of Europe's leading financial institutions with a consolidated balance sheet total of €608 billion. Poland is Commerzbank's second market of business activity after Germany.

MOVEN
(USA)

with Brett King
founder of Moven and author of *Bank 3.0*

Brett King became globally known for his ideas about the future of banking with the release of his seminal book Bank 2.0 *in 2010. After lecturing and travelling globally and talking with banks and investors about his vision, he realised that there was a major opportunity to launch a new bank concept based on mobile smartphone innovations. As a result, King began building the backing for his new bank, Moven, in 2011 and achieved a soft launch early in 2013.*

What is Moven and the background to it?

Moven started as a concept back in July 2010 when I was out on the road doing the book launch for *Bank 2.0*. I did a big presentation to a group of Venture Capital firms, movie producers and entrepreneurs out in Los Angeles, and they grilled me for about an hour on my vision of the future of banking. I kept talking about how mobile was going to be the game changer. More importantly, the fact that traditional banks had not recognised the value of mobile yet. This got me thinking that there was obviously an opportunity for someone to create an Amazon or Facebook of banking, based on mobile. Traditional banks respond slowly to these types of changes in distribution.

I went home after that meeting and immediately registered the company name "Move and Bank", or Movenbank for short. The whole start of this concept was about how Gen Y would use a bank account, and so the name is meant to reflect that the bank has to be mobile and show our orientation to be a Gen Y bank account.

Then I put together a team and we started prototyping. We decided to drop the name "bank", as it proved difficult to get our heads around why we would need a bank licence, and in the end we determined it just isn't that cool being a bank. We also found that we and our customers just started referring to ourselves as "Moven" during meetups, so it made more sense over time to call our concept that—Moven.

It's also a case of practicalities. As a start-up, there's only so much you can do at one time, and so we focused on the emerging digital customers and mobile rather than the back-end banking and charter. That made sense as the banking area was detailed, technical and complex. We felt it better to get started by partnering a bank for the core processing and build a great front-end customer experience rather than have to divide our attention on also building a core, which are plentiful in the US market.

Has that been the biggest challenge: the bank processing area?
There have been quite a few challenges along the way. For example, we had secured our first round of funding in the summer of 2012 in order to get everything ready for an early 2013 launch. We had found a bank partner and a payments processing partner. We chose the processor on its ability to provide real-time analytics and feedback on how people were spending. That meant a processor that could capture data off the back of each transaction, and at the time there were only two processors in the whole of the United States that could handle that sort of requirement. We chose TxVia, which

was one of those two. Just six weeks before our launch, TxVia was acquired by Google and Google determined that it did not want any third parties on the TxVia platform as the company wanted to use it exclusively for the Google Wallet. For us, that meant finding another processor weeks before the launch—it was a huge blow. By the time we found another processor, the bank partner we had chosen decided that it had changed strategy and had other priorities in the timeline, and we basically no longer fitted into its schedule and would have to endure a delay. So you can imagine our issue, with just six weeks to go we had lost the ability to process a payment via MasterCard or leverage a deposit account. That could have been the moment that signalled the end of the Moven project right there, but we were fortunate in that we managed to turn it around and, within three months, found an alternative bank partner and processor. That rapid turnaround meant we could still launch in April 2013, trialling the service with friends and family of the company, before opening to the first public customers at the beginning of June.

How have customers reacted since the launch?

Well it is early days, as we are still in beta product mode, but the reactions have been very positive generally. For example, we had New York's Channel 4 recently interview us and one of the early adopters about the product, and one of our customers, told them that Moven "makes saving money as easy as spending every day". That sort of response is typical and is due to the feedback loop we built into the product that tells you about your spending behaviours every time you transact. That mechanism and tool provides a very different view of money and how you use your money from a typical debit card or checking account. To get people talking about that and how they have found the money management tool has changed the way they think about spending and saving is all about what we are trying to achieve.

We had another customer whose purse was stolen, and she hadn't realised that it had been stolen until she got her Moven alert for the next transaction on her smartphone. Every receipt for any purchase is logged on the Moven app in real time and pushed to the phone. It was only when she was alerted that a transaction had been made from the Moven receipt notification that she realised her purse was missing. She was able to shut down and block use of all of her cards from our app in real time, straightaway, as a result.

This is the beauty of mobile, in that mobile is making banking more secure and also more informative. In this case, she was protected from the fraudster the moment that they made their first transaction, due to the alerts, blocks and capabilities of the app. It's also proof that people really are more likely to remember where their mobile is 24/7 while their wallet or purse is becoming more and more irrelevant.

And it also means that you are simplifying the whole experience of dealing with money.
Yes. When we started out, our aim was to reinvent the model of banking and make it simpler but also smarter. If you look back at the way banks work historically, over the past century, you would have started with a passbook in the mid-1900s, then a chequebook maybe in the 1960s and today you have a debit card. The passbook origins of banking gave you quite a lot of visibility about your money. You would walk into a branch, take the cash out, see the balance change in the passbook and you would know exactly how much money you had left to spend in your account. With a debit card, you don't have that visibility today. That's why people need to check their balance all the time as they don't know how near or far away they are from being overdrawn or overexposed financially. Credit card companies have really worked hard to exploit that lack of visibility of money. The ignorance of the customer about their financial position is what card issuers use to get the customer into a borrowing position and then charge them fees on that credit use. That's the revenue model.

At Moven, we work the opposite way. We want our customers to have the maximum visibility of their money and how they are using it. This is because we want Moven to be the primary financial application for our customers, not just an app on the back of their existing accounts. But our objective is not necessarily to get you to switch banks but to use our app to monitor your spending and saving. Having said that, over time as customers use our discretionary spending tools within Moven, people are switching more of their spend and using our service more and more often. Moven gives you a unique view of your money and how you are spending and saving, and that creates a strong behavioural imperative. As you tap and pay, you get a real-time balance check and summary of transactions related to that category and class of spending. You get the receipt on the phone telling you how much you spent with that merchant today and over the past month, and how that compares with your general spending on those sort of services. Whether you have spent more or less this month and that's great for telling you what you have done.

The thing is that most banks would not intuitively have reached the mobile experience that we have created. The traditional view of most banks is to have a debit or credit card that creates fees and generates customer activity for pure revenue purposes. It's not intuitive for a bank to then turn around and say to customers "stop spending money and save more". Their products and culture are geared in the opposite direction. The more money the customer spends, the more revenue and profit the bank makes. We take a different view—build a product that helps customers spend less money and they'll be your biggest fans, and they'll still generate revenue while telling others how cool your app is!

So when we talk about simplifying banking, we really mean to provide transparency of money.

Absolutely, that's our secret sauce. What we are realising is that there's a value exchange that occurs between the service provider (Moven in this case) and the customer as a result. If you look at one of our target segments, the Gen Y audience, they have no patience over a lack of visibility on fees. That's why the prepaid market has exploded in the United States, as it overcomes the hidden fees, overdrafts and surprises. We provide the things that customers like—instant feedback, mobile-focused thinking and features like sending money via Facebook—but there are no "gotcha" moments, no surprises and nothing hidden. We make it all visible and put the customer in control. That's the key and that value exchange creates trust with the consumer.

In the past, banks earned trust by being safe with money. Now, customers want more than that. They want a trusted relationship. And the mobile can provide a unique platform for this. In fact, we see the mobile becoming more and more of an advisory tool, giving you information and context about your life, your money, your spending and saving. That component of advice, brand advocacy and trust are all intertwined. If you don't have transparency and you don't give visibility on what you're charging and why you're charging, then you will never get that trusted relationship or capability to connect with the customer. It's an interactive relationship via a mobile app which is where we see the customer connection, not via the traditional operations, products and structures.

Could banks do what you're doing?

Undoubtedly, banks will try to copy some of the things we're doing and the way we provide information and context through the mobile app, that's the easy part. But bank culture will block a lot of these developments as it is counterintuitive for a traditional organisation. When I talk to banks about how we give our customers visibility on their spending and that leads them to reduce spending over time, most banks say to me, "Why would you want to do that? That would be throwing away revenue." Of course, these banks see the current model where revenue comes from interchange, and they are locked into that view. The reality is that people are still going to spend money, and they will put more money with you if you are totally transparent and open. That's our model and that's what we are seeing happening in the market reality during the early days of the customers using the product.

Over the first 90 days of customers using the product, we saw a shift of 18 to 20 per cent of their share of wallet from other bank accounts to Moven because of that factor. In fact, we're seeing two things happening. One is that banks are attempting to copy our positioning. We started with the phrase

"Spend, Save and Live Smarter", and we're seeing that language being used by a heap of other banks now, although they are not offering services in the same way. The second thing is that we are being approached by banks all of the time, asking if they can use Moven's platform to interface with their bank to provide our service to their customers, and we are exploring those sorts of partnerships for the future too.

Finally, where will Moven be moving in the future?

When you think about where Moven fits, once we become a customer's primary app for managing their spending and saving every day, providing information, context and advice to go with that, the next step aims to answer a different problem. Right now, the main play with the app is real-time feedback as you spend and save. The bigger question is: Should I buy this? Can I afford it? And that's the question we aim to answer in our new version of the Moven app, which is being released in November 2013. We are trying to get customers to use Moven to help them make purchase decisions, not just reflecting on what they have already spent and purchased. We are making this unique connection for our customers with their money, on a real-time basis, and being able to service customers and their financial needs as they arise—contextually. Banking based on providing you value as you need it, with transparency and helpful advice in real time every day via your smartphone. On that basis, we don't believe banks that lead with a branch or a dumb, zero-feedback plastic debit card can even come close to competing with our offering.

ABOUT BRETT KING

Brett King is a global bestselling author, a well-known futurist and speaker, the host of the "BREAKING BANK$" Radio Show on Voice America (an Internet Talk Radio Network with over nine million monthly listeners) and the founder of the start-up Moven. King was voted American Banker's Innovator of the Year in 2012 and was nominated by Bank Innovation as one of the top 10 "coolest brands in banking". Bank 3.0 (in 8 languages) has topped the charts in the United States, the United Kingdom, China, Canada, Germany, Japan and France since its release late in 2012. His latest book, Breaking Banks, is due out early 2014 with Wiley.

ABOUT MOVEN

Moven is an app that provides real-time updates on purchases and analysis of spending to help customers achieve financial wellness. It is one of the first mobile-centric banking platforms and is described by Wired magazine as "the bank of the future". The company's focus is to give financial control and insight to motivate customers to make smarter spending decisions and save more. Moven's customers are generally technologically savvy consumers, who suffer from money anxiety and struggle to manage their finances.

M-PESA
(Kenya)

with John Maynard

senior business development manager for M-PESA at Vodafone Group

Mobile payments have taken off massively over the past few years, with the most notable success being M-PESA in Kenya. Launched in March 2007, with an expected one million customers after the first year, the system far exceeded expectations and now has over 17 million registered accounts, representing nearly one account for every adult in Kenya. However, the system has not been as successful overseas. What constituted M-PESA's success in Kenya and where will it go next?

Perhaps you can give a little background to start with as to why M-PESA has been so successful in Kenya and why Vodafone got into this space?
The product originally came into existence as a result of a pilot we operated in Kenya with its original conception dating back to 2004 to 2005. Back then, Nick Hughes, who worked in Vodafone Group's Corporate Social Responsibility Unit, was looking at how to pilot mobile telephone payments for social inclusion and microfinance.

Being in Corporate Social Responsibility, it was difficult to get access to Vodafone's product development engine, which focused on more mainstream products. However, Nick was able to get agreement that if he could secure external funding, the project would be supported. He had a conversation with the UK's Department for International Development (DFID) and that led to an application for funding from Challenge Fund. The application was approved and was awarded £1 million, which Vodafone matched in terms of manpower, staff and marketing materials, and that started the pilot in Kenya in 2006 to 2007.

The pilot was operated by Safaricom, the Vodafone affiliate in Kenya, with the objectives of producing something that was affordable, would work with existing handsets and could be operated easily by the local savings and credit cooperative societies (SACCOs),[37] the microfinance institutions that exist out there.

It achieved some of those objectives except that it proved too difficult to customise the product to match the disparate systems that the individual SACCOs used to monitor their cash-in and cash-out methods on a daily basis. They were all just too different. But one thing that had been included almost as a by-product of the original pilot was the ability for individual customers to send money directly to each other. That resonated with the customers who tried it out and from there the decision was made that it would be the primary focus of the product.

M-PESA was launched in March 2007 and, by the end of the first year, we had 2.5 million customers, far beyond original expectations.

I heard the frictions internally in Kenya helped the launch.

Take a look at how Michael Joseph set up the operation.[38] He ran Safaricom and took it from a small mobile operator to a large one in Kenya through a

---

37 The SACCO movement in Kenya is the largest in Africa and among the top 10 globally. With over Ksh 230 billion (US$ 2.5 billion) in assets and a savings portfolio estimated at Ksh 190 billion (US$ 2.2 billion), the SACCO movement in Kenya constitutes a significant proportion, about 20 per cent, of the country's domestic savings. SACCOs have thus become a vital component of Kenya's economic and social development.

38 Michael Joseph was the CEO of Safaricom Limited from July 2000, when the company was relaunched as a joint venture between Vodafone UK and Telkom Kenya, until his retirement in November 2010. During his tenure, he steered the company from a subscriber base of less than 20,000 to over 16.71 million subscribers.

reputation of excellent customer care and customer service. The challenge for a mobile operator in operating a mobile money service is to convince customers that they can trust their money with them. Some mobile operators have sharp practices, such as rounding minutes up or aggregating billing to the highest numbers. Michael positioned Safaricom very much as a trusted brand and business. Michael as an individual also had a very good reputation with the people of Kenya and the customer care processes of Safaricom assured customers that if they put their money into Safaricom, they could also get it out again.

I've also read that it is a charitable system?[39]

It is a profitable venture, not a charitable system. Around 17 per cent of Safaricom's total revenues come from M-PESA, which is bigger than SMS and data combined. We make money from the network but so do our agents in the network. We have 40,000 agents in Kenya and believe that we have created about 50,000 jobs. Those agents are also making money, enough money to employ people as a result.

Why is that success not repeated in other countries?

We were lucky in Kenya. We launched at the right time and the availability of the product during the turmoil following the elections of 2007 to 2008 helped Kenyans out—M-Pesa was the safest way to send cash or buy airtime. I don't think we'll see that success repeated so quickly elsewhere. Having said that, we've got 32 million customers registered worldwide (M-PESA is live in seven markets), and if you look at Tanzania, it shows an example of a market that has taken longer to get there but is now just as important. We have around 80 per cent market share in Kenya and about 40 per cent in Tanzania. They've got ten million registered customers for mobile payments, the entirety of their base, and around three million

---

39　Safaricom is not allowed to earn interest on the money stored so instead gives interest earnings to a charitable M-PESA foundation.

are active mobile payments users now. As we have reached critical mass, transaction volumes have gone through the roof, particularly in the last twelve months.

Does that mean the Vodafone plan is to offer M-PESA services to all of Africa and other emerging markets over time?

We will launch in the markets where we think it's a good fit and that's a combination of the markets themselves saying that the timing is right to offer the product and the regulatory environment enabling us to do so.

On a general point, our view is that if you fast-forward five years, you will see every local mobile operator in the developing world offering a mobile money product, where it's allowed by regulation. If you look back, you had Smart Communications and Globe Telecom in the Philippines offering mobile money products for nearly a decade, and there have been other schemes in Korea for example, but M-PESA really re-energised interest in mobile money systems.

What we were able to show with the success in Kenya is that it was possible to reach out far beyond the existing financial systems and bank structures by leveraging the scale of the mobile airtime distribution networks. That's why, by 2009, if you were a mobile operator and were anywhere near Africa, you had to be looking to offer some form of mobile money scheme.

Looking at that restructuring, the banks have not been that supportive of such schemes, have they?

It's been a bit of a rollercoaster in terms of bank relationships to be honest. When we launched, they weren't really sure what we were doing and didn't believe it would work. After our initial success, many banks saw what we were doing as a threat, and if you look across the world, regulators at that time were implementing regulation to prevent the operating model you see in Kenya.

Where we are now, the bank relationships are much better. They now recognise that, whilst our system increased competition amongst the banking sector, they have also increased the number of bank accounts they have.

When we launched in Kenya in 2007, there were just 2.5 million bank account holders in the country. Now, there are more than nine million. That's a good thing. When you look at the Central Bank's need for more financial inclusion and what the banks themselves are looking for, which is to increase their customer base, it's a good indication that the introduction of a payment system like M-PESA can bring wider benefits across the economy.

Does that mean the M-PESA style service will always be a pure mobile payments service or do you think it might upscale into full banking over time?

I think there's always going to be a step-off point between the level of products we can offer versus the products banks can offer. We are not a bank. We have not got a banking licence. We have no intention of getting one and that means there are some services, like interest-bearing savings accounts or offering credit, that we cannot offer by ourselves. Where there is demand for these services, we will look to partner existing banks.

What about the other way round? Will you take mobile payments from the developing markets into the developed ones and, if so, when?

For sure. If you look at the recent announcements from Barclays with Pingit and O2 with their wallet service in the United Kingdom, these are good indicators of what's coming down the line and selfishly, personally, I cannot wait. Being able to pay my window cleaner or school lunch fees without scrabbling around the house for change is a future I can't wait for.

ABOUT JOHN MAYNARD

John Maynard was part of the commercial and strategy team working on M-PESA, Vodafone's mobile money transfer product. Prior to joining the M-PESA team, Maynard was product manager for a number of Vodafone products, including premium rate SMS, adult content bar and consumer email solutions. Since this interview took place in 2013, Maynard subsequently joined the UK Payments Council to develop the United Kingdom's mobile payments strategy.

ABOUT M-PESA

M-Pesa (*M* is for "mobile" and *pesa* is Swahili for "money") is a mobile phone-based money transfer and microfinancing service for Safaricom and Vodacom, the largest mobile network operators in Kenya and Tanzania. Currently the most developed mobile payment system in the world, M-Pesa allows users with a national ID card or passport to deposit, withdraw and transfer money easily with a mobile device. Today, M-PESA has over 32 million customers who can deposit or withdraw money from an account linked to their mobile phone through any of 60,000 agents. The service is live in seven markets, including India, Afghanistan and Fiji.

SIMPLE
(USA)

with Shamir Karkal
CFO and co-founder of Simple

Simple, originally known as Simplebank, launched in the United States at the end of 2011, with the aim to simplify banking and give customers what they really want and need from a bank. Designed with the user experience through the mobile Internet at its core, Simple has gained significant customer and media coverage. Is it truly innovative and inspiring or purely adding icing to the banking cake?

What is Simple and the background to it?

Simple started about four years ago when my co-founder Josh reached out to me and sent me an email saying "let's start a retail bank". I was working for McKinsey in Europe at the time and this was a surprising idea, but something that seemed interesting. So Josh and I started brainstorming and we rapidly realised that big banks in the United States make money out of confusing the customer with complexity. Large banks have mainly grown through acquisition over the past thirty years whilst the business model for community banks is to survive on their interest margins. The thing is today that large banks in the United States make most of their money through fees and charges. Overdraft fees, late payment fees and more. All of those charges apply when a customer makes a mistake. The banks therefore have no incentive to help customers deal with their money better, as that's how banks make money, and customers make a large number of mistakes with their money. The incentive structure of the banking industry in the United State is therefore set up to punish customers. We thought that if we could bring a better user interface and business model to the customer, then that would change things, and that has been the whole thinking behind Simple.

Have you found in this process that there is frustration with the banks?
We have found that there is an enormous level of frustration with traditional banks. We did not even have a true sense of the depth of that frustration when we started. That is probably because Josh and I both came from business school as software engineers, and we saw problems with our own personal banking needs. So we knew *we* had frustrations but we didn't know that this was common to everyone. One of the first things we did, for example, was put up a Simple website early in 2010, just stating that we were planning to launch a better, simpler bank. We did not say what we were going to do, but just to register your email address if you were interested. That was it. Within four months of putting up that website, we had over 20,000 people leave their email addresses. That was without any marketing or anything. Just Josh and I tweeting the weblink. So many people signed up, and we didn't know them, so we started emailing them asking about their experiences with banking. What did they like? What didn't they like? How would they change things? We started having conversations with these people, and before we knew it, we had ideas from about 10,000 people. One of the reactions was that they had already found us very engaging by the basic fact that we had responded to them with an email. Really? You find it amazing that I just sent you an email? The answer was yes because they didn't get that

sort of interest or response from their bank. The level of service that people were getting from banks appeared to be zero and, what there was had been automated as far as possible, so to get some form of human engagement with a bank via email was already setting us apart. Some people even sent us seven-page-long emails. One particular customer, a couple who regularly travel to Africa, decided to sit down one Saturday evening and write down everything that they didn't like about banking today. That was why it was seven pages long!

We all know that there is some inefficiency in service from existing banks, so how come there aren't more Simples out there?

This is because it's a regulated oligopoly. In 2012, the Big Four US banks generated over $300 billion in revenues between them. They each have over $1 trillion in assets and control over 40 per cent of the deposit market between them. In credit cards, they control over 80 per cent of the market. Just four of them. So you have these four gigantic behemoths that pretty much control the market, and then you have this tail of around 6,500 community banks and 6,000 credit unions that have a few thousand customers each on average. They are so small that they do not have the ability to invest and change anything. In fact, they cannot compete with the dollars that the Big Four put into technology so even though their heart is in the right place, their pockets are not deep enough. They do not have the resources to change the market and the big banks have the resources but do not have the incentive to change the system. Getting a bank charter and just getting into the industry is also a big barrier. Ask an entrepreneur if he wants to start a bank, and then tell him it will take about five years before he will be able to on-board his first customer. That entrepreneur will go away and start a business somewhere else.

Is it easier now, as you have started up?

It is certainly easier to innovate today thanks to the barriers of technology breaking down, but it is more than that. In our case, there were a lot of factors that came together. You need to have the right combination of the right people, the right investor and the right idea, and we had all of that. The financial crisis was also a great trigger. Before the crisis, there was this feeling that if you walked into a bank and it had a big marble hall with someone in a suit and everything was nice and bright and shiny, then it was secure and stable. Big bank equalled safety, and there was an implicit trust in the bank due to this. The financial crisis has pretty much destroyed all of that. In fact, big banks are now seen as being less safe than small banks as they can systemically fail. People are now a lot more willing to consider switching banks as a result, and safety does not come from being a big bank but from having the FDIC insurance at the bottom of the page. So people are a lot more willing to switch now that they understand that, with a much greater focus on getting good service. Ten years ago, when Check21 was first being considered, you could not do the sort of service that can be offered today, such as remote deposit via smartphone. People tried, but the innovators then found it challenging because the industry was not there, the infrastructure was not there, the regulatory structure was not there and the customer base was not there. Today, that is all different. Our median customer age is around 26 for example, so most of our customers grew up with the Internet and everything online. They're on Twitter and Facebook, and they wonder why the banks' interface with them is so much worse than any other mobile or online experience they have.

But you are not actually offering full banking are you, just a front end to traditional banking?

Well not quite. Everyone who uses Simple has to open an account with us. Every customer who comes to our site signs up for an interest-bearing checking account that has, for all intents and purposes, the same capabilities as any other interest-bearing checking account in the United States. What is different about us is that we have thought through the customer experience and designed it with modern technology to help our customers manage their finances. It has not been thought through in terms of maximising our fee revenues—in fact we do not generate any fee revenues—but has been designed for customers who do banking on mobile phones. There are small features like our map of money that shows you your balances and takes away all the forthcoming billing, savings and transactions to be processed to show you what is safe to spend. We do the maths, rather than leaving the customer to do it. It's a simple feature, but knowing what is safe to spend avoids making mistakes, and mistakes are what used to generate bank fees. That is what we are changing. We are trying to show people where and when their money is flowing in and out of their account, and making it easy to save and spend. It's seamless. It's creating simple behavioural rules that the customer can control around spending goals, budgeting and alerts, and enabling them to have this managed for them simply and easily.

What are the unique aspects of Simple and its offer?
There are a range of things we have built into the user experience that are different to the usual bank offer. The mobile app is head and shoulders above anything else in the market, and that's not me saying this but our customers. One of our customers, for example, was tweeting how she had just switched from Bank of America to Simple and Bank of America reached out and said, "Hey, we've had an app for years." She tweeted back saying she knew that, had tried it and it sucked compared to ours. She then tweeted a further six or seven tweets explaining why. This is because most banks just take Internet banking and stick it on a smartphone rather than thinking about what they can actually do with the smartphone to improve the customer experience. It's a bit like if you go to any modern website such as Twitter, Facebook and Quora, and they just suck you in. Now compare that with a bank's website; bank websites are often unusable by comparison. This is because the banks designed their services for a world dominated by branches, and they view the mobile and the Internet as just a statement delivery rather than a service delivery. So we targeted creating a website and mobile experience that is fully integrated and simple. For example, entering a username and password

on a smartphone is a pain so we use a PIN for access as it's far quicker and easier. We added other authentication to the process however, such as two-factor authentication. We have added other features, such as how you spend and on what. We can tell you exactly how many coffees you have purchased this month from a store if you used the Simple account or card to pay for that coffee. We can give you huge depth of knowledge of your spending and saving habits and how they are working. This is the intelligence we built into the design to provide a fantastic customer experience.

What have been the tangible results for Simple since its launch?

We have had an amazing reaction since our launch, in every way. You can check out our twitterfeed or Facebook page if you want to see. We are growing fast and have tens of thousands of customers today. We are seeing heavy customer usage coming through and really seeing an engaged customer base. What has been particularly satisfying is that we give customers tools, such as how much is safe to spend, and seeing customers using those tools has been incredible. I'll give you an example. We have a goals feature for the service. This allows customers to create goals that they are striving to achieve—a deposit for a house, money for paying for education through college, saving for a car or a holiday and so on. When it was launched, we just put it out there and didn't really market it at all. We then analysed what was happening with that feature and saw that customers have this habit where when they have a lot of money in their account, they feel rich, but if they have a little, they feel poor. That's fairly obvious but, by using the goal-setting process which is purely driven by the balance in their account, they can see their true balance after paying for their goals, rather than the pure balance of what they have on that day. This way, they don't have these irrational spending days because they feel rich as they have pre-allocated monies towards goals. This means that the balance in their account is less driven by their monthly income cycle and more by their actual spending and savings needs. This is a key feature that, without any marketing, we found many customers using.

There are other banks like you that we are seeing today, such as Moven. Do you see these as threats or complementary?

They are complementary as this is a small industry with a small number of new guys competing with a few giants. We do not see ourselves competing with these other guys like Brett at Moven, as we would all lose if that were the case. We are not trying to take Moven's customers or Google's, but the big banks that have millions of customers. We want a piece of that customer base and to show them that there's a better way of managing their money. There's a whole wave of innovation coming downstream focused on doing that, including Moven, but we're ahead of most people. So this is not a win/lose situation but a win/win if we can all get there.

And, in the future, how do you see the landscape and what will have changed?

We are constantly innovating. That is the most important part of our ethos. I don't know what we will be doing five years from now but we will continue to be innovating. Our core mission and vision will not change. We will stay customer centric and customer aligned, and focused on designing the best customer experience in the banking industry. That is our core. We will add new features and new technologies as we see them, as long as they leverage and support that vision. So we will add services that make it easier to transfer money into and out of an account, and to interact with your balances and goals. There was a wave of innovation in the last big technology change to banking in the late 1990s when the Internet came around, but none of them really changed anything. That is partly because of customer apathy and partly because there was not something fundamentally different. I do not believe we have that situation today. Today, combining the financial crisis with the mobile financial revolution creates a major and unique inflexion point to change things. That is what we are going to do. We are going to see a new Amazon for banking, and we wonder why that has not happened yet. The main reason why it has not happened is that banking is far more challenging for the reasons we discussed earlier: capital, structure, backing, investment, scale and ability to compete with the big incumbents. We are going to change that as we think that it is all ripe for change, and that is where we are targeted.

ABOUT SHAMIR KARKAL

Shamir Karkal is a software engineer turned finance and banking expert. Prior to Simple, Karkal was a consultant with McKinsey & Co. specialising in strategy consulting for financial institutions in Europe, the Middle East and the United States. He has a bachelor's degree in computer science, a master's in information technology and an MBA from Carnegie Mellon University.

ABOUT SIMPLE

Simple offers a bank account that has all the tools needed to manage money built right in to make managing personal finances effortless. The company believes that making wise spending and saving choices should be easy, and often even fun. All the tools customers need to manage their money are built right into the account, where they're most effective. The funds in a Simple account are held by their partner bank, Bancorp. Simple provides everything else, including the Simple Visa Card, powerful iOS and Android apps, a highly designed web interface and full customer support. Simple was acquired by BBVA in February 2014 for $117 million.

SWIFT
(global)

with Kosta Peric

head of the SWIFT Innotribe innovation programme

SWIFT stands for the Society for Worldwide Interbank Financial Telecommunication, a member-owned cooperative through which the financial world conducts its business operations with speed, certainty and confidence. More than 9,000 banking organisations, securities institutions and corporate customers in 209 countries trust SWIFT every day to exchange millions of standardised financial messages. In 2009, SWIFT launched Innotribe—an initiative to find new ideas and new projects and then establish the infrastructure that will enable them to grow.

What does innovation mean to SWIFT?

First and foremost, innovation is about encouraging and promoting entrepreneurship at SWIFT and also encouraging and promoting entrepreneurship in the financial community surrounding SWIFT. So we have a double objective: internal to SWIFT and in the community around SWIFT. So Innotribe is enabling collaborative innovation. We are big believers in the open innovation concept and want to engage with our staff, people in the banks, partners and all the people surrounding SWIFT to formulate ideas and get these ideas to us in the first stage and then, second, to be able to do something about these ideas. So that, in a nutshell, is what we are all about.

So you are not trying to create innovation yourselves but trying to capture ideas, or are you trying to do both?
No, we are a relatively small team of ten and our goal is not to do innovation. We could not do that with a ten-person team. That is not our objective—to do innovation. Our objective is to facilitate and enable innovation within the company and the community.

How has Innotribe changed over the past three years?
There are two things. One on the content and one on the process. On the content side, we have been very successful at forecasting and bringing to the table the topics that are relevant to our community, such as cloud and mobile. These have been very progressive as part of Innotribe and are now part of the mainstream, so we are now focusing on other areas like social data and media, digital identity and Big Data. This means that there is a process of us spotting the trends and bringing them in for discussion and debate and, where appropriate, they then move into the mainstream.

The other interesting aspect is how Innotribe's process has changed. When we started at SIBOS Hong Kong in 2009, we were a totally new thing and more of a sideshow. Over the years, we have since nurtured our image and are now something to be reckoned with, even though we still focus on the things that are on the longer horizons. It is something that is now counted with both within SIBOS and outside SIBOS.

Talking about SIBOS and the SWIFT community, the main audience is operational—does innovation really figure on their radar?

Yes. The best metaphor to use to explain this is to think of our core business of transactions as a castle. The castle is good, solid, has thick walls and is there to stay to generate the core business. In the castle, you can do innovation as well but it is more of an incremental nature. So what we do with Innotribe is to tell people how to think about what is outside of the castle, or outside of the box if you like, and things that might be important down the road. So although we have lots of operational people in the community, this mental picture is important to them as well as they realise that just doing business as usual is not enough. Business as usual and cost reduction and other areas do not consider the future and securing your future. That is why they see this as important now.

In particular, at SIBOS 2012, people of a more senior and more strategic nature were attracted to Innotribe too, and that's important.

But senior people aren't interested if innovations are not actionable, so are actions being taken by these people afterwards?

I've seen a couple of things in this area. One is that the community itself has decided that they need actionable ideas which is why we have created the Innotribe Incubator, which has received funds for €5 million from the SWIFT community in 2012. There we have concrete and powerful ways to act and have run six Incubator projects this year. The second example is that we have seen several decision makers from banks join us at the start-up competition at SIBOS. This is where people can pitch their new ideas to the decision makers of the banks and see how many ideas they can action out of that.

I'm aware of the Incubator and start-up programmes. Do you have specific objectives against these?

The way we measure success is that we are not at the point where we can judge based on revenues, even though two of the six Incubator projects invested in during 2012 will bring revenues to SWIFT next year. Mostly, we measure our success based on our capability to process and act upon ideas. This is because many ideas look good on paper but, when we sit down and progress them through our process, we discover they are not such good ideas. We expect the failure rate in the Incubator to be high for example, so our success rate is measured more by the number of things we can set in motion than the things that come to fruition. As we continue the Incubator programme through 2012 and 2013, I would expect some bottom-line hard benefits and revenues to come out of these projects both for SWIFT and our banking community. For example, the Extended Business Activity Monitoring (EBAM) project should bring benefits and revenues down the line.

It is difficult to measure success when you have no business case or proof points for innovation, as innovation is meant to be new, isn't it?
It's very difficult to come up with business cases for innovation. I've seen this throughout my career, in that I was a product manager before and if you ask a product manager to come up with a business case, you are asking that person to lie. There is no way that they can predict the future, especially for ideas that are new, so you just have to try them out. So I would say there is no way you can be innovative if you don't experiment, and experiments imply failure. When you fail, you should learn from these failures while other ideas may fail but will morph and become viable through trial and error. So what you really need is to try things and have a capacity internally for trying out things.

Just out of interest, what justified introducing the innovator programme Innotribe within SWIFT?
The global financial crisis was one reason, but not the only one. We have a business at SWIFT that is concentrated so, when the crisis hit, it was important to see how we could diversify our revenue stream. Another reason was more cultural following the appointment of Lázaro Campos as CEO in

2008. He is a big believer in innovation from a cultural change perspective. Our people and people around us, he believes, should see SWIFT as an innovative company that can take them into the future, not just as a banking cooperative processor of payments but as a leader. Innovation for the financial community is using SWIFT for other things than just messaging, and that is a key driver here.

The third driver is that we should always keep asking the banks if they are going to be doing all of this again, where all the banks are running their own home banking systems, their own corporate banking systems and such like. Shouldn't there be more ways to pool resources and make use of the SWIFT cooperative than there is now? This is especially important as we move towards mobile payment services and more, and this is what drove the Innotribe programme in terms of proving that SWIFT could be used for much more than just messaging.

What do you see as the big things happening in the future from a financial innovation viewpoint?

I know for a fact that the new economies and new values that we discuss within Innotribe are driven by social media. Social media is creating new currencies and new economic models, and this will be very big and very important in the two to three years downstream from now. The question for the banks is how will they position themselves in this new world of peer-to-peer currencies in social media? That is going to be a key question for banks in innovation for the next few years.

The other area is what I call strong AI. This is a modern way of looking at AI. The old way was mechanical and thought of as expert systems. Today, we have this enormous computational power in our hands, and we should make a big splash around this for the next four or five years.

So social data, social media, alternative currencies and peer-to-peer payments will dominate for the near term, and then big data and AI in four or five years from now.

And for your Innotribe programme, what's in the future?

For our own programme, we will try to have more start-up competitions, which we started at SIBOS in 2011. We would like to have three or four of those.

Innotribe also talked about "Banks for a Better World" in 2012, and that's had a strong take-up in our community. It's a hotspot as it moves us away from purely talking about technology innovations to instead talk more about the perceptions and sentiments about banking and how to improve the governance, operation and support for the industry. That's got strong interest.

When you combine the future of money, the future of banking and banks for a better world as three topic areas, you see a strong interest in this.

We will also run more around the Incubator, and then we have a few more ideas around ways to innovate Innotribe, but I'll keep that in my pocket for now.

ABOUT KOSTA PERIC

Having joined SWIFT in 1990, Konstantin (Kosta) Peric was appointed head of Innovation in 2007. In this role, his main responsibility was to lead a team whose main mission is to enable collaborative innovation within the financial industry. This division is also the driving force behind Innotribe. Peric was previously head of Securities Market Infrastructures in the sales division, where he was responsible for negotiating and acquiring key strategic programmes. Since this interview, Peric has left SWIFT to run the microfinance initiative for the Bill and Melinda Gates Foundation.

ABOUT INNOTRIBE

Innotribe is SWIFT's initiative to leverage the collective intelligence of its community in order to find new ideas and new projects, and then establish the infrastructure that will enable them to grow. The Incubator is a new mechanism created by Innotribe to facilitate exploration of innovative ideas in a collaborative way: it is a framework to enable collaborative innovation at a level up from the "proofs of concept" already facilitated by Innotribe. The Innotribe Start-up Challenge was designed to introduce the most promising FinTech and financial services start-ups to SWIFT's community of more than 9,700 banking organisations, securities institutions and corporate customers in 209 countries.

THE CURRENCY CLOUD
(global)

with Michael Laven
chief executive of The Currency Cloud

Cloud computing has been around for a while but still suffers from extreme views, with some considering cloud to just be Amazon Web Services whilst others see it as a way of leveraging new forms of business models. Michael Laven, CEO of The Currency Cloud, is one of the latter visionaries and is changing the game in cross-border payments by building a cloud-based offer for currency movements and offering this as a low-cost, transparent service to consumers and small businesses.

What is The Currency Cloud?

There is a huge volume of cross-border transactions that are well served for the large, multinational firms, but a major, untapped and underserved market for the cross-border payments needs of smaller firms. The Currency Cloud is a start-up company in the world of cross-border payments that addresses these companies' needs. We believe that the need to make cross-border payments has become globally ubiquitous. There are more and more firms that need transactions across borders than ever before. Meanwhile, the companies and systems to serve those firms have not transformed, especially the services for smaller firms. These firms do not have the ease of access, ease of use, access to good pricing or simplicity and transparency that bigger firms have. The Currency Cloud is, therefore, built as a technology platform that will bring a world of currencies with simplicity and low cost to a whole range of businesses that did not have it before. We have around a hundred clients accessing our payments platform through our API, and interfacing their business applications directly into the currency markets through our platform.

I assume you are a cloud-based service, with a name like The Currency Cloud?

We are a Software-as-a-Service (SaaS) based platform, and make a distinction between online platforms that you might get from your bank, where you are connected through a screen to the bank's platform, and what we are doing. We are enabling online applications, including payroll, enterprise resource planning (ERP), invoicing, corporate treasury and more, through a connection to ourselves. We are then connected to multiple liquidity providers, banks, which provide us with sources of hedging and currency pools, as well as multiple payment networks. These are banking and proprietary payments networks.

Through the cloud nature of our platform, it allows us to bring together a whole range of liquidity providers for small business clients that they would not otherwise have available to them. We also bring a whole range of payments networks that they would not otherwise have available to them. Finally, we also provide them with a connection to their business applications through the API.

Therefore, from the perspective of our customers, they will often be a user of a bank. What they will do today is have their payables or receivables system running, and then they need to do something across borders. What they will have to do is stop using that system, come out of that system, go to another screen or pick up the telephone to connect to their bank and then perform the transaction. As they do the transaction with their bank, the bank will often process that transaction through their own proprietary network.

What we do is ensure that they do not have to be faced with these breaks in processing by integrating all cross-border payments through our API into their business flow. We also bring a whole world of connectivity for the individual customer to a range of different sources of liquidity providers and payment platforms that are optimised for those customers. The cloud nature of our service provides this very large network of currency transactions and payment services that we connect back to the customer.

Would this work for someone who is using Infosys' Finacle application for example?

We have actually provided one client with integration with the Infosys Finacle product. In this case, the bank accounts managed using the Finacle application are linked to our platform for all currency networking, and the reconciliations and reporting and responses from the market go back into the Finacle back-end from our platform. The way we look at it is that, through the cloud, we are connecting individual users with their bank accounts to a whole series of currencies and payment services that would otherwise be unavailable to them.

How are you defining "cloud" in this case?

The way that we are talking about cloud is that there is a vast network of providers in the world of currency. In general, when you are dealing with a specific broker or a specific bank, you are dealing through their proprietary network. You may end up sending something through SWIFT, but it starts usually with someone's proprietary network. That network may be good for some areas but will be suboptimal in others. If you then take the cloud nature of what we are doing, it is transparent to you as the customer as to where the services are coming from, and you suddenly have access to a range of services that we make available to you through The Currency Cloud. We go out to the individual currency markets to perform transactions, and my platform connects all of that. This is therefore not an Amazon-style cloud service, where you use compute power to increase volume flows. In our case, the transactions are going to take place in multiple areas of the financial markets. One place may be better for Latin American currency, another place may be better for the dollar or the euro, another place may be better for liquidity providers or rates, and another for Asian currencies. That's the sort of thing that an individual consumer does not have access to, but we do as we provide sources of currency and liquidity for our customers. Also, one payment platform may do a good job of providing local payments in Europe, another one may do it better in Latin America. It's the same sort of thing and what we are doing is providing access to a global market for each individual customer through our platform.

What are the typical challenges people raise with you when you talk about this sort of service?

The issues are around the security of using us as a cloud provider but this is not a major challenge. You have to bear in mind that we are working in markets that are highly regulated and we ourselves are highly regulated within those markets. We are regulated by the Financial Services Authority in the United Kingdom for example and have the same KYC and AML requirements, and all the things that come downstream from being exposed to that. How we provide our service does not absolve us from any of those requirements, and we have to ensure that the connections we make as part of our platform have the same rigour with their processes. So the first issue raised with us is normally a compliance issue, and we have the same management and regulatory compliance requirements as any other financial provider. The second question would normally then be the security of the transactions themselves and the third is data security.

We work with a number of banks and a whole series of other regulated financial firms, as well as those who are non-regulated. Not a single one of these firms has had a question or issue with the security of the financial transactions or the security of the customer data. In general, the data we hold is only the compliance and regulatory data we need to hold.

For example, one of the specific banks we can identify is FIDOR Bank in Germany (*see* the interview with FIDOR Bank CEO Matthias Kröner), which uses The Currency Cloud to power its e-wallet. This bank uses a cloud service like ours when it improves the customer experience. Bear in mind that we don't see its individual customers within our service, rather the bank uses our currency services over the cloud to power its e-wallet. So we don't have a relationship with an individual FIDOR customer, but with FIDOR overall.

What do you think cross-border currency movements will be like in the future?

I came to this firm having spent a number of years in the capital markets where the cost of a currency transaction in any major currency has gone down to be priced at basis points rather than percentage points. The banking and payments market has not followed this model or delivered this level of pricing yet because it has just been too difficult. There are a number of breaks in the process where you have to phone and where things are not automated. We want to see a future world where there is currency fluency in most major currencies, where businesses will transact with a level of automation and trust across multiple currencies in the same way that they do today in domestic currencies. That means that the currency payment itself moves from a brokered relationship that everyone understands today. That is a zero sum relationship however, with a fixed spread. I make my margin and you get yours. That will move to more of a service-oriented relationship, where there's a small cost of doing business and it is fluent across currencies and it becomes easy. The world needs to go that way, as there is such a large requirement for this across so many small- to medium-sized firms globally. For these firms in the future, the banking or brokeraged relationship just won't get there and won't work because what is needed is a multicurrency fluency across multiple businesses and that's the future structure. In terms of business model, it means that the markets will always be pricing based on market movements, we won't get away from that as there will still be multiple currencies in use. However, the difference will be that the customer will not see that as an obstacle, and will not feel it is priced too high, as there will be transparency in the system. The cost of accessing those markets will also become nominal and will be looked at as more of a service than as a speculative gamble in what should be a daily transaction.

How would you summarise this future world?

Currencies should be easier, simpler and more transparent to use, and it is by applying technology using a cloud-based mentality that will make all of those things occur. In other words, you cannot get the simplicity, transparency and automation unless you change the technical paradigm at the same time.

ABOUT MICHAEL LAVEN

Michael Laven is the CEO of London-based The Currency Cloud, whose mission is to transform the world of cross-border payments through XBP, its simple and fully automated payments platform. From 2004 to 2011, he was the chief operating officer of Traiana which built a post-trade foreign exchange network connecting over 500 banks, brokers and trading platforms and processing millions of transactions per day. Traiana was acquired by ICAP, a UK brokerage, in 2008.

Laven has had an extensive career in building and leading venture-backed financial technology companies in Silicon Valley and London. He has a BA in Anthropology from Wesleyan University, an MA in International Affairs from the School for International Training and an M.Ed. from Harvard University.

ABOUT THE CURRENCY CLOUD

Launched in 2012, The Currency Cloud offers cross-border payments as a service that is transparent, fast and trusted. The Currency Cloud platform delivers its service through payments firms, financial services firms and e-commerce firms globally. More than 40,000 corporates and consumers already have access to the service, and more than 100 platform partners and customers are using Connect API and the Client Application.

ABOUT THE AUTHOR

CHRIS SKINNER is best known as an independent commentator on the financial markets through the Finanser (www.thefinanser.com) and chair of the European networking forum the Financial Services Club, which he founded in 2004. The Financial Services Club is a network for financial professionals and focuses on the future of financial services through the delivery of research, analysis, commentary and debate and has regular meetings in London, Edinburgh, Dublin and Vienna. He is also chief executive of Balatro Ltd, a research company, and a co-founder of the website Shaping Tomorrow, as well as a regular commentator on BBC News, Sky News and Bloomberg about banking issues.

Prior to founding Balatro, Chris was vice president of Marketing and Strategy for Unisys Global Financial Services and strategy director with NCR Financial Services. These roles sparked Chris's specialisation in the future of financial services after he created the Global Future Forum at Unisys and the Knowledge Lab at NCR.

Chris is the author of ten books, with a recent series of seven published by Searching Finance that cover everything from the credit crisis through payments to social media in finance. He is also the author of books about European regulations covering the Markets in Financial Instruments Directive and the Payment Services Directive.

He is a judge for many industry awards programmes including the Card Awards and the Asian Banker's Retail Excellence Awards. As well as having worked closely with leading banks such as HSBC, the Royal Bank of Scotland, Citibank and Société Générale, Chris is also a contributor to the World Economic Forum.

Chris is known for regular speaking and keynote presentations at leading industry forums. Through these keynotes, he has presented alongside many other leading world figures including Gary Hamel, Michael Porter, Richard Branson, Lou Gerstner, Meg Whitman and Bill Gates.

He studied at Loughborough University in the United Kingdom and holds a Bachelor of Science in Management Sciences alongside a Diploma in Industrial Studies. He is a Fellow of the British Computer Society, a Fellow of the Institute of Management Services, an Associate of the Chartered Insurance Institute and a Chartered Insurance Practitioner.

More can be discovered about Chris Skinner at http://thefinanser.co.uk/fsclub/chris-skinner/